D0398677

CYBER WAR WILL NOT TAKE PLACE

THOMAS RID

Cyber War Will Not Take Place

OXFORD
UNIVERSITY PRESS

Oxford University Press, Inc., publishes works that further
Oxford University's objective of excellence
in research, scholarship, and education.

Oxford New York
Auckland   Cape Town   Dar es Salaam   Hong Kong   Karachi
Kuala Lumpur   Madrid   Melbourne   Mexico City   Nairobi
New Delhi   Shanghai   Taipei   Toronto

With offices in
Argentina   Austria   Brazil   Chile   Czech Republic   France   Greece
Guatemala   Hungary   Italy   Japan   Poland   Portugal   Singapore
South Korea   Switzerland   Thailand   Turkey   Ukraine   Vietnam

Copyright © 2013 by Oxford University Press

Oxford is a registered trade mark of Oxford University Press in the UK
and certain other countries.

Published by Oxford University Press, Inc
198 Madison Avenue, New York, New York 10016

Published in the United Kingdom in 2013 by C. Hurst & Co. (Publishers) Ltd.

www.oup.com

Oxford is a registered trademark of Oxford University Press

All rights reserved. No part of this publication may be reproduced,
stored in a retrieval system, or transmitted, in any form or by any means,
electronic, mechanical, photocopying, recording, or otherwise,
without the prior permission of Oxford University Press.

Library of Congress Cataloging-in-Publication Data
Rid, Thomas, 1975–
Cyber war will not take place / Thomas Rid.—1st edition.
p.   cm.
Includes bibliographical references and index.
ISBN 978-0-19-933063-8 (alk. paper)
1. Information warfare. 2. Information warfare—History. 3. Information warfare—
Political aspects. 4. Cyberspace—Security measures. I. Title.
U163.R53 2013
355.4—dc23
2013014740

Printed in India
on Acid-Free Paper

CONTENTS

Preface   vii
Acknowledgments   xi
The Argument   xiii

1. What is Cyber War?   1
2. Violence   11
3. Cyber Weapons   35
4. Sabotage   55
5. Espionage   81
6. Subversion   113
7. Attribution   139
8. Beyond Cyber War   163

Notes   175
Bibliography   199
Index   207

PREFACE

The threat of cyber war has captured the popular imagination. Hollywood was quick to realize and express these fears for us. Films like *Wargames* (1983) or, more recently, *Die Hard 4.0* (2007) trod the obvious narrative path: dark forces mobilizing arcane and complex computer networks to wreak havoc, holding entire nations hostage and unleashing nuclear war by hacking into the Pentagon's vast and powerful computer systems. Such fears have always touched a deep nerve. Most of us use computers but don't really understand how hardware and software interact. A powerful embodiment of the pervasive human angst of losing control to technology itself was HAL, Stanley Kubrick's terrifying, all-controlling machine aboard a spaceship in *2001: A Space Odyssey* (1968). As more and more of us as well as more and more things go online, such fears cut deeper than ever.

Most people, young and old, carry a smart phone in their pocket at all times. And a great many have become addicted to connectivity, incessantly, sometimes furtively, checking their email and social media feeds—at the dinner table, on the beach, under the table at business meetings, and not just dull ones. An entire generation has grown up who believe that their personal and professional well-being depend on digital devices and constant connectivity. If you are fiddling with your touch screen before your morning coffee is ready, the chances are that you intuitively understand that almost everything that enables the rest of your day is controlled by computers: the water that flows from the tap, the electricity plant that powers your kettle, the traffic lights that help you cross the street, the train that takes you to work, the cash machine that gives you money, the lift that you use in the office, the plane that gets you to Berlin or Delhi or New York, the navigation system you will use to find your way around a less familiar city, and much more besides. All these features of life are now commonplace, and unremarkable—as long as they work. Just as commonplace and insidious is the all-pervasive fear that malicious actors lie in wait, at all hours, to assault and crash these computers and the software they run, thereby bringing entire societies to their knees. Water will stop flowing, the lights go out, trains derail, banks lose our financial records, the roads descend into chaos, elevators fail, and planes fall from the sky. Nobody, this adage has it, is safe from the coming cyber war. Our digital demise is only a question of time.

These fears are diverting. They distract from the real significance of cyber security: in several ways, cyber attacks are not creating more vectors of violent interaction; rather they are making previously violent interactions less violent. Only in the twenty-first century has it become possible for armed forces to cripple radar stations and missile launchers without having to bomb an adversary's air defense system and kill its personnel and possibly civilians in the process. Now this can be achieved through cyber attack. Only in the twenty-first century did it become possible for intelligence agencies to exfiltrate and download vast quantities of secret data through computer breaches, without sending spies into dangerous places to bribe, coerce, and possibly harm informants and sources first. Only in the twenty-first century can rebels and insurgents mobilize dedicated supporters online and get thousands of them to take to the streets, without spreading violence and fear to undermine the government's grip on power.

The ubiquitous rise of networked computers is changing the business of soldiers, spies, and subversives. Cyberspace is creating new—and often non-violent—opportunities for action. But these new opportunities come with their own sets of limitations and challenges, applicable equally to those trying to defend against new attack vectors as much as those seeking to exploit new technology for offensive purposes. This book explores the opportunities and challenges that cyberspace is creating for those who use violence for political purposes, whether they represent a government or not.

The rise of sophisticated computer incursions poses significant risks and threats, and understanding these risks and threats and developing adequate responses to mitigate them is of critical importance—so a short word on the evolving cyber security debate is appropriate here: the debate on cyber security is flawed, and in many quarters its quality is abysmally low. The larger debate takes place in technology journals, magazines, on specialised web forums, and of course in the mainstream media as well as in academia and on blogs and microblogs. It takes place at countless workshops and conferences that bring together representatives from the private sector, governments, intelligence agencies and the military, as well as hackers and scholars from a variety of academic disciplines. It happens publicly as well as behind closed doors and in classified environments. No doubt: a number of deeply versed experts from various backgrounds regularly produce high-quality research output on cyber security, and this book could not have been written without using their good work. But the wider one moves in political or military circles, in think tanks, parliaments, ministries, and military academies, the lower seems the density of genuine experts and the higher pitched the hyperbole. The policy debate's lagging quality is neatly illustrated by the emergence of an odd bit of jargon, the increasing use of the word "cyber" as a noun among policy wonks and many a uniformed officer. As in, "I'm interested in cyber," or, "What's the definition of cyber?," as one civil servant once asked me in sincerity after I recommended in a presentation in the Houses of Parliament *not to use* that empty yet trendy buzzword as a noun. Note that computer scientists, programmers, or software security experts do not tend to use "cyber" as a noun, neither do technology journalists nor serious scholars. I've come to be highly distrustful of "nouners," as all too often they don't seem to appreciate the necessary technical details—the phenomenon can be observed widely in Washington, but also in London, Paris, Berlin, and elsewhere. Improving the quality of the debate is all the more crucial. The public deserves a far better informed, more nuanced, and more realistic debate than that which has taken place hitherto. The public also deserves better thought-out and executed policies and legislation on cyber security.

Cyber War Will Not Take Place was written with the ambition of offering the reader a solid yet accessible contribution to this debate, an attempt to help consolidate the discussion, attenuate some of the hype, and adequately confront some of the most urgent security challenges. The book is designed to be a resource for students, analysts, and journalists. The expert debate on cyber security, as well as taught courses on cyber security, is spread across various academic disciplines, the most important of which are political science and computer science, with legal studies and sociology not far behind. Readers from either discipline will, I hope, find this book insightful: engineers, geeks, and technology enthusiasts may benefit from the strategic bird's-eye-view; policy analysts and sociologists may gain something from its accessibly presented technical details; and students from either field may appreciate both. However, no single author can even hope to cover the full spectrum of cyber security, as the long vote of thanks in my acknowledgments makes clear. To make the book more approachable, its nine chapters can be read as stand-alone essays, each of which presents its own questions, argument and set of micro-case studies to illustrate specific points.

As for the sources used in this book, the most stimulating debates on recent cyber security developments are occurring not in scholarly journals but on a significant number of technology blogs and other websites that cannot be described as blogs. Some of the most important longer papers and reports are also not published in journals that can be cited according to established academic conventions, but on websites of companies and sometimes individuals. I generally cite the commonly used details: author name, title, publication forum, and date of publication. Readers will be able to find these sources through a quick Google search. Only items that may be harder to locate come with a URL. But because many URLs are clunky as well as short-lived, I decided to provide a bitly.com-link with statistics instead, for instance,[1] http://bitly.com/OtcuJx+. This link will take the reader to a bitly.com page that shows the full link, the date it was first used, and more usage statistics—even when that link has expired.

ACKNOWLEDGMENTS

The idea for this book goes back to an article with the same title published in January 2012 in the *Journal of Strategic Studies*. Joe Maiolo and Tom Mahnken were superb editors. They gave this text added exposure by making it the journal's first article to be published online, months ahead of the actual print issue. Michelle Philipps from Taylor & Francis then decided to lift the article over the paywall, making it openly accessible. Thanks also to Blake Hounshell and Susan Glasser for publishing a shorter version of the initial JSS article in *Foreign Policy* magazine. Parts of the chapter "Cyber-Weapons" were co-authored with my colleague Peter McBurney, professor at the Department of Informatics at King's College London, and were initially published under that title. Adrian Johnson and Emma De Angelis, editors at *The RUSI Journal*, decided to feature the provocative article in the February 2012 issue of their fine outlet. A hat tip goes to Dan Dieterle, the first of many bloggers to cover "Cyber War Will Not Take Place" when the argument was still in its infancy, and to Bruce Schneier, who recommended the initial article to a wider audience than I dared hope.

Several colleagues have helped develop the analysis, sometimes by pointing out arcane details or references that I could not have discovered myself, and sometimes without agreeing with some of the book's arguments. I would like to thank, in alphabetical order, Dmitri Alperovitch, David Betz, Joel Brenner, Jeffrey Carr, Richard Chirgwin, Ron Deibert, Adam Elkus, Emily Goldman, David Grebe, Clement Guitton, Michael Hayden, Marc Hecker, Eli Jellenc, Pavan Katkar, Daniel Kuehl, Herbert Lin, Joe Maiolo, Peter McBurney, Gary McGraw, Daniel Moore, Richard

ACKNOWLEDGMENTS

Overill, David Omand, Dale Peterson, Tim Stevens, John Stone, Ron Tira, Michael Warner, Matthew Waxman, Martin Zapfe, and those who cannot be named as well as three anonymous reviewers. Michael Dwyer at Hurst had the foresight to recommend expanding the initial article into a full-length book. Working with him and his team at Hurst, especially Jon de Peyer and Tim Page, was a pleasure.

The Department of War Studies at King's College London is a most stimulating place to write and teach, thanks to many colleagues from different disciplines, especially with the Department of Informatics down the hall on the 6th floor on the Strand. The brilliant students in my 2012/13 *Cyber Security* module were a true inspiration. This book could not have been written anywhere else. For funding I am grateful to the Office of Naval Research and the Minerva Program of the US Department of Defense. I would also like to thank the University of Konstanz, especially Wolfgang Seibel and Fred Girod, for giving me the opportunity to conceptualize the rough outline of this book in the quiet and delightful surroundings of the Seeburg in Kreuzlingen in the summer of 2011.

A very special thank you goes to Annette, who added pink and much else.

THE ARGUMENT

In the mid-1930s, inspired by Europe's political descent into the First World War over the tragic summer of 1914, the French dramatist Jean Giraudoux wrote a famous play, *La guerre de Troie n'aura pas lieu* (The Trojan War Will Not Take Place). The English playwright Christopher Fry later translated its two acts in 1955 as *Tiger at the Gates*.[1] The plot is set inside the gates of the city of Troy. Hector, a disillusioned Trojan commander, tries to avoid in vain what the seer Cassandra has predicted to be inevitable: war with the Greeks. Giraudoux was a veteran of 1914 and later worked in the Quai d'Orsay, or French Foreign Office. His tragedy is an eloquent critique of Europe's leaders, diplomats, and intellectuals who were, again, about to unleash the dogs of war. The play premiered in November 1935 in the Théâtre de l'Athénée in Paris, almost exactly four years before the dramatist's fears would be realized.

Judging from recent pronouncements about cyber war, the world seems to be facing another 1935-moment. "Cyberwar Is Coming!" declared the RAND Corporation's John Arquilla and David Ronfeldt in 1993.[2] It took a while for the establishment to catch on. "Cyberspace is a domain in which the Air Force flies and fights," announced Michael Wynne, the US secretary of the Air Force, in 2006. Four years later the Pentagon leadership joined in. "Although cyberspace is a man-made domain," wrote William Lynn, America's deputy secretary of defense, in a 2010 *Foreign Affairs* article, it has become "just as critical to military operations as land, sea, air, and space."[3] Richard Clarke, the White House's former cyber czar, invokes calamities of a magnitude that make 9/11 pale in comparison and urges taking several measures "simultaneously and now to avert a cyber war disaster."[4] In February 2011, the then CIA Director Leon Panetta warned the House Permanent Select Committee on Intelligence: "The next Pearl Harbor could very well be a cyber attack."[5] Panetta later repeated this dire warning as head of the Pentagon. In late 2012, Mike McConnell, George W. Bush's director of national intelligence until 2009, warned darkly that America could not "wait for the cyber equivalent of the collapse of the World Trade Centers."[6] Yet while US politicians were warning of digital doom, America's covert operators were busy unleashing a highly sophisticated computer worm, known as Stuxnet, to wreck the Iranian nuclear enrichment program at Natanz. One much-noted investigative article in *Vanity Fair* concluded that the event foreshadowed the destructive new face of twenty-first-century warfare, "Stuxnet is the Hiroshima of cyber-war."[7]

But is it? Are the Cassandras on the right side of history? Has cyber conflict indeed entered the "fifth domain" of warfare? Is cyber war really coming?

This book argues that cyber war will not take place, a statement that is not necessarily accompanied with an ironical Giraudouxian twist. It is meant rather as a comment about the past, the present, and the likely future: cyber war has never happened in the past, it does not occur in the present, and it is highly unlikely that it will disturb our future. Instead, the opposite is taking place: a computer-enabled assault on violence itself. All past and present political cyber attacks—in contrast to computer crime—are sophisticated versions of three activities that are as old as human conflict itself: sabotage, espionage, and subversion. And on closer examination, cyber attacks help to diminish rather than accentuate political violence in three discrete ways. First, at the technical high-end, weaponized code and complex *sabotage* operations enable highly targeted attacks on the functioning of an adversary's technical systems without *directly* physically harming the human operators and managers of such systems. Even more likely are scenarios of code-borne sabotage inflicting significant financial and reputational damage without causing any physical harm to hardware at all. Secondly, *espionage* is changing: computer attacks make it possible to exfiltrate data without infiltrating humans first in highly risky operations that may imperil them. Yet, paradoxically, the better intelligence agencies become at "cyber," the less they are likely to engage in cyber espionage narrowly defined. And finally *subversion* may be becoming less reliant on armed direct action: networked computers and smartphones make it possible to mobilize followers for a political cause peacefully. In certain conditions, undermining the collective trust and the legitimacy of an established order requires less violence than in the past, when the state may have monopolized the means of mass communication. This applies especially in the early phases of unrest.

But offensively minded tech-enthusiasts should hold their breath. For these changes in the nature of political violence come with their own limitations. And these limitations greatly curtail the utility of cyber attacks. Using organized violence and putting trained and specialized personnel at risk also has unique benefits that are difficult or impossible to replicate in cyberspace. And again these limitations apply to all three types of political violence in separate ways. First, for subversives, new forms of online organization and mobilization also mean higher membership mobility, higher dependency on causes, and less of a role for leaders who may impose internal cohesion and discipline, possibly by coercive means. Starting a movement is now easier, but succeeding is more difficult. Second, using pure cyber espionage without human informers creates unprecedented difficulties for those trying to put data into context, interpret the intelligence, assess it, and turn it into political (or commercial) advantage. Getting data is now easier, but not using them. Finally, at the technical high-end, it is a massive challenge to use cyber weapons as instruments in the service of a wider political goal, not just in one-off and impossible-to-repeat sabotage stints that are more relevant to geeks with a tunnel view than to heads of states with a bird's-eye perspective.

The book's argument is presented in seven chapters. The first chapter outlines what cyber war is—or rather what it would be, were it to take place. Any attempt to answer this question has to start conceptually. An offensive act has to meet certain criteria in order to qualify as an act of war: it has to be instrumental; it has to be political; and, most crucially, it has to be violent, or at least potentially violent. The second chapter considers the altered meaning of violence in the context of cyber attacks. The third chapter examines an increasingly popular idea, "cyber weapons," and discusses the potential as well as the limitations of code-borne instruments of harm. The book continues by exploring some frequently cited examples of offensive and violent political acts in cyberspace case by case. The fourth chapter considers *sabotage*. To date, the world has not experienced a major physically destructive attack against highly vulnerable and badly secured industrial control systems, such as power plants, the electricity grid, or other critical utilities—this chapter offers an explanation for this conspicuous absence (or perhaps delay), and assesses the real risk of potentially crippling future attacks on a developed society's infrastructure. Chapter five scrutinizes *espionage* by means of computer network attack. In many ways, cyber espionage represents a paradox: it is almost always a non-violent form of network breach that is also the most fundamental and potentially game-changing threat to developed nations, mostly for economic reasons rather than for reasons of national security, strictly and narrowly defined. Chapter six explores perhaps the most widespread form of activism and political violence in cyberspace, *subversion*. Technology, it finds, has lowered the entry costs for subversive activity but it has also raised the threshold for sustained success. Chapter seven assesses the attribution problem, an issue that has been at the root of cyber security. If attribution is recognized for what it is, as a political rather than a technical problem, then it becomes possible to see that the problem itself is a function of an attack's severity. The conclusion offers a summary and hopes to take the debate beyond the tired and wasted metaphor of "cyber war."[8]

1

WHAT IS CYBER WAR?

Carl von Clausewitz still offers the most concise and the most fundamental concept of war. Sun Tzu, a much older strategic thinker, often made a showing in the debate on information warfare in the 1990s. But the ancient Chinese general and philosopher is better known for punchy aphorisms than systematic thought—long sections of his book, *The Art of War*, read like a choppy Twitter-feed from 500 BC. Sun's modern Prussian nemesis offers a far more coherent and finely tuned toolset for rigorous analysis. Clausewitz's concepts and ideas, although limited in many ways, continue to form the core vocabulary of professionals and experts in the use of force. Clausewitz identifies three main criteria any aggressive or defensive action that aspires to be a stand-alone act of war, or may be interpreted as such, has to meet all three. Past cyber attacks do not.

The first element is war's violent character. "War is an act of force to compel the enemy to do our will," wrote Clausewitz on the first page of *On War*.[1] All war, pretty simply, is violent. If an act is not potentially violent, it's not an act of war and it's not an armed attack—in this context the use of the word will acquire a metaphorical dimension, as in the "war" on obesity or the "war" on cancer. A real act of war or an armed attack is always potentially or actually lethal, at least for some participants on at least one side. Unless physical violence is stressed, war is a hodgepodge notion, to paraphrase Jack Gibbs.[2] The same applies to the idea of a weapon. In Clausewitz's thinking, violence is the pivotal point of all war. Both enemies—he usually considered two sides—would attempt to escalate violence to the extreme, unless tamed by friction, imponderables, and politics.[3]

The second element highlighted by Clausewitz is war's instrumental character. An act of war is always instrumental, and to be instrumental there has to be a means and an end: physical violence or the threat of force is the *means*; forcing the enemy to accept the offender's will is the *end*. Such a definition is "theoretically necessary," Clausewitz argued.[4] To achieve the end of war, one opponent has to be rendered defenseless. Or, to be more precise, the opponent has to be brought into a position, against their will, where any change of that position brought about by the continued use of arms would only bring more disadvantages, at least in that opponent's view. Complete defenselessness is only the most extreme of those positions. Both opponents in a war use violence in this instrumental way, shaping each other's behavior, giving each other the law of action, in the words of the Prussian philosopher of war.[5] The instrumental use of means takes place on tactical, operational, strategic, and political levels. The higher the order of the desired goal, the more difficult it is to achieve. As Clausewitz put it, in the slightly stilted language of his time: "The purpose is a political intention, the means is war; never can the means be understood without the purpose."[6]

This leads to the third and most central feature of war—its political nature. An act of war is always political. The objective of battle, to "throw" the enemy and to make him defenseless, may temporarily blind commanders and even strategists to the larger purpose of war. War is never an isolated act, nor is it ever only one decision. In the real world, war's larger purpose is always a political purpose. It transcends the use of force. This insight was famously captured by Clausewitz's most famous phrase, "War is a mere continuation of politics by other means."[7] To be political, a political entity or a representative of a political entity, whatever its constitutional form, has to have an intention, a will. That intention has to be articulated. And one side's will has to be transmitted to the adversary at some point during the confrontation (it does not have to be publicly communicated). A violent act and its larger political intention must also be attributed to one side at some point during the confrontation. History does not know of acts of war without eventual attribution.[8]

One modification is significant before applying these criteria to cyber offenses. The pivotal element of any warlike action remains the "act of force." An act of force is usually rather compact and dense, even when its components are analyzed in detail. In most armed confrontations, be they conventional or unconventional, the use of force is more or less straightforward: it may be an F-16 striking targets from the air, artillery barrages, a drone-strike, improvised explosive devices placed by the side of a road, even a suicide bomber in a public square. In all these cases, a combatant's or an insurgent's triggering action—such as pushing a button or pulling a trigger—will immediately and directly result in casualties, even if a timer or a remote control device is used, as with a drone or a cruise missile, and even if a programmed weapon system is able to semi-autonomously decide which target to engage or not.[9] An act of cyber war would be an entirely different game.

In an act of cyber war, the actual use of force is likely to be a far more complex and mediated sequence of causes and consequences that ultimately result in violence and casualties.[10] One often-invoked scenario is a Chinese cyber attack on the US homeland in the event of a political crisis in, say, the Taiwan Straits. The Chinese could blanket a major city with blackouts by activating so-called logic-bombs that had been pre-installed in America's electricity grid. Financial information could be lost on a massive scale. Derailments could crash trains. Air traffic systems and their backups could collapse, leaving hundreds of planes aloft without communication. Industrial control systems of highly sensitive plants, such as nuclear power stations, could be damaged, potentially leading to loss of cooling, meltdown, and contamination[11]—people could suffer serious injuries or even be killed. Military units could be rendered defenseless. In such a scenario, the causal chain that links somebody pushing a button to somebody else being hurt is mediated, delayed, and permeated by chance and friction. Yet such mediated destruction caused by a cyber offense *could*, without doubt, be an act of war, even if the means were not violent, only the consequences.[12] Moreover, in highly networked societies, non-violent cyber attacks *could* cause economic consequences without violent effects that *could* exceed the harm of an otherwise smaller physical attack.[13] For one thing, such scenarios have caused widespread confusion, "Rarely has something been so important and so talked about with less clarity and less apparent understanding than this phenomenon," commented Michael Hayden, formerly director of the Central Intelligence Agency (CIA) as well as the National Security Agency (NSA).[14] And secondly, to date all such scenarios have another major shortfall: they remain fiction, not to say science fiction.

If the use of force in war is violent, instrumental, and political, then there is no cyber offense that meets all three criteria. But more than that, there are very few cyber attacks in history that meet only *one* of these criteria. It is useful to consider the most-quoted offenses case by case, and criterion by criterion.

The most violent "cyber" attack to date is likely to have been a Siberian pipeline explosion—if it actually happened. In 1982, a covert American operation allegedly used rigged software to cause a massive explosion in Russia's Urengoy-Surgut-Chelyabinsk pipeline, which connected the Urengoy gas fields in Siberia across Kazakhstan to European markets. The gigantic pipeline project required sophisticated control systems for which the Soviet operators had to purchase computers on open markets. The Russian pipeline authorities tried to acquire the necessary Supervisory Control and Data Acquisition software, known as SCADA, from the United States but were turned down. The Russians then attempted to get the software from a Canadian firm. The CIA is said to have succeeded in inserting malicious code into the control system that ended up being installed in Siberia. The code that controlled pumps, turbines, and valves was programmed to operate normally for a time and then "to reset pump speeds and valve settings to produce pressures far beyond those acceptable to pipeline joints and welds," recounted Thomas Reed, an official in the National Security Council at the time.[15] In June 1982, the rigged valves probably resulted in a "monumental" explosion and fire that could be seen from space. The US Air Force reportedly rated the explosion at 3 kilotons, equivalent to a small nuclear device.[16]

But there are three problems with this story. The first pertains to the Russian sources. When Reed's book came out in 2004, Vasily Pchelintsev, a former KGB head of the Tyumen region where the alleged explosion was supposed to have taken place, denied the story. He surmised that Reed might have been referring to an explosion that happened not in June but on a warm April day that year, 50 kilometers from the city of Tobolsk, caused by shifting pipes in the thawing ground of the tundra. No one was hurt in that explosion.[17] There are no media reports from 1982 that would confirm Reed's alleged explosion, although regular accidents and pipeline explosions in the USSR were reported in the early 1980s. Later Russian sources also fail to mention the incident. In 1990, when the Soviet Union still existed, Lieutenant General Nikolai Brusnitsin published a noteworthy and highly detailed small book, translated as *Openness and Espionage*. Brusnitsin was the deputy chairman of the USSR's State Technical Commission at the time. His book has a short chapter on "computer espionage," where he discusses several devices that Soviet intelligence had discovered over previous years. He recounts three different types of discoveries: finding "blippers" inserted into packages to monitor where imported equipment would be installed; finding "additional electronic 'units' which have nothing to do with the machine itself," designed to pick up and relay data; and finding "gimmicks which render a computer totally inoperative" by destroying "both the computer software and the memory."[18] Brusnitsin even provided examples. The most drastic example was a "virus," the general wrote, implanted in a computer that was sold by a West German firm to a Soviet shoe factory. It is not unreasonable to assume that if the pipeline blitz had happened, Brusnitsin would have known about it and most likely written about it, if not naming the example then at least naming the possibility of hardware sabotage. He did not do that.

A second problem concerns the technology that was available at the time. It is uncertain if a "logic bomb" in 1982 could have been hidden easily. Retrospectively analyzing secretly modified software in an industrial control system three decades after the fact is difficult to impossible. But a few generalizations are possible: at the time technology was far simpler. A system controlling pipelines in the early 1980s would probably have been a fairly simple "state machine," and it would probably have used an 8-bit micro-controller. Back in 1982, it was most likely still possible to test every possible output that might be produced by all possible inputs. (This is not feasible with later microprocessors.) Any hidden outputs could be discovered by such a test—an input of "X" results in dangerous output "Y."[19] Testing the software for flaws, in other words, would have been rather easy. Even with the technology available at the time, a regression test would have needed less than a day to complete, estimated Richard Chirgwin, a long-standing technology reporter.[20] In short, in 1982 it was far more difficult to "hide" malicious software.

Thirdly, even after the CIA declassified the so-called Farewell Dossier, which described the effort to provide the Soviet Union with defective technology, the agency did not confirm that such an explosion took place. If it happened, it is unclear if the explosion resulted in casualties. The available evidence on the event is so thin and questionable that it cannot be counted as a proven case of a successful logic bomb.

Another oft-quoted example of cyber war is an online onrush on Estonia that began in late April 2007. At that time Estonia was one of the world's most connected nations; two-thirds of all Estonians used the Internet and 95 per cent of banking transactions were done electronically.[21] The small and well-wired Baltic country was vulnerable to cyber attacks. The story behind the much-cited incident started about two weeks before 9 May, a highly emotional day in Russia when the victory against Nazi Germany is remembered. With indelicate timing, authorities in Tallinn decided to move the two-meter Bronze Soldier, a Russian Second World War memorial of the Unknown Soldier, from the center of the capital to its outskirts. The Russian-speaking population, as well as neighboring Russia, was aghast. On 26 and 27 April, Tallinn saw violent street riots, with 1,300 arrests, 100 injuries, and one fatality.

The street riots were accompanied by online commotions. The cyber attacks started in the late hours of Friday, 27 April. Initially the offenders used rather inept, low-tech methods, such as ping floods or denial of service (DoS) attacks—basic requests for information from a server, as when an Internet user visits a website by loading the site's content. Then the assault became slightly more sophisticated. Starting on 30 April, simple botnets were used to increase the volume of distributed denial of service (DDoS) attacks, and the timing of these collective activities became increasingly coordinated. Other types of nuisances included email and comment spam as well as the defacement of the Estonian Reform Party's website. Estonia experienced what was then the worst-ever DDoS. The attacks came from an extremely large number of hijacked computers, up to 85,000, and they went on for an unusually long time, for three weeks, until 19 May. The attacks reached a peak on 9 May, when Moscow celebrates Victory Day. Fifty-eight Estonian websites were brought down at once. The online services of Estonia's largest bank, Hansapank, were unavailable for ninety minutes on 9 May and for two hours a day later.[22] The effect of these coordinated online protests on business, government, and society was noticeable, but ultimately remained minor. The only long-term consequence of the incident was that the Estonian government succeeded in getting NATO to establish a permanent agency in Tallinn, the Cooperative Cyber Defence Centre of Excellence.

A few things are notable about the story. It remained unclear who was behind the attacks. Estonia's defense minister as well as the country's top diplomat pointed their fingers at the Kremlin, but they were unable to muster evidence, retracting earlier statements that Estonia had been able to trace the IP addresses of some of the computers involved in the attack back to the Russian government. Neither experts from the Atlantic Alliance nor from the European Commission were able to identify Russian fingerprints in the operations. Russian officials described the accusations of their involvement as "unfounded."[23]

Keeping Estonia's then-novel experience in perspective is important. Mihkel Tammet, an official in charge of ICT for the Estonian Ministry of Defense, described the time leading up to the launch of the attacks as a "gathering of botnets like a gathering of armies."[24] Andrus Ansip, then Estonia's prime minister, asked, "What's the difference between a blockade of harbors or airports of sovereign states and the blockade of government institutions and newspaper web sites?"[25] It was of course a rhetorical question. Yet the answer is simple: unlike a naval blockade, the mere "blockade" of websites is not violent, not even potentially; unlike a naval blockade, the DDoS assault was not instrumentally tied to a tactical objective, but rather to an act of undirected protest; and unlike ships blocking the way, the pings remained anonymous, without political backing. Ansip could have asked what the difference was between a large popular demonstration blocking access to buildings and the blocking of websites. The comparison would have been more adequate, but still flawed for an additional reason: many more actual people have to show up for a good old-fashioned demonstration.

A year later a third major event occurred that would enter the Cassandra's tale of cyber war. The context was the ground war between the Russian Federation and Georgia in August of 2008. The short armed confrontation was triggered by a territorial dispute over South Ossetia. On 7 August, the Georgian army reacted to provocations by attacking South Ossetia's separatist forces. One day later, Russia responded militarily. Yet a computer attack on Georgian websites had started slowly on 29 July, weeks before the military confrontation and with it the main cyber offense, both of which started on 8 August. This may have been the first time that an independent cyber attack has taken place in sync with a conventional military operation.[26]

The cyber attacks on Georgia comprised three different types. Some of the country's prominent websites were defaced, for instance that of Georgia's National Bank and the Ministry of Foreign Affairs. The most notorious defacement was a collage of portraits juxtaposing Adolf Hitler and Mikheil Saakashvili, the Georgian president. The second type of offense was denial-of-service attacks against websites in the Georgian public and private sectors, including government websites and that of the Georgian parliament, but also news media, Georgia's largest commercial bank, and other minor websites. The online onslaughts, on average, lasted around two hours and fifteen minutes, the longest up to six hours.[27] A third method was an effort to distribute malicious software to deepen the ranks of the attackers and the volume of attacks. Various Russian-language forums helped distribute scripts that enabled the public to take action, even posting the attack script in an archived version, war.rar, which prioritized Georgian government websites. In a similar vein, the email accounts of Georgian politicians were spammed.

The effects of the episode were again rather minor. Despite the warlike rhetoric of the international press, the Georgian government, and anonymous hackers, the attacks were not violent. And Georgia, a small country with a population of 4.6 million, was far less vulnerable to attacks than Estonia; web access was relatively low and few vital services like energy, transportation, or banking were tied to the Internet. The entire affair had little effect beyond making a number of Georgian government websites temporarily inaccessible. The attack was also only minimally instrumental. The National Bank of Georgia ordered all branches to stop offering electronic services for ten days. The main damage caused by the attack was in limiting the government's ability to communicate internationally, thus preventing the small country's voice being heard at a critical moment. If the attackers intended this effect, its utility was limited: the foreign ministry took a rare step, with Google's permission, and set up a blog on Blogger, the company's blogging platform. This helped keep one more channel to journalists open. Most importantly, the offense was not genuinely political in nature. As in the Estonian case, the Georgian government blamed the Kremlin. But Russia again denied official sponsorship of the attacks. NATO's Tallinn-based cyber security center later published a report on the Georgia attacks. Although the onrush appeared coordinated and instructed, and although the media were pointing fingers at Russia, "there is no conclusive proof of who is behind the DDoS attacks," NATO concluded, "as was the case with Estonia."[28]

The cyber scuffles that accompanied the street protests in Estonia and the short military ground campaign in Georgia were precedents. Perhaps the novelty of these types of offenses was the main reason for their high public profile and the warlike rhetoric that surrounded them. The same observation might be true for another type of "cyber war," high-profile spying operations, an early example of which is Moonlight Maze. This lurid name was given to a highly classified cyber espionage incident that was discovered in 1999. The US Air Force coincidentally discovered an intrusion into its network, and the Federal Bureau of Investigation (FBI) was alerted. The federal investigators called the NSA. An investigation uncovered a pattern of intrusion into computers at the National Aeronautics and Space Administration (NASA), at the Department of Energy, and at universities as well as research laboratories, which had started in March 1998. Maps of military installations were copied, as were hardware designs and other sensitive information. The incursions went on for almost two years. The Department of Defense (DoD) was able to trace the attack to what was then called a mainframe computer in Russia. But again: no violence, unclear goals, no political attribution.

Yet the empirical trend is obvious: over the past dozen years, cyber attacks have been steadily on the rise. The frequency of major security breaches against governmental and corporate targets has grown. The volume of attacks is increasing, as is the number of actors participating in such episodes, ranging from criminals to activists to the NSA. The range of aggressive behavior online is widening. At the same time the sophistication of some attacks has reached new heights, and in this respect Stuxnet has indeed been a game-changing event. Yet despite these trends the "war" in "cyber war" ultimately has more in common with the "war" on obesity than with the Second World War—it has more metaphorical than descriptive value. It is high time to go back to classic terminology and understand cyber offenses for what they really are.

Aggression, whether it involves computers or not, can be criminal or political in nature. It is useful to group offenses along a spectrum, stretching from ordinary crime all the way up to conventional war. A few distinctive features then become visible: crime is mostly apolitical, war is always political; criminals conceal their identity, uniformed soldiers display their identity openly. Political violence (or "political crime" in criminology and the theory of law) occupies the muddled middle of this spectrum, being neither ordinary crime nor ordinary war. For reasons of simplicity, this middle stretch of the spectrum will be divided into three segments here: subversion, espionage, and sabotage. All three activities may involve states as well as private actors. Cyber offenses tend to be skewed towards the criminal end of the spectrum. So far there is no known act of cyber "war," when war is properly defined. This of course does not mean that there are no political cyber offenses. But all known political cyber offenses, criminal or not, are neither common crime nor common war. Their purpose is subverting, spying, or sabotaging.

In all three cases, Clausewitz's three criteria are jumbled. These activities need not be violent to be effective. They need not be instrumental to work, as subversion may often be an expression of collective passion and espionage may be an outcome of opportunity rather than strategy. And finally: aggressors engaging in subversion, espionage, or sabotage do act politically; but in sharp contrast to warfare, they are likely to have a permanent or at least a temporary interest in avoiding attribution. This is one of the main reasons why political crime, more than acts of war, has thrived online, where non-attribution is easier to achieve than water-proof attribution. It goes without saying that subversion, espionage, and sabotage—digitally facilitated or not—may accompany military operations. Both sides may engage in these activities, and have indeed done so since time immemorial. But the advent of digital networks had an uneven effect. Understanding this effect requires surveying the foundation: the notion of violence.

2

VIOLENCE

On 6 September 2007 the Israeli Air Force bombed the construction site of a nuclear reactor at Dayr ez-Zor in Northern Syria. To prepare the air raid, a secret Israeli agency neutralized a single Syrian radar site at Tall al-Abuad, close to the Turkish border. To do so, the Israelis probably used computer sabotage. This intrusion achieved something that would previously have required the physical destruction of radar installations, damaging property, potentially hurting or killing some of the system's operators, and possibly innocent civilians: a missile strike or an infiltration of Special Forces teams to blow up the site would have been the conventional alternative. So the outcome of the cyber attack was in some ways equivalent to that of a physical attack: a disabled air defense system. But was the cyber attack violent?

Any serious discussion of cyber war necessarily rests on a foundation. This foundation is our understanding of the nature of violence, and by extension our understanding of violence in cyberspace. And as with cyber war and cyber weapons, understanding the nature of violence in cyberspace means understanding the nature of the former phenomenon first. Only then can the key questions be tackled: what is violence in the context of cyber attacks? Does the notion of violence change its meaning when it is applied to cyberspace? The answer therefore depends on where a line is drawn between a violent act and a non-violent act, and on what we consider to be violence and what we do not consider as violence. This understanding of violence also forms the foundation for our understanding of political, economic, military, and especially ethical considerations of all cyber attacks, be they violent or otherwise.

This chapter puts forward a simple argument with a twist: most cyber attacks are not violent and cannot sensibly be understood as a form of violent action. And those cyber attacks that actually do have the potential of force, actual or realized, *are bound to be violent only indirectly.* Violence administered through cyberspace is less direct in at least four ways: it is less physical, less emotional, less symbolic, and, as a result, less instrumental than more conventional uses of political violence. Yet cyber attacks, be they non-violent or in very rare cases violent, can achieve the same goal that political violence is designed to achieve: namely, to undermine trust, and specifically collective social trust in specific institutions, systems, or organizations. And cyber attacks may undermine social trust, paradoxically, in a more direct way than political violence, by taking a non-violent shortcut. Moreover, they can do so by remaining entirely invisible.

The argument is outlined in four short steps. The chapter starts by considering the various media through which violence can be expressed. Secondly the crucial role of the human body in committing as well as receiving acts of violence will be discussed. The chapter then briefly clarifies the concept of violence, in juxtaposition to power, authority and, most importantly, force, highlighting the symbolic nature of instruments of force. The argument finally discusses trust and the most important limitation as well as the most important potential of cyber attacks.

Violence is conventionally administered in one of three ways—through force, through energy, or through agents. A new fourth medium is code, which is bound to be more indirect—if it is to be included as a separate medium at all. The first two categories are borrowed from physics, the third from chemistry and biology. The first instance—force—is the most obvious. In physics, force is described as an influence that changes the motion of a body, or produces motion or deformation in a stationary object. The magnitude of force can be calculated by multiplying the mass of the body by its acceleration, and almost all weapons combine physical mass with acceleration, be it a fist, a stone, a pike, a bullet, a grenade, even a missile. The second medium—energy—is perhaps somewhat less obvious at first glance, but is almost as old as the use of mechanical force to coerce, hurt, or kill other human beings. Fire, heat, and explosions are used as powerful and highly destructive media of violence. Sun Tzu, the ancient Chinese author of *The Art of War*, had a chapter on "attack by fire."[1] Less common uses of energy at war include the use of electricity, for instance in Tasers, or lasers. Agents are the third medium of violence. Some weapons rely neither on physical force nor on energy, but on agents to do the work of harming the target. The most obvious examples are biological weapons and chemical weapons—after all, such agents do not have to be fired in an artillery shell or missile, which physically thrusts them into a target perimeter to deliver the deadly payload. The agent does the harm. Weaponized agents impair the human organism and lead to injury or death: anthrax, endospores that cause respiratory infection, and in a high number of infections ultimately respiratory collapse; mustard gas, a chemical agent, causes blisters, burns, and is strongly carcinogenic.

Any discussion of violence in the context of cyber attacks needs to start by recognizing some basic philosophical insights. In contrast to almost all instruments that may be used for violent effect, code differs in two notable ways. The first basic limitation is that code-caused violence is indirect: it has to "weaponize" the target system in order to turn it into a weapon. Code doesn't have its own force or energy. Instead, any cyber attack with the goal of physical destruction, be it material destruction or harming human life, has to utilize the force or energy that is embedded in the targeted system or created by it. Code, quite simply, doesn't come with its own explosive charge. Code-caused destruction is therefore *parasitic on the target*. Even the most sophisticated cyber attack can only physically harm a human being by unleashing the violent potential that is embedded in that targeted system. This could be a traffic control system, causing trains or planes to crash; a power plant that may explode or emit radiation; a dam that may break and cause a devastating flash flood; a pipeline that may blow up; hospital life support systems that may collapse in emergency situations; or even a pacemaker implanted in a heart patient that could be disrupted by exploiting vulnerabilities in its software. Yet so far, no such scenario has ever happened in reality. Lethal cyber attacks, while certainly possible, remain the stuff of fiction novels and action films. Not a single human being has ever been killed or hurt as a result of a code-triggered cyber attack.

Computer code can only directly affect computer-controlled machines, not humans. At first glance the way a biological virus harms a system may be compared to the way a computer virus—or other malware—harms a computer system. Jürgen Kraus, a German student, coined this metaphoric comparison, and the term computer virus itself, in 1980. In his MA dissertation, "Reproduktion bei Programmen," Kraus argued that self-reproducing programs would be inconsequential if they did not reside inside the memory of a computer: "Only inside the computer, and only if the program is running, is a self-reproducing program in a position for reproduction and mutation."[2] Kraus then pointed to an important difference: a biological virus could start its own reproductive process, but a computer virus would rely on activation through the operating system. The most crucial difference was so obvious to Kraus that he didn't have to mention it: biological viruses can only affect biological systems; computer viruses can only affect machines that rely on code. Put simply, a biological virus cannot directly harm a building or vehicle, and a computer virus cannot directly harm a human being or animal.

Finally, one special hypothetical case of a parasitic cyber attack should be mentioned. Many modern weapon systems, from artillery guns to naval drones, are controlled by software, by computer code. An increasing number of such systems will be equipped with varying degrees of autonomous decision-making capabilities in the future. The International Committee of the Red Cross has recognized this trend and has already started considering possible adaptations to the law of armed conflict. Yet caution is warranted. Code that is a built-in component of a weapon system should not be seen as part of a cyber attack—otherwise the concept would lose its meaning: every complex weapon system that uses computers in one way or the other would then count as a form of cyber attack. That would not make sense. But there is one exception: an automated complex weapon system becoming the target of a breach. If weaponized code can only unlock physical destruction by modifying a targeted system, then the perfect target system is one that gives the attacker maximum flexibility and maximum potential for damage: in theory, an armed remotely controlled aircraft, such as a Predator or Reaper drone, is a far more attractive target for a cyber attack than a power plant or an air-traffic control system. In such a scenario, the aggressor would not merely weaponize a clunky system that was never designed to be a weapon—the attackers could actually "weaponize" a weapon. In practice, however, such an episode has never happened and indeed is difficult to imagine. The only incident on record that comes close to such an attack occurred in late June 2012: researchers from the University of Texas at Austin's Radionavigation Laboratory hijacked a small surveillance drone during a test-flight in a stadium in Austin, Texas. The academics "spoofed" the drone's GPS system by infiltrating the machine's navigation device with a signal that was more powerful than the one received from satellites used for legitimate GPS navigation. This meant that the scholars could override the drone's commands and thus control its flight path. The device they used allegedly cost only $1,000 to build, Fox News reported.[3] A far better-known incident is a questionable example: in the first days of December 2011, a CIA-operated American Lockheed Martin RQ-170 Sentinel drone fell into Iranian hands near the city of Kashmar, in the country's north-east. An anonymous Iranian engineer who worked on analyzing the captured drone claimed that electronic warfare specialists had spoofed the drone's GPS navigation.[4] After a ten-week review of the incident the CIA reportedly found that a faulty data stream had caused operators to lose contact with the drone, rather than Iranian interference or jamming.[5] While spoofing is technically possible, it is very unlikely that such an attack could succeed against a more complex armed military drone in the field: the controls are likely to be encrypted, altitude can be a problem, and deceiving a GPS receiver is not the same as infiltrating the control system that can unleash a military drone's deadly missiles against specified targets.

The human body, the previous pages argued, is not directly vulnerable to cyber attack, only indirectly. But the human body, in several ways, is the foundation of violence. It enables both the act of attacking and of being attacked. Understanding this foundational role of the human body is necessary to see the emotional limitations of code-borne violence, as well as the symbolic limitations of cyber attack.

Taking the human body as the starting point for political theory has a long tradition, especially among political philosophers concerned with the phenomenon of violence and how to overcome it. The human body's vulnerability is its most notable feature in most such considerations of political theory. Thomas Hobbes and his reflections on the vulnerability of the unprotected human existence probably come to mind first. The driving force for all political organization is the universal weakness of all humans and their resulting dependence on protection. The opening paragraph of Chapter 13 of *Leviathan* deserves to be read in full:

Nature has made men so equall, in the faculties of body, and mind; as that though there bee found one man sometimes manifestly stronger in body, or of quicker mind then another; yet when all is reckoned together, the difference between man, and man, is not so considerable, as that one man can thereupon claim to himselfe any benefit to which another many not pretend, as well as he. For so as to the strength of the body, the weakest has the strength enough to kill the strongest, either by secret machination, or by confederacy with others, that are in the same danger with himselfe.[6]

This equalizing vulnerability forms the conceptual basis for Hobbes's famous state of the war of all against all, and the normative basis for the social contract to overcome the resulting "natural" state of anarchy. This state of war, and the absence of political order, prevents all meaningful social development and civilization. The consequence, in Hobbes's most famous words, would be "continuall feare, and danger of violent death," which would inevitably make the life of man "solitary, poore, nasty, brutish, and short."[7] Self-help, therefore, needed to be rejected and violence taken away from man, monopolized,[8] and given to the collective, the "commonwealth." It is important to note that this basic insight forms the continued foundation of most contract theory, legal theory, and indeed the modern notion of the state.[9]

Wolfgang Sofsky, a more recent German political theorist, is also noteworthy in this context. The political philosopher wrote a highly inspiring work about violence, entitled *Traktat über die Gewalt* (Pamphlet on Violence).[10] The book is especially useful in the context of the present inquiry because, like cyber attacks, it ignores the state's frontiers, and does not limit itself to internal or external violence. For Sofsky, whether domestically or internationally, the body is the center of human existence. It is because of man's bodily existence that all humans are *verletzungmächtig*, able to hurt, and *verletzungsoffen*, able to be hurt.[11] The body, in other words, is the first instrument of violence, and it is the first target of violence. The two sides—the active and the passive; aggression and protection; offense and defense—will be considered in turn.

The body is the first and foremost *target of violence*. Even if more advanced weapons are designed to destroy buildings, bunkers, or barricades, their ultimate aim always remains the human body. Appreciating this foundation is crucial. The experience of physical violence at the hands of a criminal or an enemy is a life-changing event for the survivor that transcends the moment of aggression. It stays with the victim. Sofsky puts this in drastic but appropriate language. Somebody else's death may leave a painful hole in the social fabric of a family, village, or country. But the situation is different for the survivor of a violent attack. Depending on the attack's intensity, the victim has made personal acquaintance with a life-changing event, with possibly permanent injuries, physical as well as psychological ones. Sofsky:

> Pain is the material portend of death, and fear [of pain] is ultimately only an offspring of the fear of death. Pain forces man to feel what ceases to be felt in death, the tenuousness of the body, the destruction of the mind, the negation of existence. The survivor knows this in his flesh. He feels that dying has begun.[12]

Violence, like serious illness, confronts individuals with the fragility of their existence, with the proximity of death. Anyone who has spent time in a war zone, even if they were spared a personal encounter with violence, understands this existential dimension. The strong bonds of friendship forged in war zones are an expression of this existential and highly emotional experience. Individual violence can literally break down an individual, cause irreversible trauma, and end his or her existence—political violence, likewise, can break down a political community, cause deep collective trauma, and even upend its existence entirely. Therefore, Sofsky concluded, "no language has more power to persuade than the language of force."[13]

From this follows the second major limitation: violence administered through cyberspace is not only indirect and mediated; it is also likely to have less emotional impact. Due to its intermediary and roundabout nature, a cyber attack is unlikely to release the same amount of terror and fear as a coordinated campaign of terrorism or conventional military operations would produce. A coordinated cyber attack that produces a level of pain that could sensibly be compared to that which a well-executed air campaign can inflict on a targeted country is plainly unimaginable at present.[14] And here a comparison with airpower may be instructive: the use of airpower has historically been overestimated again and again, from the Second World War to Vietnam to the Persian Gulf War to the Kosovo campaign to Israel's 2006 war against Hezbollah. In each instance the proponents of punishment administered from the air overestimated the psychological impact of aerial bombardments and underestimated the adversary's resilience—and it should be noted that being bombed from the air is a most terrifying experience.[15] Against this background of consistent hopefulness and overconfidence, it is perhaps

17

not surprising that it was air forces, not land forces, that first warmed to "cyber" and started to maintain that their pilots would now "fly, fight and win"[16] in cyberspace, the much-vaunted "fifth domain of warfare,"[17] next to land, sea, air, and space. The use of cyber weapons that could inflict damage and pain comparable to the pummeling of Dresden, London, Belgrade, or Beirut at the receiving end of devastating airpower is, at present, too unrealistic even for a bad science fiction plot.

When the first casualty is caused by a cyber attack—and a "when" seems to be a more appropriate conjunction than an "if" here—there is no question that the public outcry will be massive, and depending on the context, the collective fear could be significant. But after the initial dust has settled, the panic is likely to subside and a more sober assessment will be possible. The likely finding will be that, to paraphrase Sofsky, in cyberspace the language of force just isn't as convincing. Another reason for the limitations of instruments of violence in cyberspace, or cyber weapons, is their symbolic limitation. To appreciate the symbolism of weapons, the key is again the body.

The body is also the first *instrument of violence*, the first weapon. Here the "first" doesn't indicate a priority, but the beginning of an anthropological and ultimately a technical development that is still in full force. Three things are constantly increasing: the power of weapons, the skills needed to use them, and the distance to the target. Needless to say, it is the deadly ingenuity of the human mind that devised most weapons and optimized the skills needed to use them and to build them. Yet it was the bare body that was man's first weapon, and all instruments of violence are extensions of the human body. Examples of simple weapons, such as a club, a knife, or a sword, can help illustrate this unity between user and instrument. Martial artists trained in the delicate techniques of fencing or kendo, a Japanese form of sword-fighting, will intuitively understand that the purpose of intensive training, mental as well as physical, is to make the weapon's use as natural as the use of one's arms or legs, and vastly more efficient. Hence expressions such as "going into the weapon," "becoming one" with it, or "feeling" it. Such expressions are not just familiar to fencers, archers, or snipers. The unity between the fighter and his or her weapon is not limited to the relatively simple, traditional instruments of harm. It also applies to more complex weapon systems. The F-15 pilot or the artillery gunner equally accumulate large numbers of hours in flight or on range in order to routinize the use of these instruments of harm. The goal is that the pilot does not have to think about the basics any more, even in more complex maneuvers under high stress, and instead is able to focus on other aspects of an operation. The plane, ultimately, becomes an extension of the pilot's body as well. And the more complex a weapon, the more its use becomes the prerogative of specialists in the use of force who are trained to operate it.

Technology affects the relationship between violence and the human body in an uneven way: technology drastically altered the instruments of violence—but technology did not alter the foundation, the ultimate vulnerability of the human body. Technology can physically remove the perpetrator from the inflicted violence, but technology cannot physically remove the victim from the inflicted violence. If the bare human body is the instrument of harm, it is a fist or foot that will hit the victim's body. If the instrument of harm is a blade, the knife will cut the victim's skin. An arrow will hit its victim's shoulder from a small distance. A sniper's bullet will tear tissue from hundreds of yards. A shell's detonation will break bones from miles away. A long-range missile can kill human beings across thousands of miles, continents away. Man can delegate the delivery of violence to an artifact, to weapon systems, but the reception of violence remains an intimately personal, bodily experience. The complexity, the precision, and the destructive power of weapon systems, as well as the degree of specialization of those operating them, have been growing continuously.

This ever-increasing power of offensive weapons highlights the symbolic role of instruments of violence—and the third major limitation: using cyber weapons for symbolic purposes. The well-trained body of a boxer or wrestler is a symbol of his or her strength, even outside the ring, outside a fight. The sword is traditionally used as a symbol of glory, martial prowess, and social status. Showing weapons, consequently, becomes a crucial part of their use and justification. In Yemen, for instance, the *jambeeya*, a traditional dagger worn like a giant belt-buckle, is still a man's most visible symbol of social standing. In New York City and elsewhere, a police officer with a holstered gun imposes more respect than an unarmed sheriff. In Beijing, military parades are perhaps the most obvious spectacle literally designed to show the state's imposing power. There is even an entire range of military operations largely executed for the purpose of display. Examples can be found on strategic and tactical levels: deploying major assets, such as a carrier strike group, at strategically significant points, or merely a patrol, be it marching, driving, sailing, or flying.[18] Most explicitly, airpower may be deployed in so-called "show of force" operations, such as a deliberately low flyover by a military aircraft, designed to intimidate the enemy tactically. As the power of weapons increases along with the required skills of their users and the distance they can bridge, the need for symbolism increases as well: displaying weapon systems and threatening their use, in many situations, becomes more cost-efficient than using them. Politically and ethically the symbolic use of weapons is also strongly preferable. Nuclear weapons are the most extreme expression of this trend. But cyber assets are different. Showing the power of cyber weapons is vastly more difficult than showing the power of conventional weapons, especially if the purpose is to administer a threat of force, not actually using force itself. Exploit code cannot be paraded on the battlefield in a commanding gesture, let alone displayed in large city squares on imposing military vehicles. In fact, publishing dangerous exploit code ready to be unleashed (say, for the sake of the argument, on the DoD's website) would immediately lead to patched defenses and thus invalidate the cyber weapon before its use. Using cyber weapons, for instance to fire a warning shot in the general direction of a potential target once for a show-of-force operation, comes with a separate set of problems. The next chapter will explore some of these limitations in more detail. The argument here is that displaying force in cyberspace is fraught with novel and unanticipated difficulties.

So far, three limitations of violence in cyberspace have been introduced: code-induced violence is physically, emotionally, and symbolically limited. These limitations were straightforward and highlighting them did not require significant conceptual groundwork. This is different for both the most significant *limitation* of cyber attacks[19] and their most significant *potential*. To bring both into relief, a more solid conceptual grounding in the political thought on violence is required. (Note to readers: this book caters to a diverse audience, those interested in conflict first and in computers only second, and to those interested primarily in new technologies and their impact on our lives. For readers from either group, political theory may not be the first reading choice. Yet especially those readers with a practical bent are encouraged to engage with the following pages. These conceptual considerations are not introduced here as a scholarly gimmick. Indeed theory shouldn't be left to scholars; theory needs to become *personal knowledge*, conceptual tools used to comprehend conflict, to prevail in it, or to prevent it. Not having such conceptual tools is like an architect lacking a drawing board, a carpenter without a metering rule, or, indeed, a soldier without a rifle.)

Political violence is always instrumental violence, violence administered (or threatened) in the service of a political purpose, and that purpose is always to affect relationships of trust. Violence can either be used to establish and to maintain trust, or it can be used to corrode and to undermine trust. Terrorism, for instance, is a means to undermine a society's trust in its government. Violence can be used to maintain or re-establish trust, for instance by identifying and arresting criminals (or terrorists), those who broke the social contract by using force against other citizens and their property. The political mechanic of violence has two starkly contrasting sides, a constructive and a destructive side, one designed to maintain trust, the other designed to undermine trust. The two are mutually exclusive, and will be considered in turn. Only then can the utility of cyber attacks be considered respectively.

A brief word on trust is necessary here. Trust is an essential resource in any society.[20] Perhaps because of this towering significance, trust and trustworthiness are highly contested concepts in political theory. Because trust is so important yet so abstract and contested, concisely defining the use of the term is crucial for the purposes of the present argument. Political thought distinguishes between two rather different kinds of trusting: trust should first be understood as an interpersonal relationship between two individuals.[21] Examples are the kind of trust relationships that exist between me and my brother, between you and your plumber, or between a customer and a taxi driver. Such relationships of trust are always directed towards an action: my brother may trust me to take care of his daughter while he's away; you trust your plumber to fix the bathroom boiler while you are at work; and a traveler trusts the cabbie to go the right way and not rob them. The second kind of trust refers to a collective attribute rather than to an individual's psychological state: the trust that individuals collectively place into institutions.[22] Such an institution can be a bank, a solicitor, an airline, the police, the army, the government, or more abstract entities like the banking system or the legal order more generally. Again, such relationships of institutional trust are related to an activity or service: customers trust their bank not to steal money from them, they trust airlines to maintain and operate planes properly, and citizens trust the police to protect them when necessary. At second glance, interpersonal trust and institutional trust are connected. You are likely to trust your plumber not because he's such a trustworthy person per se, but because you know that law enforcement in England or France or Germany is set up in a way that, if he betrays your trust, he will face legal punishment. Something similar applies to the taxi ride. Consequently, an astute traveler looking out for a taxi ride across Cairo just after the 2011 revolution, with law and order having partly collapsed, is likely to place far less trust into the orderly behavior of a random cab driver. This means that trustworthy and stable legal institutions only enable interpersonal trust between individuals who may represent those institutions or be bound by them.[23]

Focusing on trust significantly broadens the horizon of the analysis of political violence. At the same time it offers a more fine-grained perspective on the purpose of an attack, and this increased resolution is especially useful when looking at various kinds of cyber attacks. The goal of an attack—executed by code or not, violent or not—may be more limited than bringing down the government or challenging its legitimacy in a wholesale fashion. Not all political violence is revolutionary, not all activists are insurgents, and not all political attacks are violent. The goal of an attack may be as distinct as a specific policy of a specific government, a particular business practice of a particular corporation, or the reputation of an individual.

Violence, in the hands of the established order, is designed to maintain social trust. To appreciate the depth of this insight, consider three well-established maxims of political theory. First, violence is an *implicit* element of even the most modern legal order. Any established political order comes with a certain degree of violence built-in—consolidated states, after all, are states because they successfully maintain a monopoly over the legitimate use of force. Any legal order, to use the language of jurisprudence, is ultimately a coercive order.[24] One of the most inspiring writers on this subject is Alexander Passerin d'Entrèves, a twentieth-century political philosopher from the multi-lingual Aosta Valley in the Italian Alps. In his book, *The Notion of the State*, the political philosopher discusses the state and its use of force at length. "The State 'exists' in as far as a force exists which bears its name," he wrote, referring to the tacit nature of the potential threat of force that is the subtext and foundation of any rule of law. "The relations of the State with individuals as well as those between States are relations of force."[25] One of Hobbes's most famous quotes captures this tacit presence of force in the authority of the law, "Covenants, without the sword, are but words."[26]

This tacit violence, secondly, *becomes power*. And it is trust that turns violence into power. To be more precise: social trust, ultimately, relies on the functioning of the rule of law, and the rule of law in turn relies on the state effectively maintaining and defending a monopoly of force, internally as well as externally. This thought may appear complex at first glance, but it forms the foundation of the modern state. In fact this question is at the root of much of a vast body of political theory, a body of literature dedicated, in Passerin d'Entrèves's words, to the long and mysterious ascent that leads from force to authority, to asking what transforms "force into law, fear into respect, coercion into consent— necessity into liberty." It is obviously beyond the capacity of the present analysis to go into a great level of detail here. But a short recourse to a few of the most influential political thinkers will help make the case that trust is a critically important concept. Again Hobbes:

> The Office of the sovereign, be it a monarch or an assembly, consisteth in the end, for which he was trusted with the sovereign power, namely the procuration of the safety of the people.[27]

Collective trust in the institutions of the state is one of the features that turn violence into power. John Locke, a philosopher of almost equal standing to Hobbes in the history of Western political thought, captured this dynamic eloquently. For Locke, trust is an even more central concept:

> [P]olitical power is that power which every man having in the state of Nature has given up into the hands of the society, and therein to the governors whom the society hath set over itself, with this express or tacit trust, that it shall be employed for their good and the preservation of their property.[28]

Force, when it is used by the sovereign in order to enforce the law, ceases to be mere violence. By representing the legal order, force becomes institutionalized, "qualified" in Passerin d'Entrèves's phrase, "force, by the very fact of being qualified, ceases to be force" and is being transformed into power.[29]

Thirdly, political violence—whether in its raw form or in its tacit, qualified form as power—is *always instrumental.* "Violence can be sought only in the realm of means, not of ends," wrote Walter Benjamin, an influential German-Jewish philosopher and literary critic. His essay, *Critique of Violence,* published in the author's native German as *Kritik der Gewalt* in 1921, is a classic in the study of violence.[30] Benjamin also pointed to a fundamentally constitutional character of violence, its "lawmaking" character. "People give up all their violence for the sake of the state," Benjamin writes, in agreement with realist political theorists and positivist legal thought.[31] He then distinguishes between a "law-preserving function" of violence and a "lawmaking function" of political violence.[32]

While there is some consensus on a theory of war, and certainly on a theory of law, there is little consensus on a theory of violence—although both war and law employ force and ultimately violence. Perhaps not surprisingly, a significant amount of political thought on violence—like on war and law—comes from philosophers and political thinkers who were German, or at least German-speaking. The German word for violence is *Gewalt.* This is not surprising for two reasons: one, because the country's history was exceptionally violent, especially during the nineteenth and the first half of the twentieth century, when most landmark texts were written. Its authors include Karl Marx, Max Weber, Walter Benjamin, Hannah Arendt, and Carl Schmitt, all of whom wrote classics in sociology and political science. But it also includes authors like Carl von Clausewitz, who wrote one of the founding texts of the theory of war, *On War,* and Hans Kelsen, whose œuvre includes one of the founding texts of jurisprudence, *The Pure Theory of Law. Gewalt,* a word that does not translate directly into English, plays a key role in all of these texts. It is indeed a forceful concept. This leads to the other reason for the prevalence of German authors in this field: the German language "qualifies" violence from the start—or more precisely, it never disqualified *Gewalt,* it never distinguished between violence, force, and power. *Gewalt* can be used as in *Staatsgewalt,* the power of the state, or as in *Gewaltverbrechen,* violent crime. These basic concepts of classical political theory bring into relief the most important limitation as well as the most important potential of cyber attacks.

The utility of cyber attacks—be they violent or non-violent—to establish and maintain trust is crucially limited. First, violent cyber attacks, or the threat of violent cyber attacks, are unlikely to ever be an implicit part of a legal order. Neither espionage, nor sabotage or subversion, has the potential to maintain let alone establish a coercive order. Domestic surveillance may be used as a supplemental and highly controversial tool for that purpose, but not as the actual instrument of coercion. From this follows, secondly, that the notion of "cyberpower," properly defined, is so shaky and slippery as to be useless. The notion of *Cybergewalt*, in other words, doesn't make a lot of sense at present. Hence, thirdly, code-borne violence is hugely limited in its instrumentality: it has little to no trust-maintaining potential, and may only contribute to undermining trust. This limiting insight at the same time points to the most signifi-cant potential of cyber attacks: cyber attacks can achieve similar or better effects in a non-violent way.

Political violence is also a means of eroding trust. The perpetrators of political violence, especially in its most extreme form, terrorism, almost always clamor for publicity and for media attention, even if no group claims credit for an attack. The rationale of maximum public visibility is to get one crucial statement across to the maximum number of reci-pients: see, your government can't protect you, you can't trust the state to keep you safe. This logic of undermining a government's trustwor-thiness applies in two scenarios that otherwise have little in common. One is indiscriminate terrorist violence where random civilians are the victims, including vulnerable groups, such as the elderly, women, and children. All political violence, but especially the most brutal indiscrimi-nate kind, also sends a message that is likely to cross the militants' inte-rest: we don't discriminate, we're brutal, we don't respect the life of innocents. But in the heat of violent internal conflict, the utility of progressively undermining the population's trust in the government outweighs these reputational costs. The other scenario is regular, state-on-state war. When one country's army goes to war against another country's armed forces, one of the key objectives is to undermine the link between the population and its own government. That link is a form of institutional trust. Clausewitz famously described the population as one of the three elements of a "fascinating trinity" (the other elements being the government and the army). The population, the Prussian philoso-pher of war wrote, is the source of passion and the energy that is required to sustain a nation's war effort. Therefore, if the majority of the popula-tion loses faith in its government's and army's ability to prevail, then public opinion and morale will collapse. This dynamic does not just apply to democracies, but to all political systems, albeit in different ways. Modern armed forces, not unlike militant groups, are therefore seeking to maximize the public visibility of their superior firepower.[33] In both regular and irregular conflict, for generals and terrorists, one of the main goals is to convince opinion leaders in a country's wider population that their present regime will be unable to resurrect and maintain its monopoly of force—either externally or internally.

Cyber attacks can undermine an institution's trustworthiness in a non-violent way. Here the context matters greatly. Of course the use of political violence is not the only way to undermine trust in a government, an institution, a policy, a company, or somebody's competence. It is not even the most common method, nor is it the most efficient or most precise one. Violence is merely the most extreme form of political attack. In liberal democracies, such as the United States, most forms of non-violent political activism and protest are not just legal, but are also considered legitimate, especially in hindsight, for instance the civil rights movement in the United States. But even extreme forms of activism and political speech are protected by the American Constitution's First Amendment.[34] In less liberal political communities, certain forms of non-violent political activism will be illegal. The more illiberal a system, the more non-violent dissent will be outlawed (the chapter on subversion below will explore this problem in more detail).

Cyber attacks, both non-violent as well as violent ones, have a significant utility in undermining social trust in established institutions, be they governments, companies, or broader social norms. Cyber attacks are more precise than conventional political violence: they do not necessarily undermine the state's monopoly of force in a wholesale fashion. Instead they can be tailored to specific companies or public sector organizations and used to undermine their authority selectively. The logic of eroding trust by means of cyber attack is best illustrated with examples. Four examples will help extract several insights.

The first and most drastic is the DigiNotar case, a hacking attack on a computer security company. DigiNotar used to be a leading certificate authority based in the Netherlands, initially founded by a private lawyer in cooperation with the official body of Dutch civil law notaries. Certificate authorities issue digital certificates, and DigiNotar was founded to do so for the Dutch government as well as commercial customers. In cryptographic terms, the certificate authority is a so-called trusted third party, often abbreviated as TTP, and effectively acts as a provider of trust between two other parties. It does so by certifying the ownership of a public key by the named "subject" (the owner) of the certificate. A browser usually displays the presence of a certified website by a small green lock or other green symbol on the left side of the browser's address bar. All mainstream browsers were configured to trust DigiNotar's certificates automatically. Significantly, some of the Dutch government's most widely used electronic services relied on certificates issued by the compromised firm, for example the country's central agency for car registration, Rijksdienst voor het Wegverkeer, or DigiD, an identity management platform used by the Dutch Tax and Customs Administration to verify the identity of citizens online by using the country's national identification number, the *Burgerservicenummer*. Given the nature of DigiNotar's services as a certificate authority—trust was its main product—it was by definition highly vulnerable to cyber attack.

That attack happened on 10 July 2011.[35] The self-styled "Comodo Hacker" gained access to the firm's computer systems and, over the next ten days, issued more than 530 fraudulent certificates, including certificates pretending to be from Google, Skype, and Mozilla, but also from major Western intelligence agencies, such as the CIA, the Mossad, and the British MI6.[36] Nine days later, on 19 July, DigiNotar's staff had detected an intrusion into its certificate infrastructure, but the firm did not publicly disclose this information at the time. The company revoked all the fraudulent certificates it detected, about 230 in total, but that meant that it failed to revoke more than half of the fraudulent certificates.[37] At least one certificate was then used for so-called man-in-the-middle attacks against users of Gmail and other encrypted Google services. By intercepting the traffic between Google and the user, unknown attackers were able to steal passwords and everything else that these unsuspecting users typed or stored in their account. The Dutch security firm did not usually issue certificates for the Californian search giant. But the fact that Google had no business relationship with the issuer of the certificate did not make the attack any less effective—all mainstream browsers, from Firefox to Chrome to Internet Explorer, accepted DigiNotar's faked certificate as credible anyway. Only six weeks later, on Saturday, 27 August, one user in Iran noticed something was wrong. Alibo, as he chose to call himself, was running the latest version of Google's Chrome browser and noticed an unusual warning when he checked his emails on Gmail. Just two months earlier, in May 2011, Google added the "public key pinning" feature to its browser. This meant that Google essentially "hard-coded" fingerprints for its own web services into Chrome. Chrome then simply ignored contrary information from certificate authorities, and displayed a warning to users.[38] Alibo saw this warning and posted a question on a Google forum that Saturday, "Is this MITM to Gmail's SSL?" he asked in broken geek jargon, referring to a man-in-the-middle attack and a common encryption format, secure socket layer.[39]

The reaction came quickly. After all, this was the first time that the malicious use of a fake certificate on the Internet had come to light, as was pointed out by the Electronic Frontier Foundation, a group that protects civil liberties online.[40] By Monday, Internet Explorer, Firefox, and Chrome had been updated, and patched versions rejected all of DigiNotar's certificates and displayed a warning to the user. "Browser makers Google, Mozilla and Microsoft subsequently announced that they would permanently block all digital certificates issued by DigiNotar, suggesting a complete loss of trust in the integrity of its service," *Wired* magazine reported. The affair, and the Dutch certificate authority's handling of the breach, fatally undermined the trust that its users and customers had placed in the firm. The Dutch Ministry of the Interior even went so far as to announce that the government of the Netherlands was no longer able to guarantee that it was safe to use its own websites. On 20 September 2011, DigiNotar's owner, VASCO, announced that the company was bankrupt.

The hack was highly significant. It enabled a deluge of second-order attacks. When a certificate is used, the browser sends a request to a responding server at the certificate issuing company by using a special Internet protocol, the Online Certificate Status Protocol, or OCSP, to obtain a certificate's revocation status. The protocol reveals to the responder that a particular network host is using a particular certificate at a particular time. The first fake *.google.com certificate status request came on 27 July, seventeen days after the certificate had been issued. A week later, on 4 August, the numbers of requests to DigiNotar's OCSP responders "massively" surged, the official investigation found. The affected users, Google reported, were mostly in Iran.[41] The suspicion was that Iranian dissidents, many of whom trusted Google for secure communications, had been targeted in the attack.[42] Around 300,000 unique IPs requesting access to Google were identified, with more than 99 per cent coming from Iran. Those that did not come from Iran were mainly due to Iranian users hiding behind a proxy server abroad. This means that somebody in Iran was trying to spy on more than a quarter of a million users in a very short period of time.[43] The question of who that somebody was remains unanswered. The initial attack on DigiNotar may be the work of a single hacker. The infamous Comodo Hacker, named after an earlier attack on a company called Comodo, described himself as a 21-year-old student of software engineering in Tehran—and a pro-establishment patriot.[44] In an interview with *The New York Times* shortly after the notorious attack, he claimed to revere Ayatollah Ali Khamenei and despise Iran's dissident Green Movement. Comodo Hacker chose that particular certificate authority from a larger list of such companies because it was Dutch, he told the *Times*.[45] The allegedly angry student blamed the Dutch government for the murder of more than 8,000 Muslims in Srebrenica in 1995 during the Bosnian War:

> When Dutch government, exchanged 8000 Muslim for 30 Dutch soldiers and Animal Serbian soldiers killed 8000 Muslims in same day, Dutch government have to pay for it, nothing is changed, just 16 years has been passed. Dutch government's 13 million dollars which paid for DigiNotar will have to go *directly* into trash, it's what I can do from KMs [kilometers] away! It's enough for Dutch government for now, to understand that 1 Muslim soldier worth 10000 Dutch government.[46]

This justification is somewhat dubious. It is more likely that DigiNotar simply offered "low-hanging fruit," a term malware experts often use when referring to easy-to-pick and obvious targets. An audit immediately after the hack found that the compromised firm lacked even basic protection: it had weak passwords, lacked anti-virus shields, and even up-to-date security patches. What the industry calls "bad hygiene" enabled the consequential breach. As late as 30 August, F-Secure, a cutting-edge Finnish security firm, discovered several defacements to less often visited parts of DigiNotar's website, some of which were more than two years old and related to older hacks committed by other groups.[47] It is therefore likely that DigiNotar had a reputation for being an easy target among hackers. The question of whether or not the hacker acted on his own initiative is of secondary importance. The online vigilante openly admitted that he shared his information with the Iranian government. "My country should have control over Google, Skype, Yahoo, etc.," the alleged Comodo Hacker told *The New York Times* by email. "I'm breaking all encryption algorithms and giving power to my country to control all of them." It is highly likely that the spying surge after 4 August was the result of Iranian government agencies or their representatives, possibly ISPs, spying on unsuspecting citizens using Gmail, an email service popular among techy users for its high security standards.

The DigiNotar case offers a triple example of how cyber attacks can undermine trust: first, the trust in the Dutch certificate authority DigiNotar was fatally destroyed, leading straight to bankruptcy for the company. Secondly, because the Dutch government relied on the company's credibility, its own trustworthiness received a temporary hit, which the Ministry of the Interior tried to limit by being transparent about the crisis.

A second example also involves a joint public–private target set, the infamous cyber attacks against Estonia's government and some private sector companies in May 2007. The perpetrators, likely Russians with a political motivation, most certainly did not anticipate the massive response and high public visibility that their DDoS attacks received. Estonia's political leadership was taken aback by the attack and scrambled for an appropriate response, both practical and conceptual. "The attacks were aimed at the essential electronic infrastructure of the Republic of Estonia," said Jaak Aaviksoo, then Estonia's new minister of defense:

> All major commercial banks, telcos, media outlets, and name servers—the phone books of the Internet—felt the impact, and this affected the majority of the Estonian population. This was the first time that a botnet threatened the national security of an entire nation.[48]

One of the questions on Aaviksoo's mind at the time was if he should try to invoke Article 5 of the North Atlantic Treaty, which guarantees a collective response to an armed attack against any NATO country. Ultimately that was not an option as most NATO states did not see a cyber attack as an "armed attack," not even in the heat of the three-week crisis. "Not a single Nato defence minister would define a cyber-attack as a clear military action at present," Aarviksoo conceded, adding: "However, this matter needs to be resolved in the near future."[49] One Estonian defense official described the time leading up to the launch of the attacks as a "gathering of botnets like a gathering of armies."[50] Other senior ministers shared his concern. Estonia's foreign minister at the time of the attack was Urmas Paet. From the start, he pointed the finger at the Kremlin: "The European Union is under attack, because Russia is attacking Estonia," he wrote in a statement on 1 May 2007, and added: "The attacks are virtual, psychological, and real."[51] Ansip, the prime minister, was already quoted above: "What's the difference between a blockade of harbors or airports of sovereign states and the blockade of government institutions and newspaper web sites?"[52] Ene Ergma, the speaker of the Estonian parliament with a PhD from Russia's Institute of Space Research, preferred yet another analogy. She compared the attack to the explosion of a nuclear weapon and the resulting invisible radiation. "When I look at a nuclear explosion and the explosion that happened in our country in May," Ergma told *Wired* magazine, referring to the cyber attack, "I see the same thing. Like nuclear radiation, cyber warfare doesn't make you bleed, but it can destroy everything."[53] The panic was not confined to the small Baltic country. In the United States, hawkish commentators were alarmed at what they saw as a genuine, new, and highly dangerous threat. Ralph Peters, a retired Army intelligence officer and prolific hawkish commentator, published a red-hot op-ed in *Wired* two months after the Estonia attack. He accused the Department of Defense of underestimating a novel and possibly devastating new threat:

> [T]he Pentagon doesn't seem to fully grasp the dangerous potential of this new domain of warfare. If you follow defense-budget dollars, funding still goes overwhelmingly to cold war era legacy systems meant to defeat Soviet tank armies, not Russian e-brigades.[54]

The United States could face a devastating surprise attack, Peters held, an attack that could make Pearl Harbor look like "strictly a pup-tent affair," he wrote, borrowing an expression from Frank Zappa's song "Cheepnis."

In hindsight, these comparisons and concerns may appear overblown and out of sync with reality. But they should not be dismissed as hyperbole too easily. Aaviksoo's and Ansip's and Peters's concerns were genuine and honest—they are expressions of a successful erosion of trust in previous security arrangements. It is important to point out—especially against the background of all these martial analogies—that both the DigiNotar hack and the Estonian DDoS were non-violent. Yet they effectively undermined public trust in a company and in a country's ability to cope with a new problem. In the one case the erosion of trust was terminal (DigiNotar filed for bankruptcy); in the other case it was temporary: a few years after the attack Estonia had better defenses, better staff, and excellent skills and expertise on how to handle a national cyber security incident.

Therefore, thirdly, examining the only possibly violent cyber attack to have taken place in the wild—Stuxnet—is instructive.[55] Even this one cyber attack that created a certain amount physical destruction, albeit directed against technical equipment, had a strong psychological element. It was intended to undermine trust, the trust of scientists in their systems and in themselves, and the trust of a regime in its ability to succeed in its quest for nuclear weapons. When Stuxnet started successfully damaging the Iranian centrifuges, the Iranian operators did not know what was happening for more than two years. The operation started long before Barack Obama was sworn in as president in January 2009, possibly as early as November 2005. Independent security companies would discover the malicious code only in June 2010. The original intention was to cause physical damage to as many of the Iranian centrifuges as possible. But the American–Israeli attackers probably knew that the physical effect could be exploited to unleash a much more damaging psychological effect: "The intent was that the failures should make them feel they were stupid, which is what happened," an American participant in the attacks told *The New York Times*.[56] The rationale was that once a few machines failed, the Iranian engineers would shut down larger groups of machines, so-called "stands" that connected 164 centrifuges in a batch, because they distrusted their own technology and would suspect sabotage in all of them. In the International Atomic Energy Agency, a powerful UN watchdog organization based in Vienna, rumors circulated that the Iranians had lost so much trust in their own systems and instruments that the management in Natanz, a large nuclear site, had taken the extraordinary step of assigning engineers to sit in the plant and radio back what they saw to confirm the readings of the instruments.[57] Such confusion would be useful to the attackers: "They overreacted," one of the attackers revealed, "And that delayed them even more."[58] The Iranians working on the nuclear enrichment program began to assign blame internally, pointing fingers at each other, even firing people. Stuxnet, it turned out, was not a stand-alone attack against the self-confidence of Iranian engineers. It is important to note that the Stuxnet operation was probably designed to remain entirely clandestine.

The best trust-eroding effect would have been achieved if Iran's engineers and leaders had not realized that their work was being sabotaged at all. The most effective cyber attacks may be those that remain entirely secret.

A most curious follow-on cyber assault occurred on 25 July 2012, and provides an insightful fourth example of undermining trust. A rather unusual type of attack struck two of Iran's uranium enrichment plants: some computers shut down, while others played "Thunderstruck," an aggressive and energetic song by the Australian rock band AC/DC. An Iranian scientist based at the Atomic Energy Organization of Iran, AEOI in short, had taken the initiative and reached out to Mikko Hypponen, the prominent and highly respected head researcher of the Finland-based anti-virus company F-Secure. Hypponen confirmed that the emails came from within the AEOI:

> I am writing you to inform you that our nuclear program has once again been compromised and attacked by a new worm with exploits which have shut down our automation network at Natanz and another facility Fordo near Qom.[59]

F-Secure couldn't confirm any details mentioned in the email. The anonymous Iranian scientists apparently quoted from an internal email that the organization's "cyber experts" had sent to the teams of scientists. The email mentioned a common tool for finding vulnerabilities and developing exploit code, Metasploit, and that the mysterious attackers allegedly had access to the AEOI's virtual private network (VPN). The attack, the scientist volunteered, shut down "the automation network and Siemens hardware." He then revealed the most curious element that hundreds of media articles had seized on after Bloomberg first reported the news of the email published on F-Secure's blog:

> There was also some music playing randomly on several of the workstations during the middle of the night with the volume maxed out. I believe it was playing "Thunderstruck" by AC/DC.[60]

Some caution is in order. The only report from the episode comes from an Iranian scientist who volunteered this information to an anti-virus company. It is also unclear if the attack should be seen as the latest incident in a series of US-designed cyber attacks that may have started with Stuxnet. At first glance, literally blasting an attack in the face of the Iranian engineers stands in stark contrast to clandestine attacks like Stuxnet or Flame, which were sophisticated pieces of spying software—

but then, maybe the attackers didn't expect news of the AC/DC blast to leak out, embarrassing the Iranians publicly. So either way it was not a surprise when Fereydoun Abbasi, the head of the AEOI, disputed the attack a few days later: "Who seriously believes such a story? It is baseless and there has never been such a thing," Abbasi said in a statement to the Iranian ISNA news agency.[61] The story may well be a hoax. But it should not be dismissed out of hand. AC/DC, after all, seem to be a favorite soundtrack for American warriors in battle; during the war in neighboring Iraq in 2004, for example, the Marines blasted into Fallujah to the loud riffs of AC/DC's "Hells Bells."[62] It would be plausible to assume that the operation was part of a larger psychological campaign of attrition, designed to undermine the Iranian engineers' trust in their systems, their skills, and their entire project, in a blow-by-blow fashion. News consumers in Europe or the United States may not seriously believe such a story—but Abbasi's engineers, if it happened, would certainly wonder what else the mysterious attackers were able to do, after yet another entirely unpredicted attack hit their systems.

Violence administered through weaponized code, in sum, is limited in several ways: it is less physical, because it is always indirect. It is less emotional, because it is less personal and intimate. The symbolic uses of force through cyberspace are limited. And, as a result, code-triggered violence is less instrumental than more conventional uses of force. Yet, despite these limits, the psychological effects of cyber attacks, their utility in undermining trust, can still be highly effective.

This chapter opened by asking if the Israeli cyber attack on the Syrian air defense system in August 2007 was violent or not. Against the background of this analysis, the answer is clear: it was not violent. Only the combined airstrike on the soon-to-be-finished nuclear reactor was violent. But the cyber attack on its own achieved two effects that previously would have required a military strike: first, it neutralized the threat of the Syrian air defense batteries. This was a significant achievement that enabled a stealthier and possibly faster and more successful air incursion. But the second effect is possibly even more significant: the cyber attack helped undermine the Syrian regime's trust in its own capabilities and the belief that it could defend its most critical installations against future Israeli attacks. Bashar al-Assad's government subsequently decided not to restart Syria's enrichment program, so this second less tangible result may have had the more sustainable effect.

3

CYBER WEAPONS

In the days and hours leading up to the afternoon of 19 March 2011, air force planners in France, Britain, and several other NATO countries were frantically preparing an imminent bombing campaign against military targets in Libya. In Washington on that same March weekend an unusual discussion took place between the Department of Defense and the White House. Should America deploy its cyber arsenal against Libya's air defense system?[1] After the Pentagon's generals and geeks had briefed the president on the options, he ultimately decided that the time was not ripe for cyber weapons.

This behind-the-scenes episode is part of a much larger debate about offensive cyber weapons. In September 2011, William Lynn, the US Deputy Secretary of Defense, warned, "If a terrorist group does obtain destructive cyberweapons, it could strike with little hesitation."[2] In January 2012, the Department of Defense announced its plans to equip America's armed forces for "conducting a combined arms campaign across all domains—land, air, maritime, space, and cyberspace."[3] To counter a novel arms race, China and Russia, among others, have suggested discussing forms of "cyber arms control" to restrict new forms of military conflict in cyberspace.

But the debate and those trying to turn it into policy are getting ahead of themselves. Some fundamental questions on the use of force in cyberspace are still unanswered; worse, they are still unexplored: what are cyber "weapons" in the first place? How is weaponized code different from physical weapons? What are the differences between various cyber attack tools? And do the same dynamics and norms that govern the use of weapons on the conventional battlefield apply in cyberspace?

Cyber weapons span a wide spectrum. That spectrum, this chapter argues, reaches from *generic but low-potential tools* to *specific but high-potential weaponry*. A didactically useful comparison helps illustrate this polarity. Low-potential "cyber weapons" resemble paintball pistols: they may be mistaken for real weapons, they are easily and commercially available, used by many to "play," and getting hit is highly visible—but at closer inspection these "weapons" will lose some of their threatening character. High-potential cyber weapons could be compared with sophisticated fire-and-forget weapon systems such as modern anti-radar missiles: they require specific target intelligence that is programmed into the weapon system itself, notable investments for R&D, significant lead-time, and while they open up entirely new tactics they also create novel limitations. This distinction brings into relief a two-pronged hypothesis that stands in stark contrast to some of the debate's received wisdoms. Maximizing the destructive potential of a cyber weapon is likely to come with a double effect: it will significantly *increase* the resources, intelligence, and time required to build and to deploy it— and increasing a cyber weapon's potential is likely to *decrease* significantly the number of targets, the risk of collateral damage, and the coercive utility of cyber weapons.

The chapter's argument is presented in three steps. The chapter begins by outlining what cyber weapons are in conceptual terms. Then I suggest a way to class cyber attack tools by discussing the most important empirical cases on record. Thirdly the chapter explores why even some sophisticated and effective instruments of electronic attack *cannot* sensibly be called a cyber weapon. The chapter closes by pointing out how cyber weapons confront us with three problems. These three problems will largely define the future development and use of weaponized code.

Weapons are, simply put, instruments of harm. Since the dawn of time, humans have used weapons to hunt prey and each other. Weapons range from the nuclear warhead to the bare human body trained in martial arts, their utility ranging from destroying an entire city to protecting one single person. Yet practitioners as well as scholars often seem to take the meaning of the term "weapon" for granted. Remarkably, even the US *Department of Defense Dictionary of Military and Associated Terms*, an authoritative 550-page compendium that defines anything from *abort* to *Zulu time*, has no definition for *weapon*, let alone for cyber weapon.[4] For the purposes of this book, a weapon can be defined as *a tool that is used, or designed to be used, with the aim of threatening or causing physical, functional, or mental harm to structures, systems, or living things*. This general definition is an essential building block for developing a more precise understanding of cyber weapons.

The term cyber weapon is much broader than cyber war. Cyber war is a highly problematic, even a dangerous, concept. An act of war must be instrumental, political, and potentially lethal, whether in cyberspace or not.[5] No stand-alone cyber offense on record meets these criteria, so "cyber war" remains a metaphor for the time being. Not so in the case of cyber weapons. Weapons are not just used in war. Arms are used for a wide range of purposes: to threaten others, for self-defense, to steal, to protect, to blackmail, to police, to break into buildings, to enforce the law, to flee, to destroy things, and even to train, to hunt, and for sports and play. Weapons, of course, may also be used to make war, and some more complex weapons systems are exclusively developed for that purpose, for instance warships or anti-aircraft guns. But most weapons are neither designed for warfare nor used in wars. This is true also for cyber weapons. Therefore, while it is counterproductive and distracting to speak about *cyber war*, it can be productive and clarifying to speak about *cyber weapons*. Yet conceptual precision remains a problem— "There is currently no international consensus regarding the definition of a 'cyber weapon'," lamented the Pentagon in November 2011, elegantly distracting from the problem that there is no consensus inside the DoD either.[6] For the purposes of this book, a cyber weapon is seen as a subset of weapons more generally: as *computer code that is used, or designed to be used, with the aim of threatening or causing physical, functional, or mental harm to structures, systems, or living beings*.

A psychological dimension is a crucial element in the use of any weapon, but especially so in the case of a cyber weapon, in two ways: the first psychological dimension is *the offender's intention to threaten harm or cause harm to a target*. An instrument may be expressly designed as a weapon, like a rifle, or repurposed for use as a weapon, as in using a hammer to threaten or hit somebody.[7] Simple as well as complex products can be used both for peaceful purposes and as arms. In the case of sole-purpose weapon systems as well as in the case of repurposed items, a tool is actually used as a weapon when an actor *is intending to use it as such*; whether harm is successfully inflicted or not is of secondary concern. A rifle, for instance, may be used to threaten; it may malfunction; or the bullet may miss the target. But in all cases the arm has been used because an attacker was intending to use it as such in a given situation.

The same logic applies to cyber weapons. An illustration of this is a remarkable event that took place at the Sayano-Shushenskaya hydroelectric plant in Russia. Keith Alexander, a general at the head of America's National Security Agency as well as of US Cyber Command, used the incident in a speech to highlight the *potential* risks of cyber attacks.[8] With a height of 245 meters and a span of 1 kilometer, the Shushenskaya dam is the largest in Russia, holding back the mighty Yenisei River in Khakassia in south-central Siberia.[9] Shortly after midnight GMT on 17 August 2009, a 940-ton turbine, one of ten 640 megawatt turbines at the plant, was ripped out of its seat by a so-called water hammer, a sudden surge in water pressure, which then caused a transformer explosion. The turbine's unusually high vibrations had eventually worn down the bolts that kept its cover in place. Seventy-five people died in the accident, energy prices in Russia rose, and rebuilding the plant will cost $1.3bn. The ill-fated turbine 2 had been malfunctioning for some time and the plant's management was poor, but the key event that ultimately triggered the catastrophe seems to have been a fire at Bratsk power station, about 500 miles away. Because the energy supply from Bratsk dropped, the authorities remotely increased the burden on the Shushenskaya plant. The sudden spike overwhelmed turbine 2, which at twenty-nine years and ten months had nearly reached the end of its predicted lifecycle of thirty years.[10] The incident would have been a powerful example of the use of a cyber weapon if intruders had intentionally caused the plant's crash through a remote command (although to plan such an attack they would have required remarkably detailed advance knowledge of the plant's long-standing maintenance deficiencies). But such an intention was absent. Intention may be the only line separating the attack from an accident.

A second psychological dimension comes into play if a weapon is used as a threat, or if its use is announced or anticipated: *the target's perception of the weapon's potential to cause actual harm*. It is important to note that the attacker may use a weapon as a threat, which may achieve the objective without actually inflicting physical harm; or the attacker may use the weapon to cause harm instantly, without threatening to do so first. Furthermore, a victim's estimation of a weapon's potential to harm is different from a victim's estimation of an attacker's potential to harm. To illustrate all this, a fictional scenario is useful: suppose an armed robber enters a bank and threatens the clerk with a paintball pistol; both the clerk *and* the robber assume that the paintball pistol is real and loaded with live bullets; money is handed over; the robber flees. Has a weapon been used? Arguably the answer is yes. This fictitious scenario is less anomalous than it may seem; it merely affords starker contrasts. The history of domestic and international armed confrontations offers plenty of examples where the aggressor's power to cause injury was vastly overestimated, both by the defender as well as by the aggressor.[11] The paintball pistol scenario inevitably leads to a seeming paradox: suppose the bank clerk noticed that the robber's pistol could only shoot paintballs. Would it still be a weapon? The answer is no. The fake firearm would have lost its threatening character and have thus ceased to be a weapon, even if the robber still believed it to be real. The conclusion: a weapon's utility critically depends on the perception of the threatened party. In every real armed confrontation, both the victim and the aggressor will hold crude theories of an arm's capability to inflict harm and their own ability to withstand or absorb this harm. These subjective estimates will necessarily vary in their accuracy when put to a violent test. The actual weapon may be more or less powerful than assumed. In the case of cyber weapons, this discrepancy is especially large: publicly known cyber weapons have far less firepower than is commonly assumed.

Cyber weapons can be grouped along a spectrum: on the generic, low-potential end of the spectrum is malicious software—malware—that is able to influence a system merely from the outside but which is technically incapable of penetrating that system and creating direct harm—resembling the proverbial paintball pistol. On the specific, high-potential end of the spectrum is malware able to act as an intelligent agent—capable of penetrating even protected and physically isolated systems and *autonomously* influencing output processes in order to inflict direct harm, thus resembling the proverbial fire-and-forget smart-bomb. In between are malicious intrusions that include generic system penetrations incapable of identifying and influencing a targeted process, but also targeted and specific intrusions capable of creating functional and even physical damage.

On the low-potential end of the spectrum is the *paintball pistol effect*. Software used to generate traffic to overload a server, for instance, is not strictly speaking physically or functionally damaging a living being, a structure, or a system; it is only temporarily slowing down or shutting down a system, without damaging it directly and immediately. Denial of service (DoS) attacks are easy to mount and relatively easy to defend against, but they are also highly visible—and for those who find themselves for the first time at the receiving end of an attack that is distributed for better effect across multiple attacking machines the experience can be distressing, and it may well create mental harm and even second-order damage: a persistent high-volume Distributed Denial of Service (DDoS) attack which may bring down a bank's website for an extended period of time; defaced websites which may seriously damage an organization's reputation; and espionage or intellectual property theft that can put a company in a less advantageous market position. But these forms of damage are second-order effects, not *direct* damage inflicted by a cyber weapon.[12] At closer inspection, the "weapon" ceases to be a weapon.

One example is Estonia's reaction to a large DDoS attack in late April 2007, which was discussed earlier. The real-life effect of the Russian-coordinated online protests on business, government, and society was noticeable, but ultimately it remained relatively minor. Yet at the time, Estonian officials and citizens were genuinely scared by the attack.

At the opposite, high-potential end of the spectrum is the proverbial fire-and-forget missile. A useful military analogy is the high-speed anti-radar missile, usually shortened to HARM, initially produced by Texas Instruments, and which is one of the most widely deployed anti-radar weapons worldwide. The missile's critical innovation is a seeker that includes an intelligent, programmable video processor, designed to recognize characteristic pulse repetition frequencies of enemy radars. This means that the weapon can be launched into a certain area where it then searches for suitable target radars, discriminating between friendly and hostile radar by band. Once an emitter is identified as hostile, the missile software's decision logic will allow it to select the highest value target and home to impact. The missile can be seen as an intelligent agent. In computer science, intelligent agents are autonomous software entities that are able to assess the environment they find themselves in, and which are capable of reacting autonomously in order to achieve a predefined goal. Such a quality is necessary to attack the most highly prized targets.

The proverbial HARM missile contrasts with proverbial paintball pistols in at least five important ways. Firstly, its objective is not just interrupting traffic at a system's ports facing the public, but getting inside and penetrating a system. Secondly, its objective is not just penetrating any system that happens to be vulnerable ("low-hanging fruit" in geek jargon) but specific systems of particular interest. Thirdly, these systems are likely to be better protected. For any cyber attacker with the goal of causing physical damage, the prime targets are likely to be industrial processes, public utilities, and civilian as well as military telecommunication networks. The computerized control systems in such installations tend to be better secured than less critical systems. Fourthly, if the goal of a stand-alone cyber attack is physical damage, rather than just enabling a conventional strike, then the target itself has to come equipped with a built-in potential for physical harm. Weaponized code, quite simply, doesn't come with an explosive charge, as chapter two explored in detail. Potential physical damage will have to be created by the targeted system itself, by changing or stopping ongoing processes. Finally, an attack agent's objective is likely to be not just shutting down a penetrated system, but subtly influencing ongoing processes in order to achieve a specific malicious goal. Merely forcing the shutdown of one industrial control system may have the undesirable effect that a fail-safe mechanism or a backup system kicks in, or operators start looking for the bug. To work as an effective weapon, the attack software may have to influence an active process in a malicious way, and if the malicious activity extends over a certain period of time this should be done in a stealthy way as well. But stealthily or overtly influencing an active process is far more complicated than just hitting the virtual off-button. Three real-world examples of weaponized code illustrate this.

In a first, contested[13] example, the CIA may have rigged the control system of a Soviet pipeline in order to cause a major explosion. The powerful 1982 explosion was not caused by a system shutdown, but by deliberately creating overpressure in a gas pipeline by manipulating pressure-control valves in an active control process. A second example is the

Israeli cyber attack that was designed to blind the Syrian air defense system. The goal was not just to shut down the entire air-defense radar station—this would have been suspicious and could have triggered an alarm or investigation—but to trick the active system to display no approaching airplanes to its operators for a limited time. Thirdly, and most famously, the worm that sabotaged Iran's nuclear program didn't just shut down the centrifuges at Natanz. Before Stuxnet started sabotaging ongoing processes, it intercepted input values from sensors, for instance the state of a valve or operating temperatures, recorded these data, and then provided the legitimate controller code with prerecorded fake input signals, while the actual processes in the hidden background were manipulated.

The two latter examples need to be examined in some detail (the pipeline explosion was already covered in chapter one). The use of weaponized code may happen in conjunction with conventional military force or may be stand-alone. One of the most spectacular examples of a combined strike is Operation Orchard, Israel's bombing raid on a nuclear reactor site at Dayr ez-Zor in Northern Syria on 6 September 2007. It appears that the Israeli Air Force prepared for the main attack by taking out a single Syrian radar site at Tall al-Abuad close to the Turkish border. The Israeli attackers combined electronic warfare with precision strikes. The Syrian electrical grid was not affected. Syria's air-defense system, one of the most capable in the world, went blind and failed to detect an entire Israeli squadron of F-15I and F-16I warplanes entering Syrian airspace, raiding the site, and leaving again.[14] Before-and-after satellite pictures of the targeted site on the Euphrates were made public by the US government. They show that the nascent nuclear facility and its suspected reactor building, which were located about 145 kilometers from Iraq, had been reduced to rubble. The coding work for the operation was probably done by Unit 8200, the largest unit in the IDF and Israel's equivalent of the NSA.[15] The technicians may have used a so-called "kill switch" embedded in the air-defense system by a contractor to render it useless.[16] The details of the operation remain classified, and therefore unconfirmed. But one thing should be highlighted here: the network attack component of Operation Orchard was probably critical for the success of the Israeli raid, and although the cyber attack did not physically destroy anything in its own right, it should be seen as an integrated part of a larger military operation. While the cyber attack on its own—without the military component—would have constituted neither an act of war nor an armed attack, it was nevertheless an enabler for a successful military strike. That was different in another, even more spectacular recent incident.

Stuxnet is by far the most sophisticated known cyber attack to date. It was a highly directed attack against specific targets, Iran's nuclear enrichment program at Natanz. The worm was an act of cyber-enabled stand-alone sabotage that was not connected to a conventional military operation. The US government's internal codename for the operation was "Olympic Games." But that name became known only after independent researchers had discovered and analyzed the malware's code for many months, usually discussing the threat under the name Stuxnet. Stuxnet caught on, and therefore this book sticks to the unofficial but publicly better-established name (it is also more elegant). There is reason to believe that Olympic Games was the codename for a larger program that included more than just the Stuxnet attack. It was probably part of a bigger operation that included at least one other publicly known intrusion software. What is certain is that Stuxnet was a multi-year campaign. The program appears to span nearly seven years, from November 2005 to June 2012.[17] It is likely that the main attack had been executed between June 2009 and June 2010, when IT security companies first publicly mentioned the worm. Stuxnet recorded a timestamp and other system information. Therefore engineers were able, in months of hard work, to outline the worm's infection history as well as to reverse-engineer the threat and to understand its purpose. The following paragraphs are intended to provide a glimpse into Stuxnet's complexity and sophistication.

The sabotage software was specifically written for industrial control systems. These control systems are box-shaped stacks of hardware without keyboards or screens. A Programmable Logic Controller, or PLC, runs the control system. An industrial plant's operators have to program the controllers by temporarily hooking them up to a laptop, most likely a so-called Field PG, a special industrial notebook sold by Siemens. These Field PGs, unlike the control system and the controller itself, run Microsoft Windows and were most likely not connected to the Internet or even to an internal network.[18]

The first complication for the attackers was therefore a feasible infection strategy. Stuxnet had to be introduced into the target environment and spread there in order to reach its precise target, which was protected by an "air gap," in not being connected to the insecure Internet and even internal networks. As a result, it is highly likely that the infection occurred through the use of a removable drive, such as a USB stick. The attack vehicle was coded in a way that allowed its handlers to connect to the worm through a command-and-control server. But because the final target was not networked, "all the functionality required to sabotage a system was embedded directly in the Stuxnet executable," Symantec observed in the updated *W32.Stuxnet Dossier*, an authoritative analysis of the worm's code.[19] The worm's injection mechanism, at least in a later version, had an aggressive design. The number of collateral and inconsequential infections was large: by the end of 2010, the worm had infected approximately 100,000 hosts in dozens of countries, 60 per cent of which were in Iran. It is possible that the worm's aggressive infection mechanism was intended to maximize the likelihood that it would end up on a Field PG used to program the PLCs in Natanz. Human agents may also have helped infiltrate the target, willingly as well as unwillingly.[20]

A second complexity was Stuxnet's "sabotage strategy," in Symantec's words. The worm specifically targeted two models of Siemens logic controllers, 6ES7–315–2 and 6ES7–417, known as code 315 and code 417. The likely targets were the K-1000–60/3000–3 steam turbine in the Bushehr nuclear power plant for code 417 and the gas centrifuges in Natanz for code 315.[21] If the worm was able to connect to such controllers, it proceeded to check their configurations in order to identify the target; if Stuxnet didn't find the right configuration, it did nothing. But if it found what it was looking for, the worm started a sequence to inject one of three payloads. These payloads were coded to change the output frequencies of specific drivers that run motors. Stuxnet was thus set up to cause industrial processes to malfunction, physically damaging rotors, turbines, and centrifuges. The attack's goal was to damage the centrifuges slowly, thereby tricking the plant's operators. The rationale was probably that damaging hardware would delay Iran's enrichment program for a significant period of time, as the requisite components cannot easily be bought on open markets.

This method relates to a third complexity, the worm's stealthiness. Before Stuxnet started sabotaging processes, it intercepted input values from sensors, such as the state of a valve or operating temperatures, recorded these data, and then provided the legitimate controller code with prerecorded fake input signals, while the actual processes in the hidden background were manipulated. The objective was not just to fool operators in a control room, but to circumvent and compromise digital safety systems. Stuxnet also hid the modifications it made to the controller code. And even before launching a payload, Stuxnet operated stealthily: it had mechanisms to evade anti-virus software, it was able to hide copies of its files on removable drives and hide its own program blocks when an enumeration was enforced on a controller, and it erased itself from machines that did not lead to the target.

The resources and investment that went into Stuxnet could only be mustered by a "cyber superpower," argued Ralph Langner, a German control system security consultant who first extracted and decompiled the attack code.[22] The Obama administration later admitted that it co-developed the sabotage malware together with Israeli experts in computer attacks. The operation's first challenge was getting the intelligence right. Each single control system is a unique configuration, so the attackers needed superb information about the specific system's schematics. "They probably even knew the shoe size of the operators," said Langner. The designs of the target system were probably stolen or even exfiltrated from Iran by an earlier piece of espionage software related to the final Stuxnet, known as the beacon. Another aspect is the threat's design itself: the code was so specific that it is likely that the attackers had to set up a mirrored environment to refine their attack vehicle, which could have included a mock enrichment facility.[23] Stuxnet also had network infection routines; it was equipped with peer-to-peer update mechanisms that seem to have been capable of communicating even with infected equipment without an Internet connection, and injecting code into industrial control systems while hiding the code from the operator. Programming such a complex agent required time, resources, and an entire team of core developers as well as quality assurance and management.[24] The threat also combined expensive and hard-to-get items: four zero-day exploits (i.e. previously unknown and hence highly valuable vulnerabilities); two stolen digital certificates; a Windows rootkit (software granting hidden privileged access); and even the first-ever Programmable Logic Controller rootkit.[25] For the time being it remains unclear how successful the Stuxnet attack against Iran's nuclear program actually was. But it is clear that the operation has taken computer sabotage to an entirely new level.

Stuxnet is also noteworthy in several other respects. One observation concerns the high amount of intelligence programmed into the weapon itself. The attack vehicle was coded in a way that allowed its handlers in Washington to connect to the worm through a command-and-control server. But because the final target was not networked, "all the functionality required to sabotage a system was embedded directly in the Stuxnet executable," Symantec observed in the *W32.Stuxnet Dossier*.[26] Another observation is that it did not create collateral damage. Cyber weapons with aggressive infection strategies built in, a popular argument goes, are bound to create uncontrollable collateral damage.[27] The underlying image is that of a virus escaping from the lab to cause an unwanted pandemic. But this comparison is misleading. Stuxnet infected a very large number of hosts—but the worm did not create any damage on these computers. In the known cases of sophisticated cyber weapons, collateral infections did not mean inadvertent collateral damage.

Another illustrative demonstration of a cyber weapon took place a few years later "on range." On range means that it happened in a testing and training environment. In an experiment in 2006, the Idaho National Laboratory tested the so-called "Aurora" vulnerability that left some North American power stations exposed to electronic attack. The test target was a $1m, 27-ton industrial diesel generator. The goal: permanently disabling the enormous machine in a controlled environment through an Internet-based cyber attack from 100 miles away. In the test, the generator started shuddering, shaking, and smoke came puffing out, ultimately disabling the green machine. The lab reportedly came up with twenty-one lines of code that "caused the generator to blow up."[28] The malicious code caused the machine's circuit breakers to cycle on-and-off in rapid succession, causing permanent damage through vibration.[29]

The line between what is a cyber weapon and what is not a cyber weapon is subtle. But drawing this line is extraordinarily important. For one it has security consequences: if a tool has no potential to be used as a weapon and to do harm to one or many, it is simply less dangerous. Secondly, drawing this line has political consequences: an unarmed intrusion is politically less explosive than an armed one that has the potential to damage buildings and injure and kill people. Thirdly, the line has legal consequences: identifying something as a weapon means, at least in principle, that it may be outlawed and its development, possession, or use made punishable. It follows that the line between a weapon and non-weapon is conceptually significant: identifying something as *not a weapon* is an important first step towards properly understanding the problem at hand and to developing appropriate responses. The most common and probably the most costly form of cyber attack aims to spy. But even a highly sophisticated piece of malware that is developed and used for the sole purpose of covertly exfiltrating data from a network or machine is *not a weapon*. Consequently, the law of armed conflict does not deem espionage an armed attack. Three noteworthy cases that may be confused with cyber weapons help make the concept more precise.

The first example of what does *not* constitute a cyber weapon is the weaponization of gadgets, rather than code. Technically sophisticated operations are well known in the world of espionage, for instance tiny listening bugs or exploding pens and cigars. Such cases figure more prominently in fiction than in reality, but occasionally they do happen. One of the best-known James Bond-style examples is the assassination of Yahya Abd-al-Latif Ayyash, aka "the engineer." Ayyash, an important bomb-maker for Hamas and Islamic Jihad, built the improvised explosive devices used in numerous suicide bombings and terrorist attacks. He had been one of Israel's most-wanted enemies. On 5 January 1999, the Shin Bet, Israel's domestic intelligence service, assassinated him by placing 15 grams of RDX, an explosive nitroamine, into the cellphone of one of Ayyash's trusted friends. Israeli agents tricked that friend's uncle and his wife, who unknowingly helped place the deadly phone at the engineer's ear, assuming they would help the Israelis eavesdrop on Ayyash, not execute him.[30]

Lesser known is the fact that Hezbollah had pulled off a similar if less sophisticated stunt in the same year, penetrating one of the IDF's most secretive and technologically sophisticated entities, Unit 8200, which allegedly helped to build Stuxnet a decade later. In early 1999, a Hezbollah cellphone with a depleted battery was found in a raid in Southern Lebanon. A military intelligence officer turned over the device to the signal intelligence unit and it was brought to the headquarters of Unit 8200 close to Glilot junction north of Tel Aviv. When two officers tried to connect the device to an appropriate charger, it detonated, severely injuring both. One lost his hand.[31] Previously harmless devices may indeed be turned into deadly weapons by secretly (or overtly) adding explosives or other harmful functions. But such militant gadgetry belongs more to the category of improvised explosive devices, IEDs, than to that of weaponized code.

The second non-weapon discussed here is intellectually more interesting: the ILOVEYOU worm, perhaps the most costly generic intrusion to date. On 4 May 2000, a new malware rapidly spread by exploiting a generic scripting engine. A 24-year-old undergraduate student in the Philippines, Onel De Guzman, had programmed the worm. Originating in Manila, it spread across the globe in one day, infecting around 45 million Windows PCs. The worm spread by sending emails to entire address books, thus pretending to be a love letter from a known and trusted person. The "Love Bug," as the media called the work, was capable of overwriting audio and picture files, replacing them with malicious code. In Britain, 30 per cent of all email servers in private companies were brought down by the volume of requests. The estimated worldwide damage exceeded $10bn. Among the infected targets were governments and defense establishments. Britain's House of Commons saw its internal communication system immobilized. The virus infected four classified internal systems in the Pentagon, according to Kenneth Bacon, then the DoD spokesperson,[32] and it was also found on around a dozen CIA computers.[33] ILOVEYOU, it is very important to note, did not exfiltrate any data to external servers. The small software did not even have a command-and-control infrastructure, but was acting in a primitively autonomous way. Yet there are instances when such generic pieces of malware could lead to physical damage. This almost happened in early 2003 in Ohio.

A third example that may be mistaken for a cyber weapon is the so-called Slammer Worm. On 25 January 2003, this highly effective worm led to a so-far unique incident at the Davis-Besse nuclear power plant in Oak Harbor, Ohio, about 80 miles west of Cleveland. The plant operated a single light water reactor. Ten months earlier, in March 2002, the station had already suffered one of America's most serious nuclear safety incidents, this one entirely unrelated to a computer flaw. Maintenance workers had discovered that borated water which had leaked from a cracked rod had eaten a football-sized hole into the reactor head. As a result, the reactor was shut down for repair works that took two years. So Davis-Besse was offline when the Slammer worm hit. The Slammer worm entered the plant through an unnamed contractor, via a simple T1 telephone line that connected the contractor's computers to the business network of FirstEnergy, the utility company that operated the plant. This T1 line, according to a later investigation, bypassed the plant's firewall. Dale Wuokko of FirstEnergy explained the bypassed firewall to the Nuclear Regulatory Commission after the incident: "This is in essence a backdoor from the Internet to the Corporate internal network that was not monitored by Corporate personnel," Wuokko wrote, "some people in Corporate's Network Services department were aware of this T1 connection and some were not."

SQL Slammer, as the worm is known, started to spread like an Internet wildfire on the early morning of Saturday, 25 January 2003, at 05:30 Greenwich Mean Time. The worm exploited a buffer overflow flaw in a widely used Microsoft SQL server. The small piece of code generates random IP addresses and then copies itself to those addresses. If the program gets lucky, and one of these addresses leads to a host that happens to be running an unpatched version of Microsoft's SQL Server, then this machine becomes infected and begins randomly spraying the web with more worms. The vulnerability used by the worm had in fact been known for half a year, and Microsoft had made a security update available six months before Slammer went viral—and to Microsoft's credit even before the vulnerability became public. But not everybody had installed the patch, including many at Microsoft and, as it turned out, the operators at Davis-Besse. In fact the plant operators didn't even know there was a patch for the vulnerability.

A few things are noteworthy about Slammer. The worm itself was tiny; its code had a mere 376 bytes and fitted inside a single Internet packet (this means the worm's code was smaller than an empty email without any text and subject line). Additionally, the worm used a specific Internet protocol that allows a computer to send a message to another computer without requiring prior communications to set up special transmission channels, other than email or browser data. An attack consisted of a single packet sent to UDP port 1434. The worm was therefore able to broadcast scans without the need for a prior response from its potential victims. This meant that each infected host blasted out single yet effective "fire-and-forget" packets that contained the worm. An infected machine with a normal Internet connection speed of 100-Mbps could realistically produce 26,000 scans per second. As a result, Slammer was the fastest worm in the history of computing.[34] When Slammer's rapid spread slowed down Internet traffic globally that morning, many computers lost all legitimate traffic *yet they were still able to send and receive the worm* because it was so small and so versatile. Analysis estimated that the worm infected more than 75,000 hosts, spraying the Internet with scans from each of those. The resulting slowdown caused computer network outages, cancelled airline flights, failures in ATM machines, and even interference with elections.[35] Davis-Besse's corporate network was affected by that global flood of confused packets and slowed down as well. The plant's business network, it soon turned out, was connected to the plant's industrial control network, which is not supposed to be the case (such connections make it easier for the plant's operators to access real-time data, but ideally these connections should be read-only). At 16:00 local time, the operators of the power plant itself noticed that the network was slowing down. Fifty minutes later, the Safety Parameter Display Unit System crashed. This system is designed to monitor a plant's safety indicators, such as coolant systems, core temperatures, and external radiation sensors.[36] Twenty-three minutes later, at 17:13, the less critical Plant Process Computer also crashed. Both systems, it should be noted, had analogue backups in place which were not affected by the rummaging worm.[37] After six hours the plant's engineers had reinstated both systems.

Three things should be noted about the Davis-Besse incident. First, Slammer's nuclear attack was concerning, but it was a miss: even if Davis-Besse had *not* been "in a safely defueled condition," as the NRC's chairman said in response to a concerned letter from a congressman, the backup systems would likely have prevented a more serious incident.[38] Second, Slammer was the precise opposite of a targeted attack. The worm's impact on Davis-Besse was entirely random, and partly the result of bad systems administration at the nuclear plant. Predicting and planning with such a unique set of coincidences would be a significant challenge for an attacker focused on a specific target or set of targets. Yet, thirdly, it should also be noted that the incident, despite these limitations, demonstrates the real risk of a catastrophic cyber attack, even the risk of an accidental cyber attack of major proportions.

So far this chapter has discussed a number of different cyber attacks, including targeted ones like Stuxnet and generic ones like Slammer. These cases bring to light a conceptual tension between highly generic and untargeted malware and highly specific and targeted malware. At closer examination, this tension gives rise to three problems that are probably unique to the offensive use of cyber weapons.

The first problem will be called *the problem of generics* here. The generic–specific tension probably has no useful equivalent in the conventional use of force. On one end of the spectrum is the highly targeted use of force, for instance by a sniper: there's only one target, one bullet, either hit or miss. On the other end of the spectrum is a highly infectious and virulent biological agent: once released, the killer virus may spread beyond the initial attacker's and anybody else's control. These comparisons are highly imperfect. But they help illustrate the problem of generics for architects of cyber weapons. In most if not all circumstances, those seeking to deploy code for political purposes would want to avoid both extremes: developing a weapon that is so specific that it may only be able to hit one specific target system. Such a one-off attack is impossible to repeat, thus limiting its threatening utility. Alternatively they would want to avoid developing a weapon that is so generic that it could spin out of control once released, threatening to create uncontrollable collateral damage. Based on the available empirical evidence, the first scenario is significantly more realistic than the second one. Yet the risks need to be properly understood.

Computer security experts of various strains do not necessarily have a good understanding of the full potential of generic intrusions. This lack of such knowledge arises from the complexity and uniqueness of most computer installations, with a bespoke mix of hardware types, networks, and software systems, including in most cases software applications that can be many years old, so-called "legacy systems." Components of these large-scale systems may be updated and exchanged on a case-by-case basis, so that the larger system and its processes are continually changing. Different parts of such a complex system may be owned, designed, operated, maintained, and administered by different organizations. This dynamic applies to modern commercial, governmental, and military installations. In fact the problem is so large that it has become a subject for research in computer science. American and European governments and other funders have sponsored research on large-scale complex IT systems. Industrial control systems fall into this category. In SCADA networks and their programmable field devices, attack vectors and configurations tend to be rather specific, so that a widely generic attack seems to be unlikely.

Yet the problem of generics remains empirically unexplored. Dale Peterson, one of the world's leading SCADA security experts, has distinguished three types of attack against industrial control systems: *simple attacks* that merely crash systems or interrupt their correct operation, for instance by exploiting a widespread lack of authentification in those systems; *moderate attacks* where attackers have intelligence on a process and learn how to damage a physical component or subsystem; and *complex attacks*, where attackers modify a process in a stealthy manner over an extended period of time. Simple attacks require less process intelligence than a complex attack. To illustrate the point, Peterson offers an example of how rogue firmware could be loaded onto the Rockwell Automation ControlLogix PLC:

> An attacker could develop and load a set of actions into the rogue firmware which could reboot the PLC, report a percentage of wrong values, issue random write commands, etc. The rogue firmware would use a pseudo-random number generator to select both the type and timing of a series of attacks, producing intermittent PLC failures. The rogue firmware could also easily be spread with a worm, making for a variety of intermittent failures across all PLCs that would be very difficult to diagnose. This is a simple attack that would require little process knowledge.[39]

Simple generic attacks against a specific set of machine configurations are possible, at least in theory. The 64,000-dollar question is where the limits are of generic higher-order attacks. Stuxnet, the most sophisticated attack on record, was extremely specific and highly targeted—the worm's collateral infections on seemingly random machines did not have any real consequences for the owners and users of those computers. But it is unclear whether the next generation of high-powered cyber weapons will be equally specific in design, although this will probably be the case. The future will likely bring the answer, either through experience or through research.

The second unique and difficult problem of cyber weapons is *the problem of intentionality*. This problem arises in unexpected ways in the context of weaponized code. The core question is when a specific attack on a specific target ceases to be—or begins to be—an instrument of a specific attacker. To answer this question, the notion of a "cyber attack" requires clarification. Cyber attack includes both non-violent events, like denial of service attacks or indeed most malware incidents that illegitimately affect a computer or a network of computers, and those attacks that can cause a violent outcome. Even (and especially) relatively short and simple malware, like the SQL Slammer worm, may propagate itself and reach targets in a generic rather than in a specific fashion. Malware, simply put, may identify potential hosts through generic scans, propagate itself through built-in infection mechanisms, infiltrate a new host, execute itself on that host (or get executed by an unknowing user), and then repeat this cycle. Such malware qualifies, in the language of agent theory, as an autonomous agent.[40] Autonomous agents act autonomously. The actions of such autonomous agents can therefore be seen as a form of attack, not merely as an accident.

But the autonomy of software agents has a problematic flipside. The Slammer Worm could indeed be compared to a biological virus, or even to a wildfire: once the worm began to spread on its own, it was literally out of control in the sense that the software was not, like other more sophisticated malware, at the leash of a command-and-control server. Even its author could not stop or contain it any longer. It spread randomly. But weapons are *instruments* of harm. If the author of an attack is unable to control the instrument of harm, then the tool's instrumentality gets progressively lost. Instrumentality means shaping an opponent's or a victim's behavior—but if the attacker has lost the ability to react to an opponent's change of behavior by adapting the use of the instrument, for instance by increasing the level of pain or by ceasing an attack, then it would be irrational for the opponent to attempt such a moderating change of behavior. It is therefore necessary to distinguish between a violent cyber attack and a cyber weapon—to qualify as a cyber attack, an incident does not necessarily have to be intentional and instrumental. ILOVEYOU's effects on the CIA and SQL Slammer's effects on Davis-Besse may qualify as cyber attacks: but although such incidents could in theory have violent effects, they have lost their instrumental character. As a result, they cannot be regarded as cyber weapons.

Taken together, the problem of generics and the problem of intentionality lead to a third problem: *the problem of learning agents.* Stuxnet is noteworthy for something it didn't do. Stuxnet was an intelligent agent, able to make simple decisions based on environmental data, but it was not a *learning* intelligent agent. One confidential study by America's national laboratories estimated that the worm set Iran's nuclear program back by one to two years. "There were a lot of mistakes made the first time," one senior US official was quoted as saying in *The New York Times*. "This was a first generation product. Think of Edison's initial lightbulbs, or the Apple II."[41] A next generation product could be able to *learn*. Learning software agents and machine learning generally have been the focus of much research attention and funding in computer science of the past decade. The defense and intelligence establishments in the United States, Britain, and Israel have traditionally been well ahead of general trends in computer science research, for instance in cryptography or distributed systems. It would be surprising if an intelligent coded weapon capable of learning had not yet been developed. A learning weapon could be able to observe and evaluate the specifics of an isolated environment autonomously, analyze available courses of action, and then take action. By doing so, learning malicious software agents would redefine both the problem of generics and the problem of intentionality in entirely unprecedented ways.

4

SABOTAGE

The world economy depends on energy. The most essential source of energy is oil and the world's biggest source of oil is Saudi Arabia. The bulk of the country's oil production is in the hands of its national oil company, Saudi Aramco. On 15 August 2012, this pivotal corporate behemoth with a workforce of about 54,000 people became the target of a cyber attack that knocked out 30,000 of its workstations, about three-quarters of the total, turning their Microsoft Windows machines into bricks that could not even be booted up.[1]

The attack could have been disastrous. The company has the largest proven crude reserves and produces more units of oil than anybody else, pumping 9.1 million barrels a day during 2011, 15 per cent more than the year before. It manages more than 100 oil and gas fields, including Ghawar Field, the world's largest oil field. The firm's reach is global. Its operations include exploration, drilling, producing, refining, distributing, and marketing oil, gas, petroleum, and other petrochemicals. Saudi Aramco is headquartered in Dhahran, a small city in Saudi Arabia's Eastern Province; the Kingdom of Bahrain is a 20-mile driving distance to the west. This geographical location contains a clue to the alleged motivation of the cyber attack that hit on 15 August, just when many employees were about go on leave for Eid ul-Fitr, the Muslim holiday that marks the end of Ramadan. A targeted computer virus managed to penetrate the company's business network and, once inside, rapidly spread through shared network connections. The malware's main function was deleting data and making the infected Windows computer unbootable by overwriting the machine's Master Boot Record files. Saudi Aramco instantly put out word that its core operations, oil exploration, production, and refinement were not affected by the attack.

Wider operations could easily have been affected. The computer systems that control plant operations and oil production on the company's oil and gas fields may have been isolated from the Internet, as Saudi Aramco claimed they were. In any case, the virus used for the attack was incapable of harming any of the systems that commonly run on Industrial Control Systems. Such SCADA systems, which control valves and pumps in remote oil installations, are not well defended and present rather easy targets for skilled attackers. So a more sophisticated attack could well have affected oil production. But even without directly affecting field operations—one must assume that almost all other business operations took a hard hit for two chaotic weeks, including general administration, human resources, customer support, marketing, etc.— the hours after the attack were "critical" and a "humongous challenge," in the words of one company insider.[2] Some of the company's websites remained offline for more than a week. Emails bounced back. Engineers feared a follow-on attack. In the end Saudi Aramco managed to put its network back online only on Saturday, 31 August, more than ten days after the initial attack.

The Aramco attack raises a number of intriguing conceptual questions. The attack was not violent, and it did not have a direct potential to be violent, as the more detailed analysis below will show. Yet the attackers managed to damage Saudi Aramco's good reputation and significantly disrupted its day-to-day business operations. Was the attack an act of sabotage? What is sabotage in general terms, and what is its purpose? Does sabotage have to be violent or potentially violent? And what is the potential of sabotage in future cyber attacks?

This chapter argues that malicious software and cyber attacks are ideal instruments of sabotage. Cyber attacks which are designed to sabotage a system may be violent or, in the vast majority of cases, non-violent. The higher the technical development and the dependency of a society on technology (including public administration, the security sector, and industry), the higher the potential for both violent and non-violent sabotage, especially cyber-enabled sabotage. This has a seemingly contradictory effect: the higher the number of activists or adversaries that choose computer sabotage over physical sabotage, the easier it will be to distinguish between violence and non-violence, and the more likely it is that saboteurs choose non-violence over violence.

The argument is unveiled in four stages. The first section will define the nature of sabotage and highlight what remains unaffected by the rise of cyber attacks. The second section will illustrate the historically deep-rooted tension between disablement and destruction, and introduce what is affected by the rise of cyber attacks. The chapter then discusses the details of a few high-profile computer-sabotage examples. It closes with some considerations on the new vulnerabilities of industrial control systems that are likely to affect the future of sabotage.

Sabotage is the deliberate attempt to weaken or disable an economic or military system. All sabotage is predominantly *technical* in nature, but it may of course use social enablers. The means used in sabotage may not always lead to physical destruction and overt violence. Sabotage may be designed merely to disable machines or production processes temporarily, and explicitly to avoid damaging anything in a violent way. *If violence is used, things are the prime targets, not humans*, even if the ultimate objective may be to change the cost–benefit calculus of decision-makers. Sabotage tends to be tactical in nature and will only rarely have operational or even strategic effects. Sabotage on its own may not qualify as an armed attack because the saboteurs may deliberately avoid open violence, they may avoid political attribution, but they always aim to be instrumental. Both avoiding excessive violence and avoiding identification may serve the ultimate goal of sabotage: impairing a technical system. Sabotage is therefore an indirect form of attack. The ultimate target of all political violence is the mind of human decision-makers, as a previous chapter has argued. Political violence against humans is designed to affect decision-makers, for instance by grabbing as much public visibility as possible. Sabotage, in contrast to the use of guns and explosives (or cyber weapons), is not ultimately focused on the human body as a vehicle to the human mind—instead, sabotage, first and foremost, attempts to impair a technical or commercial system and to achieve a particular effect by means of damaging that system.

The core ideas of sabotage have barely changed in the past century, despite the advent of sabotage by cyber attack. Looking back seventy years will illustrate this continuity. In 1944, the United States Office of

Strategic Services, the CIA's precursor organization, issued the *Simple Sabotage Field Manual*, and stamped it secret. The document was declassified in 1963. It set out in great detail how to slow down the Axis powers. The manual was mainly written as a guide to help recruit insiders working for the Axis powers who did not support the Nazis and Fascists and wanted to sabotage the war effort from within. The manual was hands-on, and recommended how to use salt, nails, candles, and pebbles as weapons, or how to slow down an organization by making meetings and bureaucratic procedures as inefficient and faulty as possible. But the manual also contained a short paragraph on the idea itself, which may help clarify the notion of sabotage held by the US intelligence community:

> Sabotage varies from highly technical *coup de main* acts that require detailed planning and the use of specially trained operatives, to innumerable simple acts which the ordinary individual citizen-saboteur can perform. … Simple sabotage does not require specially prepared tools or equipment; it is executed by an ordinary citizen who may or may not act individually and without the necessity for active connection with an organized group; and it is carried out in such a way as to involve a minimum danger of injury, detection, and reprisal.[3]

All four of the main features contained in the manual and this key paragraph still hold true in the context of twenty-first-century cyber attacks: online sabotage, firstly, still ranges from highly technical, planned, and skill-intensive operations on the one end of the spectrum to manifold simple acts that citizen-saboteurs can perform. Computer sabotage, secondly, may be executed by organized groups and even agencies representing states, or such attacks may be designed and executed by single individuals. Software attacks with the goal of sabotaging a system, thirdly, are still mostly carried out in ways that involve minimum danger of detection, attribution, and reprisal. And finally it is still uniquely skilled insiders who are the potentially most devastating enablers of sabotage, either acting on their own or as representatives of outside adversaries. These four dimensions of continuity raise the question of how sabotage has changed in the digital age.

A brief look at the concept's origins greatly helps to understand some of today's novel features. The word sabotage has a controversial history. Its origins date back to the heyday of industrialization in the nineteenth century, when workers rebelled against dire conditions in mechanized factories. Émile Pouget, a French anarchist active at the turn of the twentieth century, promoted sabotage in pamphlets and other publications. A *sabot* is a simple shoe, hollowed out from a single block of soft wood, traditionally worn by Breton peasants, and today one of the main tourist souvenirs in the Netherlands. The symbol of the wooden shoe goes back to the urban myth of French workmen throwing their wooden shoes into finely tuned moving machinery parts to clog them up. That metaphorical use of "sabotage," Pouget wrote in 1910, had already been around in street slang for decades. "Comme à coups de sabots," as if hit with wooden shoes, stood for working intentionally clumsily, slowly, without thought and skill, thus slowing down or halting the process of production.[4] The expression soon became more widespread and its metaphorical origins were forgotten, especially in cultures that didn't know the sabot. An equivalent in American English is "monkeywrenching," which refers to the comparable practice of throwing a heavy adjustable wrench into the gears of industrial machinery to damage it and keep strike-breakers from continuing work. Elizabeth Gurly Flynn, a leading organizer for the Industrial Workers of the World, a large union also known as the Wobblies, defined sabotage as "the withdrawal of efficiency:"

> Sabotage means either to slacken up and interfere with the quantity, or to botch in your skill and interfere with the quality of capitalist production or to give poor service ... And these three forms of sabotage—to affect the quality, the quantity and the service are aimed at affecting the profit of the employer. Sabotage is a means of striking at the employer's profit for the purpose of forcing him into granting certain conditions, even as working-men strike for the same purpose of coercing him. It is simply another form of coercion.[5]

Some labor activists and syndicalists explicitly understood sabotage as a way to inflict physical damage against the oppressive machinery that made their work miserable or threatened the unskilled worker's livelihood altogether by making manual labor obsolete. Pouget quotes from an article published in 1900, a few weeks ahead of an important workers' congress in Paris. In it, the *Bulletin de la bourse du travail de Montpellier* gives recommendations for sabotage:

> If you are a mechanic, it's very easy for you with two pence worth of ordinary powder, or even just sand, to stop your machine, to bring about a loss of time and a costly repair for your employer. If you are a joiner or

a cabinet maker, what is more easy than to spoil a piece of furniture without the employer knowing it and making him lose customers?[6]

The pamphlet achieved some modest fame for its clever advice on how workers could cause accidents and damage without attribution: shop-assistants may drop fabrics onto dirty ground, garment workers may ignore faults in textiles; engineers may deliberately neglect oiling the moving parts of the machines they were supposed to maintain. Sabotage was historically understood as a coercive tactic directed against property, not against people. Even when it was directed merely against machines, the question of whether restive workers should try to destroy machinery or merely disable it for a limited period of time was controversial given that the use of violence, even if only directed at machines, was a matter of some dispute among syndicalists at the time. Delaying production was one thing; destroying property was something else, something that could have dire consequences, legally as well as politically. In America, political opponents had accused the Industrial Workers of the World, popularly known as the "Wobblies," of relying mainly on crude violence to achieve their goals. Some labor organizers therefore considered it necessary to distinguish between violence on the one hand and sabotage on the other. Arturo Giovannitti, a prominent Italian-American union leader and poet, argued for the latter in the foreword to the 1913 English translation of Pouget's book *Sabotage*. Sabotage, Giovannitti wrote, was:

> Any skilful operation on the machinery of production intended not to destroy or render it defective, but only to disable it temporarily and to put it out of running condition in order to make impossible the work of scabs and thus to secure the complete and real stoppage of work during a strike.[7]

Sabotage is this and nothing but this, he added, using the language of political activism rather than the language of scholarship, "It has nothing to do with violence, neither to life nor to property."[8]

Such subtle differences made sense in theory. In practice it was often difficult to distinguish between permanent destruction and temporary disablement—for several reasons, two of which will serve to highlight the novelties of sabotage by cyber attack. The first is the difference between hardware and software. If temporarily interrupting a process required damaging hardware, then the line between violence and sabotage is hard to draw. This is illustrated by an example from the early twentieth century, when telecommunication installations became a target of sabotage. Sabotage had to target hardware, pretty simply, because software did not exist yet. During French postal and railway strikes in 1909 and 1910, for instance, saboteurs cut signal wires and tore down telegraph posts. Cutting a telegraph wire may have been intended as temporary disablement, yet it also effectively destroyed property. Distinguishing between violence and non-violence was also difficult for a second reason: the dynamics of group confrontations. Again the worker confrontations around the time of the First World War are an instructive example: many union activists knew that situations where striking workers squared off with the capitalist forces of the state could turn violent. Vincent Saint John, a miner, a Wobbly, and one of America's most influential labor leaders, made this point explicit: "I don't mean to say that we advocate violence; but we won't tell our members to allow themselves to be shot down and beaten up like cattle. Violence as a general rule is forced upon us."[9] Such concern was not necessarily unjustified. Strikes and worker demonstrations could easily intensify into violent riots. A graphic example was the Grabow Riot of 7 July 1912, a violent confrontation between unionized Louisiana sawmill workers and the Galloway Lumber Company, which left four men dead and around fifty wounded. Pre-Internet-age sabotage, in short, easily escalated into violence against machines and, in groups, against people.

Both of these difficulties largely disappear in an age of computer attack. Distinguishing violent from non-violent attacks becomes easier. Violence is more easily contained and avoided: by default, software attacks maliciously affect software and business processes—but damaging hardware and mechanical industrial processes through software attack has become far more difficult. The remit of non-violent cyber attack, as a consequence, has widened: a well-crafted cyber attack that destroys or damages data, although without interfering with physical industrial processes, remains non-violent. The Shamoon attack against Saudi Aramco of August 2012 is an ideal example. Neither hardware nor humans were physically harmed. Yet, by allegedly wiping the hard disks of 30,000 computers, the attack created vastly more delay and monetary damage for Saudi Aramco than a minor act of sabotage against machinery in one of Aramco's plants. That may have been easier to fix and conceal. The oil giant reportedly hired six specialized computer security firms to help the forensic investigation and the post-attack cleanup. Liam Murchu was involved in Symantec's research into the attack. "We don't normally see threats that are so destructive," Murchu told Reuters, "It's probably been 10 years since we saw something so destructive."[10] Non-violent cyber attacks, in short, may be more efficient, more damaging, and more instrumental than violent attacks, whether executed through cyberspace or not.

Online attacks also made it easier, or possible in the first place, to isolate sabotage from volatile group dynamics. Online sabotage, if it relies on group participation at all, is highly unlikely to escalate into real bloodshed and street violence—activists and perpetrators of code-borne sabotage, after all, may not even be physically present on a street or anywhere else. Both of these dynamics are novel. And both will be illustrated by a more detailed examination of recent cases that witnessed serious acts of sabotage administered through cyber attack.

A more granular and technical examination of the Shamoon attack is instructive. The initially mysterious outage in the then cyber-attack-ridden Middle East occurred in the otherwise calm summer month of August in 2012. This time the attack became known as "Shamoon," again because the anti-virus researchers who analyzed the software chose this name. That name, curiously, was taken from a folder name in one of the malware's strings,

C:\Shamoon\ArabianGulf\wiper\release\wiper.pdb

Shamoon simply means "Simon" in Arabic. One initial and, as it turned out, wrong suspicion was that it could be related to the Sami Shamoon College of Engineering, Israel's largest and most well-reputed engineering school. The malware came in the form of a small 900-kilobyte file that included encrypted elements. It had three functional components: a dropper, to install additional modules; a wiper, responsible for deleting files; and a reporter, to relay details back to the software's handlers. After the small file was introduced into a target network, most likely as an email attachment, it would spread via shared network connections to other machines on the same network. The software's payload was designed to destroy data. It overwrote the segment of a hard drive responsible for rebooting the system as well as partition tables and most files with random data, including a small segment of an image that allegedly shows a burning American flag.[11] As a result of the software's destructive capabilities, the US government's computer emergency response team pointed out that "an organization infected with the malware could experience operational impacts including loss of intellectual property and disruption of critical systems." The US agency in charge of responding to computer emergencies also pointed out that the software's destructive potential remained limited: "no evidence exists that Shamoon specifically targets industrial control systems components or U.S. government agencies."[12] There is equally no evidence that the software succeeded in disrupting critical systems—and this is the case despite its initial success.

A previously unknown entity, the "Cutting Sword of Justice," claimed credit for the attack against Saudi Aramco by pasting a poorly crafted message on Pastebin, a platform used by hackers to dump raided data in simple text form. First the attackers made clear what their intention was, aligning themselves with anti-oppression rebels in the countries affected by the Arab Spring:

> We, behalf of an anti-oppression hacker group that have been fed up of crimes and atrocities taking place in various countries around the world, especially in the neighboring countries such as Syria, Bahrain, Yemen, Lebanon, Egypt and …, and also of dual approach of the world community to these nations, want to hit the main supporters of these disasters by this action.

> One of the main supporters of this disasters [sic] is Al-Saud corrupt regime that sponsors such oppressive measures by using Muslims oil resources. Al-Saud is a partner in committing these crimes. It's [sic] hands are infected with the blood of innocent children and people.

With their motivation and their target set out, the Cutting Sword of Justice announced some initial action:

> In the first step, an action was performed against Aramco company, as the largest financial source for Al-Saud regime. In this step, we penetrated a system of Aramco company by using the hacked systems in several countries and then sended [sic] a malicious virus to destroy thirty thousand computers networked in this company. The destruction operations began on Wednesday, Aug 15, 2012 at 11:08 AM (Local time in Saudi Arabia) and will be completed within a few hours.[13]

This anonymous claim was most likely genuine. Symantec only learned about the new malware after this message had been posted. The security firm confirmed that the timing of 11:08 a.m. was hard-wired into Shamoon, as announced on Pastebin. Two days later the hackers followed up with a separate post, publishing thousands of IP addresses which, they claimed, belonged to the infected computers.[14] Saudi

Aramco did not respond to those claims, but Symantec assumed that the addresses did indeed belong to the Saudi oil producer.[15] Aramco later confirmed that the number of infected computers was 30,000, as claimed by the Cutting Sword of Justice. The attacks remained targeted, with probably less than fifty separate infections worldwide, most of them inconsequential. RasGas of Qatar, also one of the world's largest exporters of natural gas, was the second victim and was more seriously affected.

Shamoon was focused on the energy sector; it was designed to destroy data, and it even contained a reference to "wiper" in the above-quoted string. So was Shamoon in fact that mysterious Wiper? After all, like Saudi Arabia, the Iranian regime was highly unpopular with anti-government activists and rebels across the Arab world. The answer, however, is most likely "no." Kaspersky Lab, which did the most detailed research into Wiper, pointed out that the deletion routine is different and that the hacker group's attack against Saudi Aramco used different filenames for its drivers. Perhaps most notably, the politico-hackers made some programming errors, including a crude one. They wanted Shamoon to start thrashing Saudi files on 15 August 2012, 08:08 UTC—but their date-checking routine contained a logical flaw: the software's date-testing query would return the order to attack even when it should not, in any year after 2012 provided the month and time was before 15 August. February 2013, for instance, would therefore qualify as being before 15 August 2012. To the developers at Kaspersky Lab, this mistake was additional proof that Shamoon was a copy-cat attack by far less sophisticated hacktivists, and not a follow-on attack by the highly professional developers that had written Wiper or even Stuxnet; "experienced programmers would hardly be expected to mess up a date comparison routine," wrote Dmitry Tarakanov, one of Kaspersky's analysts.[16] It remains unclear precisely how Shamoon's authors managed to breach Saudi Aramco's networks.

Another case of Middle Eastern cyber sabotage is equally instructive. At the end of April 2012, a new and rather mysterious piece of malware appeared. Alireza Nikzad, a spokesman for the Iranian oil ministry, confirmed that an attack on data systems had taken place. Probably as a precaution, Iran took its main Persian Gulf oil terminals off the Internet. But Nikzad stressed that the attackers had failed to damage or destroy data:

This cyber attack has not damaged the main data of the oil ministry and the National Iranian Oil Company (NIOC) since the general servers are separate from the main servers, even their cables are not linked to each other and are not linked to internet service ... We have a backup from all our main or secondary data, and there is no problem in this regard.[17]

The malware posed an unusual problem to its victims and those trying to understand the new threat: the software was designed to delete not only files on the attacked computer networks, but also itself and all traces of the attack. Consequently, no samples of the malware had been available for analysis. For months, leading anti-virus companies were unable to find Wiper, prompting some outside observers to question the veracity of news reports about yet another Iran-bashing cyber attack. But Kaspersky Lab, the Russian software security firm that seems to be especially popular in countries that harbor suspicions against private American security companies, established some facts. The Russian firm was able to obtain "dozens" of hard drive images from computer systems that had been attacked by Wiper, presumably from some of its Iranian customers, either directly or with help from Russian state intelligence. A hard drive image is an exact copy of an entire hard drive at a given moment. Kaspersky Lab was able to confirm that the attack indeed took place in the last ten days of April 2012.[18] The designers of the attack had two priorities: the first was destroying data as efficiently as possible. Deleting the full contents of a large storage device, such as a hard drive several hundred gigabytes in size, can take a long time, up to several hours, depending on the capacity of the processor and other technical characteristics. So the attackers decided to craft a wiping algorithm that prioritized speed.

The attackers' second priority was stealth. Wiper's creators, Kaspersky Lab pointed out, "were extremely careful to destroy absolutely every single piece of data which could be used to trace the incidents." Yet in some cases traces did remain. Some of the attacked systems were able to recover a copy of the Windows registry hives, parts of a computer's underlying master database that are saved in separate files on the hard disk. On some of the systems analyzed by Kaspersky Lab, Wiper deleted all .PNF files in a specific Windows folder where important system files are stored (the INF folder). It deleted those files with a higher priority than other files on the system. The researchers suspected that Wiper kept its own main body in that folder as an encrypted .PNF file. Other sophisticated cyber attacks, notably Stuxnet and Duqu, also stored most of their primary files in PNF, something that is uncommon for malware. The rationale, the Russian experts reasoned, was that Wiper would wipe itself and all its malware components first, and only then proceed to delete other targeted files, including the system files that would ultimately crash the system. If Wiper had started deleting system files randomly, the chances would be significant that it would "forget" to delete itself on some machines before the operating system crashed, thus conserving all non-deleted files on the hard drive, leaving forensic traces of the malware itself behind. But this particular malware was so expertly written that no data survived in each instance where it was activated. Although Kaspersky Lab has seen traces of infections, the malware itself remains unknown, as is the software's targeting priority. Who the attacker was, and how many victims got hit, remains a matter of speculation.

Both Shamoon and Wiper had one critical limitation. They targeted large energy companies, companies that move vast quantities of oil and gas. Yet production and logistics remained unaffected by the attacks. The business network was hit, but not the industrial control network that made sure the crucial combustible fossil fuel was still pumped out of the ground and into pipelines and tankers. In December 2012, Saudi Aramco's forensic investigation into Shamoon brought to light the fact that the attackers had tried for a full month to disrupt the industrial control systems that manage the company's oil production, "The main target in this attack was to stop the flow of oil and gas to local and international markets," said Abdullah al-Saadan, the firm's vice-president for corporate planning.[19] The attack on the SCADA network was unsuccessful. More serious sabotage has to overcome this limitation.

Successful attacks on industrial control systems that cause physical damage are very rare, but real. Sabotage, which dates back to industrial confrontations in the late nineteenth century, is again going industrial in the digitized twenty-first century: today's most formidable targets are industrial control systems, also known as systems in charge of Supervisory Control and Data Acquisition. Such systems are used in power plants, the electrical grid, refineries, pipelines, water and wastewater plants, trains, underground transportation, traffic lights, heat and lighting in office buildings and hospitals, elevators, and many other physical processes. An alternative abbreviation that is sometimes used is DCS, which stands for Distributed Control Systems. DCS tend to be used to control processes in smaller geographical areas, such as factory floors, whereas SCADA systems can span entire regions, for instance in the case of pipelines or transportation grids. Both are subsets of Industrial Control Systems, or ICS. Attacking an industrial control system is the most probable way for a computer attack to create physical damage and indirectly injure or kill people.

Although "Supervisory control and data acquisition" sounds complicated, the earliest control networks were actually made up of a simple monitoring device, say a meter with a switch, and remote sensors and actuators: if the temperature in a factory tank a mile away dropped below 100 degrees, for instance, the operator would remotely switch on the boiler. As industrial production became more complex, so did the computerized control networks. Yet most industrial control systems have basic design features in common, be they oil refineries, electrical power stations, steel plants, chemical factories, or water utilities. To understand the potential of sabotage against SCADA systems, some of these basics are important.

The first part, at least from the point of view of the operator, is the so-called *human–machine interface*, often abbreviated as HMI. The community of engineers specialized in SCADA systems commonly use shorthand, and their analysis is hard to penetrate without knowing at least some of the jargon. Plant operators or maintenance personnel would mostly control the system through that interface. In modern systems the HMI is in effect a large screen showing a mimic of a plant or large apparatus, with small images perhaps showing pipes and joints and tanks, equipped with bright lights and small meters that would allow the operator to get readings on critical values, such as pressures and speeds. If a certain parameter requires action, a light may start blinking red or a meter may indicate a potential problem. A second component is the *supervisory computer system*. This is the system's brain. The supervisory computer is able to gather data and respond by sending commands back to field devices to control the process. Field devices may be on the plant floor, or actually and quite literally in the field, such as a pipeline network that spans large distances outdoors. In simpler systems, so-called Programmable Logic Controllers (PLCs) can replace a more complex supervisory computer system. Control systems and PLCs are so-called "master devices." The third set of components are Remote Terminal (or Telemetry) Units, known as RTUs in the industry jargon.

These are "slave devices" which carry out orders from their masters. These devices would sit close to motors or valves that need to be controlled. RTUs act in both directions; they transmit sensor data to the control system and transmit orders from the supervisory system to remote motors and valves.

All SCADA systems require a communication infrastructure. This communication infrastructure can be complex and costly, especially for systems that are geographically spread out over a wider area. Distances can be significant in the case of pipeline networks, water grids, and large chemical plants. Some industrial plants have to withstand extreme temperatures generated in the production process, electro-magnetic radiation, or rugged environmental conditions. The requirements for the communication hardware are not only rough but also diverse, because the industrial applications are so diverse. The companies that produce components for SCADA networks have therefore developed approximately 200 proprietary protocols, often individually. For a long time, this diverse and somewhat chaotic situation made it difficult for attackers to penetrate and understand a particular control network. A SCADA network is often connected to a company's business network through special gateways. Enabling data-links between the business network and automated production processes enables increased efficiency, better supply management, and other benefits. Such gateways provide an interface between IP-based networks, such as a company's business network or the open Internet, and the simpler, fieldbus protocol-based SCADA network that controls field devices.[20] Sometimes, especially in large networks like electricity grids, there may be unexpected links to the outside world such as phone connections or open channels for radio communication. SCADA networks are often old legacy systems, and as a result of complexity and staff turnover no single person may be able to understand the full reaches of the network. A large but ultimately unknown number of SCADA systems are connected to the Internet, also possibly without their operators' awareness.[21]

Three trends are making SCADA systems potentially more vulnerable. The first trend is standardization in communication protocols. Increasing efficiency at minimum costs also creates pressures for the operators of control systems. In a dynamic that is comparable to open-source software, open protocol standards create significant gains in efficiency. But they also make the systems more vulnerable overall. "The open standards make it very easy for attackers to gain in-depth knowledge about the working of these SCADA networks," one research paper pointed out in 2006.[22] One possibility, for instance, is that an attacker, once the network is penetrated, could observe and "sniff" communications on a network. Once malicious actors have learned more about the data and control commands, they could utilize their new knowledge to tamper with the operation. In some ways this is precisely what Stuxnet did.

The second trend that is making industrial control systems more vulnerable to outside attack is an increase in connectivity. Technically, SCADA communication systems used to be organized as point-to-multipoint "serial" communications over various channels, for example phone lines or private radio systems. But increasingly the communication within a SCADA system relies on Internet Protocols. This means that terminal servers are increasingly set up to convert serial asynchronous data (i.e. bit- or byte-oriented data) into IP or "frame relay packets" for transmission in upgraded systems. This change brings many benefits. Maintenance of devices becomes easier when these devices are easy to connect to, both from a company's business network, which connects air-conditioned office space in headquarters with noisy factory floors, and from the wider Internet, which is often the bridge to contractors and complex supply chains. This trend is amplified by the push for smart grids, which can save money by automatically moving peak production to times of cheap energy prices. Telvent is a leading industrial automation company, valued at $2bn, and a subsidiary of the giant Schneider Electric, a French international firm that employs 130,000 people worldwide. One of Telvent's main smart grid products, OASyS, is specifically designed to bridge the gap between an energy firm's enterprise network and its activities in the field that are run by older legacy systems. In the fall of 2012, Telvent reported that attackers had installed malicious software and stolen project files related to Oasys.[23] The intruders were likely to have been members of the possibly Shanghai-based "Comment Group," a large-scale cyber espionage operation allegedly linked to the Third Department of the People's Liberation Army of China.[24]

A third trend is more visibility. Search technology has made many things far easier to find, and this includes previously hard to get manuals from PLC manufacturers which may occasionally even contain hard-coded login credentials. But the biggest change in visibility is probably due to one private programmer. In 2009, the then 26-year-old John

Matherley started operating a search engine for all sorts of devices connected to the Internet. Shodanhq.com boasts of listing: "Webcams. Routers. Power Plants. iPhones. Wind Turbines. Refrigerators. VoIP Phones."[25] The platform has been dubbed the Google for hackers. Its search functionality offers to find computers based on software, geography, operating system, IP address, and other variables. Shodan's crawlers scan the Internet for the ports usually associated with mainstream protocols such as HTTP, FTP, SSH, and Telnet. On 28 October 2010, the US Department of Homeland Security warned that the resources to identify control systems openly connected to the Internet have been greatly reduced. The ICS-CERT alert pointed out that there was an "increased risk" posed by Shodan's growing database.[26] In June of the following year, Éireann Leverett, a computer science student at Cambridge University, finished his MPhil dissertation. Using Shodan, Leverett had found and mapped 10,358 Internet-facing industrial control systems, although it remained unclear how many of them were in working condition. Yet, remarkably, only 17 per cent of all systems, Leverett found, required a login authentification. When Leverett presented his findings at the S4 conference, a special event for control system specialists, many were surprised and even shocked. Some vendors started using Shodan to notify customers whose systems they would find online. One attendee who worked for Schweitzer, a PLC manufacturer, admitted the ignorance of some operators: "At least one customer told us 'We didn't even know it was attached'," he told *Wired* magazine.[27]

Yet the picture would not be complete without acknowledging the counter-trends. SCADA systems are not only becoming more vulnerable, but are also subject to several trends that make them less vulnerable. The question of security becomes a question of balance. And it may only be possible to answer that question in a case-by-case analysis. For the following three reasons industrial control systems may be getting safer, not more vulnerable. These reasons may also help explain why the world, by the end of 2012, had still not witnessed a destructive cyber attack that actually injured or killed human beings.

The first reason is closely related to more visibility: improved oversight and red-teaming. A red team, an expression common in national defense as well as in computer security, refers to a group of mock adversaries with the task of trying to test and expose an organization's or a plan's flaws and weaknesses. On 12 December 2011, for instance, a

29-year-old independent European researcher, Rubén Santamarta, blogged[28] about his discovery of a flaw in the firmware of one of Schneider's programmable logic controllers, more precisely the so-called NOE 771 module. The module contained at least fourteen hard-coded passwords, some of which were apparently published in support manuals. Before Santamarta published the vulnerabilities, he had informed the US government's computer emergency response team in charge of control systems. ICS-CERT promptly reacted. On the same day, Homeland Security published an alert pointing to the new vulnerability, and coordinated with Schneider Electric "to develop mitigations."[29] Santamarta's hack effectively resulted in considerable pressure on Schneider to fix the problem. A better-known white-hat PLC hacker is Dillon Beresford. White-hat is jargon for ethical hackers whose goal is to improve security, as opposed to black-hats who seek to exploit security flaws. Beresford, a researcher with little previous experience in control systems, uncovered critical vulnerabilities in the Siemens Simatic S7 programmable logic controllers, a widely used product.[30] The security analyst at NSS Labs gained recognition among control system experts when Siemens and the US Department of Homeland Security requested that he cancel his presentation on newly discovered Siemens S7 vulnerabilities scheduled at a hacker conference in Dallas in May 2011, TakeDownCon.[31] A number of harmless but high-profile SCADA breaches in the past years have also contributed to a sense of alarm in the control system community. A third example is Justin Clarke's exposures of vulnerabilities in RuggedCom's products, which were also highlighted by an ICS-CERT alert.[32] The pressure on the vendors kept mounting.

The second reason, partly a result of the first, is slowly improving vendor security. There are dozens of companies that produce Programmable Logic Controllers, but the worldwide market is dominated by only a few companies, with Siemens covering more than 30 per cent, Rockwell Automation just over 20 per cent, Mitsubishi at about 14 per cent, and Schneider Electric just under 10 per cent. Specific applications tend to be in the hands of specific vendors. Refineries, for instance, use mostly Honeywell, Emerson, and Yokogawa products.[33] Some of these manufacturers have a highly problematic track record in fixing flaws. Various critics had been pointing out for years, for instance, that Siemens had failed to remove critical vulnerabilities in its Simatic Step 7 and Simatic PCS 7 software. A bug in the software enabled attackers to inject a malicious dynamic-link library, a .dll file, into an unprotected Step 7 project folder. Stuxnet exploited this type of flaw to destroy the centrifuges in Natanz. Among the most prominent critics were Ralph Langner, a German engineer and early Stuxnet detective,[34] as well as Dale Peterson's team at Digital Bond, a leading consultancy on industrial control systems.[35] Digital Bond runs an active blog and one of the industry's most highly reputed conferences, the yearly S4 conference in Miami Beach. Peterson is feared by many in the control system industry for publishing far too many unpleasant details on systems that are insecure by design. But, he says, "we publish probably only about 10 per cent of what we find."[36] After years of pressure, Siemens and other PLC vendors seem to have started responding and improving the security of their products, albeit still far too slowly.

The final reason is continued, and possibly increasing, obscurity. Despite open protocols, more connectivity, and better documentation through a new search engine focused on hidden Internet-facing devices, the obscurity of systems remains a huge hurdle for successful outside attacks (but not for inside attackers). Merely gaining access to a system and even sniffing it out may not be enough to prepare a sophisticated attack, especially in highly complex industrial production processes. "You don't have the human machine interface so you don't really know what the PLC is plugged into," explained Reid Wightman, a well-known expert on industrial control systems. "I really don't know if the [device] is a release valve, an input valve, or a lightbulb." Superb intelligence is needed for success, and possibly even test-flying the attack agent in an experimental setup that resembles the original target as closely as possible. Something like this is hard to design, as Stuxnet demonstrated. As production systems become more complex, and often more bespoke, their obscurity may increase rather than decrease.

The most effective saboteur has always been the insider—a feature that remains as true in the twenty-first century as it did in the 1910s. If anything, computer sabotage has empowered the outsider vis-à-vis the inside threat, although the most violent acts of computer sabotage remain inside jobs. The reason is simple. The best-placed person to damage a machine is the engineer who built it or maintains it, the manager who designed and runs a production process, or the IT administrator who adapted or installed a software solution. It therefore comes as no surprise that sabotage manuals tend to be written largely for insiders, and this insight seems to apply to French anarchists as well as to American spies: in 1900, the bulletin of Montpellier's *Bourse de Travail* was meant to be applied on the job, by the very factory workers best placed to monkeywrench the appliances of their despised capitalist bosses. In 1944, the OSS's *Simple Sabotage Field Manual* also hoped to assist privy personnel in devising methods that would cause dithering, delay, distress, and destruction, from telegraph operators to railway engineers. In the context of cyber attacks, the insider threat is especially pertinent for complex SCADA systems. Engineers and administrators who work for a power plant or utility company know the systems best. They have the high degree of process knowledge that is required to mount an effective attack against bespoke legacy systems. If there is a risk of somebody secretly installing "logic bombs" that could be timed or activated from afar, it is the insider that poses the greatest risk.

The saboteurs' long-standing emphasis on inside knowledge has a problematic flipside, both for those trying to sabotage and for those trying to defend against sabotage: the most effective acts of industrial incapacitation require supreme access, supreme skill, and supreme intelligence regarding the target. As systems become more complex and arcane, the knowledge required to fiddle with them also becomes more complex and arcane. The result is a tenuous security advantage for the defender. Security engineers in computer science even have a technical term for this double-edged sword, "security-by-obscurity." "There is no security-by-obscurity" is a popular pejorative phrase among computer scientists. It goes back to Auguste Kerckhoffs, a nineteenth-century Parisian cryptographer and linguist. A core assumption broadly held in cryptography, known as Kerckhoffs's Principle, is widely considered incompatible with the idea of securing a system by obscuring knowledge about how to attack it.[37] Kerckoffs's idea holds that a cryptosystem must be secure even if that system's design—except the encryption key—is public knowledge. It is therefore no surprise that the notion of security-by-obscurity is looked down upon by leading cryptographers. Yet the relationship between security and obscurity is more complicated outside the narrow remit of cryptographers.[38] For engineers in charge of industrial control systems, security-by-obscurity is a fact of life, even if they don't like the idea in theory.[39]

Yet the debate about the pros and cons of security-by-obscurity misses one central point: the insider. Claude Shannon, an American pioneer in information theory, famously reformulated Kerckhoffs's Principle as "The enemy knows the system." For Shannon this statement was a theoretical assumption that may be true in exceptional cases, rather than being a factual statement. The situation is different for the saboteur who is already on his target's payroll. The insider actually knows the system. And the insider may be that enemy. The most successful sabotage operations by computer attack, including Stuxnet and Shamoon, allegedly relied on some form of inside support. Precisely what that inside support looked like remains unclear in both cases. Yet in other cases it is better documented. Three examples will illustrate this.

In early 2000, *Time* magazine reported two years after the fact that the Russian energy giant Gazprom had suffered a serious breach as a result of an insider. A disgruntled employee, Russian officials allegedly told *Time*, helped "a group of hackers" penetrate the company's business network and "seize" Gazprom's computers for several hours. The intruders could allegedly control even the SCADA systems that monitor and regulate the gas flow through the company's vast network of pipelines. Executives in the politically well-connected firm were reportedly furious when the information was made public. Fearing embarrassment, Gazprom denied reports of the incident in the Russian press. "Heads rolled in the Interior Ministry after the newspaper report came out," *Time* quoted another senior official. "We were very close to a major natural disaster."[40] A small natural disaster happened as a result of a successful breach a few years later.

The second example occurred in March and April 2000 in the Shire of Maroochy, on Queensland's Sunshine Cost in Australia. The Maroochy incident is one of the most damaging breaches of a SCADA system to have ever taken place. After forty-six repeated wireless intrusions into a large wastewater plant over a period of three months, a lone attacker succeeded in spilling more than a million liters of raw sewage into local parks, rivers, and even the grounds of a Hyatt Regency hotel. The author of the attack was 49-year-old Vitek Boden. His motive was revenge; the Maroochy Shire Council had rejected his job application.[41] At the time Boden was an employee of the company that had installed the Maroochy plant's SCADA system. The Australian plant's system covered a wide geographical area and radio signals were used to communicate with remote field devices, which start pumps or close valves. And Boden had the software to control the management system on his laptop and the knowledge to operate the radio transmitting equipment. This allowed him to take control of 150 sewage pumping stations. The attack resulted in hundreds of thousands of liters of raw sewage being pumped into public waterways. The Maroochy Shire Council's clean-up work took one week and cost $13,000, plus an additional $176,000 to update the plant's security. "Vitek Boden's actions were premeditated and systematic, causing significant harm to an area enjoyed by young families and other members of the public," said Janelle Bryant at the time, the investigations manager at the Queensland Environmental Protection Agency. "Marine life died, the creek water turned black and the stench was unbearable for residents."[42] Boden was eventually jailed for two years.[43]

Another, lesser-known ICS insider attack happened in early 2009 in a Texas hospital, the W.B. Carrell Memorial Clinic in Dallas. The incident did not cause any harm, but resulted in a severe criminal conviction. A night guard at the hospital, Jesse William McGraw, had managed to hack Carrell's Heating, Ventilation and Air Conditioning (HVAC) system as well as a nurse's computer that contained confidential patient information. McGraw then posted online screenshots of the compromised HVAC system and even brazenly published a YouTube video that showed him installing malware on the hospital's computers that made the machines slaves for a botnet that the twenty-five-year-old operated. McGraw used the moniker "GhostExodus" and proclaimed himself the leader of the hacking group "Electronik Tribulation Army," which he envisioned as a rival of Anonymous. In the early hours of 13 February 2009, the night guard-turned-hacker physically accessed the control system facility for the clinic's ventilation system without authorization, inserted a removable storage device, and ran a program that allowed him to emulate a CD/DVD drive. McGraw could have caused significant harm: "The HVAC system intrusion presented a health and safety risk to patients who could be adversely affected by the cooling if it were turned off during Texas summer weather conditions," the FBI's Dallas office argued, although summer was still a few months off.[44] But hospital staff had reportedly experienced problems with the air conditioning and ventilation system, wondering why the alarm did not go off as programmed. McGraw's screenshots revealed that the alarm notification in the hospital's surgery center had indeed been set to "inactive."[45] In March 2011, two years after his offense, McGraw was sentenced to 110 months in federal prison.[46]

A further, most curious insider incident occurred on 17 November 2011. Joe Weiss, a security consultant working in the control systems industry, published a blog post, "Water System Hack—The System Is Broken." Weiss alleged that an intruder from Russia had hacked into an American water utility, stole customer usernames and passwords, and created physical damage by switching the system on-and-off until the water pump was burned out. Minor glitches were observed for two to three months, Weiss wrote, which were then identified as a malicious cyber attack.[47] Weiss's information seems to have been based on a leaked report by the Illinois Statewide Terrorism and Intelligence Center, which was based on raw and unconfirmed data.[48] *The Washington Post* covered the story and identified the alleged attack as the first foreign SCADA attack against a target in the United States, the Curran-Gardner Townships Public Water District in Springfield, Illinois. "This is a big deal," Weiss was quoted in the paper, "It was tracked to Russia. It has been in the system for at least two to three months. It has caused damage."[49] The article did not ask why anybody in Russia would attack a single random water plant in the Midwestern United States. The FBI and the Department of Homeland Security started investigating the incident in Springfield and quickly cautioned against premature conclusions. One week later the facts were established. A contractor working on the Illinois water plant was traveling in Russia on personal business at the time and remotely accessed the plant's computer systems. The information was not entirely wrong: the plant had a history of malfunction, a pump failed, and somebody from an IP address in Russia accessed the system. Yet the incident and the misunderstanding illustrate several things: it shows how malicious intention and activity would turn an accident into an attack—but in the case of the contractor logging into the Springfield water plant from Russia that malicious intent was absent. The incident also shows how urban legends about successful SCADA attacks are created. The problem of false ICS attacks is so common that the British Columbia Institute of Technology's Industrial Security Incident Database used to have a separate category for "Hoax/Urban Legend."[50]

But it turned out to be premature and dangerous to dismiss the risk of a devastating attack against critical infrastructure and utility companies, as one hacker demonstrated in the aftermath of the Springfield water hack story. One reader of the British IT news site The Register was so incensed by the statement of a government official that he decided to take action. "My eyes were drawn, nary, pulled, to a particular quote," the angry hacker wrote in a Pastebin post a day later. One US Department of Homeland Security official had commented that, "At this time there is no credible corroborated data that indicates a risk to critical infrastructure entities or a threat to public safety."[51] This statement was highly controversial, even naïve, especially as it came from an official. "This was stupid. You know. Insanely stupid. I dislike, immensely, how the DHS tend to downplay how absolutely *fucked* the state of national infrastructure is."[52] So he decided to prove the government wrong by showing how bad the situation actually is. Using the handle pr0f, the angry reader proceeded to penetrate into the human–machine interface software of a SCADA system used by a water plant in South Houston, which serves 16,000 Texans with water. With the help of the public Shodan search engine that looks for fingerprints of SCADA systems online, pr0f allegedly found that the plant in South Houston was running the Siemens Simatic HMI software, connected to the Internet, and protected by a simple three-character password. The twenty-two-year-old unemployed hacker then made five screenshots of the human–machine interface and posted links to the files on Pastebin. The break-in took barely ten minutes. Pr0f did not do any damage and did not expose any details that could make it easy for malicious hackers to do damage, expressing his dislike of vandalism. The still unknown intruder allegedly favors hoodie sweatshirts and lives in his parents' home somewhere overseas.[53] The city of South Houston upgraded its water plant to the Siemens system long before 11 September 2001, before the debate about industrial control systems as targets had caught on. "Nobody gave it a second thought," Mayor Joe Soto told *The Washington Post*. "When it was put in, we didn't have terrorists." Soto knew that pr0f had chosen his target more or less randomly. "We're probably not the only one who is wide open," the mayor said later, "He caught everyone with our pants down."[54]

A comparable incident occurred over February and March 2012. One or multiple users from unauthorized IP addresses accessed the ICS network of an unidentified New Jersey air conditioning company, according to a memo published by the FBI.[55] The intruders used a backdoor to access the company's Tridium Niagara system, enabling them to control the system remotely. It is not known if the intruders actually changed the system settings or caused any damage. But they could have caused damage. The Niagara AX framework is installed on over 300,000 systems worldwide in applications such as energy management, building automation, telecommunications, including heating, fire detection, and surveillance systems for the Pentagon, the FBI, and America's Internal Revenue Service.[56] In the case of the New Jersey AC company, the intruder was able to access a "Graphical User Interface, which provided a floor plan layout of the office, with control fields and feedback for each office and shop area," the FBI reported. "All areas of the office were clearly labeled with employee names or area names." The incident could be traced back to two messages on Pastebin from January 2012.[57] A user with the Twitter handle @ntisec, for "anti-security," had posted a list of IP addresses, one of which led to the unidentified company. @ntisec identified himself as an "anarcho-syndicalist" who sympathized with Anonymous. He found the vulnerability through Google and Shodan by searching for ":|slot:/," he reported. @ntisec seemed surprised by the ease with which he could get to various meter readings and control panels online:

> Don't even need an exploit to get in here. Don't even have to be a hacker. No passwords what so ever.

> So how is the state of your other #SCADA systems like your electrical grid? Or traffic management?

> What about chemical industry? Or can hackers switch some stuff that sends trains to another fail?[58]

Yet the anarcho-syndicalist seemingly didn't want to live up to his declared ideology, explicitly warning fellow amateur hackers not to do anything illegal, or, as it were, anarchical:

> Be careful and don't cause rampant anarchy. They might trace you and I have warned you not to alter control states. Just have a look around to see [for] yourself how these systems affect our everyday life.[59]

The unidentified intruders apparently did exactly that: using @ntisec's public backdoor URL to gain administrator-level access to the company's industrial control systems—no firewall to breach, no password required, as the FBI noted. It is unclear if the hackers also took @ntisec's advice and didn't alter the system's control states. Either way, it seems that no harm was caused.

These incidents—Maroochy, Springfield, Houston, Carrell—are a far cry from "cyber war." None harmed any human beings, and none had a tangible political goal. Yet they are among the most serious control system intrusions on record. But it would be shortsighted to dismiss the threat of serious computer attacks: the future of computer sabotage seems to be bright and the phenomenon seems to be on the rise. In 2012, the number of malicious programs that were able to "withdraw efficiency" from companies and governments multiplied quickly. Stuxnet set a new standard for what is possible. Shodan, the search engine, has removed some obscurity by exposing a vast number of Internet-facing control systems, although the details of the various installations certainly remain obscure, thus limiting what an attacker could accomplish, but by no means preventing a successful attack. A physically harmful attack on an industrial control system is a highly likely future scenario. "Eventually, somebody will get access to a major system and people will be hurt," pr0f, the hacker who penetrated the Houston water plant, told *The Washington Post*. "It's just a matter of time." But it is important to keep these risks in perspective. Almost all acts of computer-sabotage to date have been non-violent, harming neither machines nor human beings (Stuxnet, which harmed an unknown number of machines in Iran's Natanz nuclear enrichment plant, seems to be the only known exception). Such non-violent acts of sabotage seem to be on the rise—the Saudi Aramco incident discussed in the opening paragraph of this chapter is an ideal example, not least because the attack's ICS component failed—and they clearly have the capability to undermine the trust and the confidence that consumers and citizens place in companies and governments, and in the products and services that they offer. They can also undermine the trust the executives place in their organization. Increased digitization and automation offer more and more opportunities for attackers to withdraw efficiency without actual physical destruction. In that sense sabotage in the age of computer attack is becoming less violent, not more violent.

5

ESPIONAGE

The second offensive activity that is neither crime nor war is espionage. Cyber espionage is an attempt to penetrate an adversarial computer network or system for the purpose of extracting sensitive or protected information. Two major distinctions dominate the organization as well as the study of intelligence. Intelligence agencies may either restrict themselves to collecting and analyzing information, while remaining largely passive observers—or spy agencies may also engage in operations, almost always covert operations, with the intention of concealing the entire operation (clandestine operations) or at least the identity of the sponsor. The second distinction concerns the nature of intelligence collection: it can be either *social* or *technical* in nature. That division of labor is old. In the intelligence community it is reflected in the distinction between human intelligence, HUMINT, and signals intelligence, SIGINT. Sensitive information transmitted by telecommunication is often encrypted. Espionage that takes advantage of SIGINT therefore requires the use of specialists in decryption and cryptanalysis. The field of signals intelligence is wide: it includes intercepting civilian and military radio signals, satellite links, telephone traffic, mobile phone conversations, and of course intercepting communication between computers through various data protocols, such as email and voice-over-internet-protocol. Gaining illicit access into computer networks is therefore only one, albeit a fast-growing, part of signals intelligence. Some conceptual clarity can be achieved by applying both distinctions to cyberspace: cyber espionage, for the purposes of this study, refers to the clandestine collection of intelligence by intercepting communications between computers as well as breaking into somebody else's computer networks in order to exfiltrate data. Cyber sabotage, by contrast, would be the computer attack equivalent of covert operations: infiltrating an adversarial computer system with malicious software in order to create a desired physical effect or to withdraw efficiency from a process. The level of technical sophistication required for cyber espionage may be high, but the requirements are less demanding than for complex sabotage operations. This is because espionage is not directly instrumental: its main purpose is not achieving a goal, but to gather the information that may be used to design more concrete instruments or policies. The novel challenge of code-enabled sabotage has been discussed in the previous two chapters on cyber weapons and sabotage. This chapter will focus on cyber espionage.

The most widespread use of state-sponsored cyber capabilities is for the purposes of espionage. Empirically, the vast majority of all political cyber security incidents have been cases of espionage, not sabotage. And an ever more digitized environment is vastly increasing the number of actors in the espionage business. Professionally and expensively trained agents working for governments (or large companies) have new competition from hackers and private individuals, sometimes acting on their own initiative yet providing information for a larger cause. This chapter will explore the extent of the problem and the major notable cases where details are available in the public domain: what are the most spectacular network breaches on record? How significant is the threat of electronic espionage? (Or, from an offender's point of view, how big is the opportunity for cyber espionage?) And what does this mean for intelligence agencies struggling to adapt to a new set of challenges?

The argument put forward on the following pages holds, in sharp contrast to the cyber security debate's received wisdom, that three paradoxes are *limiting* the scope of cyber espionage. The first is the *danger paradox*: cyber espionage is not an act of war, not a weapon, and not an armed attack, yet it is a serious threat to the world's most advanced economies. Experts in the use of code, to a degree, are replacing experts in the use of force—computer spying, in short, is entirely non-violent yet most dangerous. But there's a caveat: those who are placing their bets on stripping their adversaries of a competitive advantage should be careful not to overestimate the possibilities of large-scale data exfiltration. Cyber espionage's second characteristic is the *significance paradox*: although cyber espionage is perhaps the most significant form of cyber attack, it may not represent a fundamentally game-changing development for intelligence agencies—cyber espionage is a game-changer, but not for the best spy agencies. This is explained by the third seeming contradiction, which I call the *normalization paradox*: an intelligence agency taking cyber operations seriously will back these operations up with human sources, experienced informers, and expert operatives, thus progressively moving what the debate refers to as "cyber espionage" out of the realm of "cyber" and back into the realm of the traditional tradecraft of intelligence agencies, including HUMINT and covert operations. The outcome may be surprising: the better intelligence agencies become at "cyber," the less they are likely to engage in cyber espionage narrowly defined. Something comparable applies in the arena of commercial espionage.

The argument is presented in five steps. Understanding the challenge of espionage, especially industrial espionage, requires understanding the nature of transferring technical expertise. The chapter therefore opens with a short conceptual exploration: at closer view, personalized expert knowledge about complex industrial or political processes cannot be downloaded as easily as is generally assumed. Secondly, some of the major cases of cyber espionage will be explored in detail, including Duqu, Flame, and Shady Rat. Thirdly, the growing role of social media in the cyber espionage business will be examined briefly. The chapter concludes by discussing some of the inherent difficulties associated with cyber espionage: distinguishing it from cyber crime, defending against it, doing it, and estimating the damage it causes as well as its benefits.

Some conceptual help is required to understand these limitations. We can get this help from Michael Polanyi, a highly influential philosopher of science.[1] Polanyi's work inspired one of the most influential books on creativity and innovation ever written, Ikujiro Nonaka's *The Knowledge Creating Company*, published in 1995.[2] One of Polanyi's core distinctions concerns that between tacit and explicit knowledge. Tacit knowledge is personal, context-specific, and difficult to formalize and to communicate, Nonaka pointed out. It resides in experience, in practical insights, in teams, in established routines, in ways of doing things, in social interactions. Such experiences and interactions are hard to express in words. Video is a somewhat better format for transmitting such knowledge, as anybody who has tried to hone a specific personal skill—from kettlebell techniques to cooking a fish pie to building a boat—intuitively understands. Explicit knowledge, on the other hand, is codified and transmittable in formal, systematic language, for instance in an economics textbook or in a military field manual. Explicit knowledge, which can be expressed in words and numbers, is only the tip of the iceberg. That iceberg consists largely of tacit knowledge.

A bread-making machine is one of Nonaka's most instructive examples. In the late 1980s, Matsushita Electrical Company, based near Osaka and now Panasonic, wanted to develop a top-of-the-line bread-making machine. The company compared bread and dough prepared by a standard machine with that of a master baker. X-raying the dough revealed no meaningful differences. Ikuko Tanaka, the head of software development, then embedded herself with a well-known chef in Osaka International Hotel, famous for its delicious bread. Yet merely observing the head baker didn't teach Tanaka how to make truly excellent bread. Only through imitation and practice did she learn how to stretch and twist the dough the right way. Even the head baker himself would not have been able to write down the "secret" recipe—it was embedded in his long-honed routines and practices. Japanese dough and bread-making holds an important lesson for Western intelligence agencies. Tacit knowledge is a major challenge for espionage, especially industrial espionage. A Chinese company that is remotely infiltrating an American competitor's network will have difficulty—metaphorically speaking—to bake bread to their customers' delight, let alone manufacture a far more complex product like chloride-route processed titanium dioxide, as in the case of one of largest China-related conventional corporate espionage cases involving the chemical company Dupont.[3]

No doubt: economic cyber espionage is a major problem. But remotely stealing *and then taking advantage of* trade secrets by clandestinely breaching a competitor's computer networks is more complicated than meets the eye. This becomes evident if one tries to list the most significant cases where cyber espionage caused real and quantifiable economic damage of major proportions—that list is shorter and more controversial than the media coverage implies. Among the most high-profile cases are three: a remarkable case is a hack that involved the

Coca-Cola Corporation. On 15 March 2009, FBI officials quietly approached the soft drink company. They revealed that intruders, possibly the infamous "Comment Group," had hacked into Coca-Cola's networks and stole sensitive files about an attempted acquisition of China Huiyuan Juice Group. The deal, valued at $2.4 billion, collapsed three days later.[4] If the acquisition had succeeded, it would have been the largest foreign takeover of a Chinese company at the time. A second, seemingly similar British case was revealed by MI5's Jonathan Evans in mid-2012, when one UK-listed company allegedly lost a £800 million deal as a result of cyber espionage, although the details remain unknown.[5] Possibly the most consequential, but also highly controversial, example is the demise of Nortel Networks Corp, a once-leading telecommunications manufacturer headquartered in Ontario, Canada. After the troubled company entered bankruptcy proceedings and then liquidation in 2009, Nortel sources claimed that Chinese hackers and a nearly decade-long high-level breach had caused, or at least contributed to, Nortel's fall.[6] But again, details about how precisely the loss of data damaged the firm remain mysterious. Other cases of real-life costs are discussed later in this book.

Yet these brief examples already illustrate how difficult it is to analyze computer espionage cases and come to general observations. The nature of the exfiltrated data is critical: process-related knowledge (think: bread making) may reside more in routines and practices, not in reports or on hard-drives, and therefore seems to be more difficult to steal and to replicate remotely—whereas confidential data about acquisitions and business-to-business negotiations may be pilfered from top executives and exploited more easily. Only a close empirical analysis can shed light on the challenges and limitations of cyber espionage. But too often what is known publicly are merely details about the exfiltration method, not details about the exfiltrated data and on how it was used or not used. The following pages will introduce most major cases of cyber espionage and often push the inquiry right to the limit of what is known about these cases on the public domain.

Perhaps the earliest example of cyber espionage is Moonlight Maze, which was discussed in chapter one. A more consequential example is Titan Rain. Titan Rain is the US government codename for a series of attacks on military and governmental computer systems that took place in 2003, and which continued persistently for years. Chinese hackers had probably gained access to hundreds of firewalled networks at the Pentagon, the State Department, and the Department of Homeland Security, as well as defense contractors such as Lockheed Martin. It remains unclear if Chinese security agencies were behind the intrusion or if an intruder merely wanted to mask his true identity by using computers based in China. Whoever was behind Titan Rain, the numbers were eye-popping. In August 2006, during an Air Force IT conference in Montgomery, Alabama, Major General William Lord, then the director of information, services and integration in the Air Force's Office of Warfighting Integration, publicly mentioned the extent of what he believed was China's state-sponsored espionage operation against America's defense establishment. "China has downloaded 10 to 20 terabytes of data from the NIPRNET already," he said, referring to the Pentagon's non-classified but still sensitive IP router network. At the time the cyber attackers had not yet breached the Pentagon's classified networks, the so-called SIPRNET, the Secret Internet Protocol Router Network.[7] But the unclassified network contains the personal information, including the names, of every single person working for the Department of Defense.[8] That, Lord assumed, was one of the most valuable things the attackers were after. "They're looking for your identity so they can get into the network as you," Lord said to the airmen and Pentagon employees assembled at Maxwell Air Force Base.

Twenty terabytes is a lot of information. If the same amount of data was printed on paper, physically carrying the stacks of documents would require "a line of moving vans stretching from the Pentagon to the Chinese freighters docked in Baltimore harbor 50 miles away," calculated Joel Brenner, a former senior counsel at the National Security Agency.[9] And the Department of Defense was certainly not the only target, so there was more than one proverbial line of trucks stretching from Washington to Baltimore. In June 2006, for instance, America's Energy Department publicly revealed that the personal information of more than 1,500 employees of the National Nuclear Security Administration had been stolen. The intrusion into the nuclear security organization's network had happened in 2004, but NNSA only discovered the breach a year after it had happened.

In November 2008, the US military witnessed what could be the most significant breach of its computers to date. An allegedly Russian piece of spyware was inserted into a flash drive on a laptop at a base in the Middle East, "placed there by a foreign intelligence agency," according to the Pentagon's number two.[10] It then started scanning the Internet for dot-mil domain addresses. In this way the malware gained access to the Pentagon's unclassified network, the NIPRNET. The Defense Department's global secure intranet, the SIPRNET, designed to transmit confidential and secret-level information, is protected by an air gap or air wall, meaning that the secure network is physically, electrically, and electromagnetically separated from insecure networks. So once the piece of malware was on a hard drive in the NIPRNET, it began copying itself onto removable thumb drives. The hope was that an unknowing user would carry it over the air gap into SIPRNET, a problem known as the "sneakernet" effect among the Pentagon's security experts.[11] That indeed seems to have happened, and a virtual beachhead was established. But it remains unclear if the software was able to extricate information from the classified network, let alone what and how much.

"Shady RAT" is another well-known and well-executed case. It is the selection of targets that points to a specific country, but not to a specific actor within that country, and in the case of Shady RAT China is the suspect. RAT is a common acronym in the computer security industry which stands for Remote Access Tool. McAfee, the company that discovered and named the operation, ominously hinted at the enterprising and courageous features of the rat in the Chinese horoscope. The attack is relatively well documented, so it is instructive to look underneath the hood for a moment.

The attackers operated in a sequence of four steps. First they selected specific target organizations according to economic or political criteria. The second step was the actual penetration. To penetrate a company's or an organization's computers, the attackers chose specific individuals within those target organizations as entry points. The contact information and email addresses for these employees could sometimes be gleaned from LinkedIn. Based on all available information, the attacker then tailored emails to their specific recipients, complete with attachments in commonly used Microsoft Office formats, such as .PPT, .DOC, or .XLS, but also PDF files. The files contained an exploit code which, when opened, would execute and compromise software running on the recipient's computer. This spear phishing ploy was remarkably sophisticated at times. One such email, sent to selected individuals, had the subject line "CNA National Security Seminar." CNA referred to the

Alexandria-based Center for Naval Analyses. The email's body was even more specific:

> We are pleased to announce that that Dr. Jeffrey A. Bader will the distinguished speaker at the CNA National Security Seminar (NSS) on Tuesday, 19 July, from 12:00 p.m. to 1:30 p.m. Dr. Bader, who was Special Assistant to the President and Senior Director for East Asian Affairs on the National Security Council from January 2009 to April 2011, will discuss the Obama Administration and East Asia.[12]

The phishing email's content was not plucked out of thin air, but actually referred to an event that was scheduled at the CNA, and was therefore highly credible. The attached file, "Contact List.XLS," contained a well-known exploit that was still effective due to Microsoft's less-than-perfect security practices, the so-called Microsoft Excel "FEATHEADER" Record Remote Code Execution Vulnerability (detected by Bloodhound.Exploit.306).[13] If the recipient's computer had not installed Microsoft's latest security updates, a clean copy of the Excel file would open as intended by the user, in order to avoid suspicion. But by clicking the file the user also opened a Trojan. One possible tell-tale sign of this particular exploit, Symantec reported, was that the MS Excel application would appear unresponsive for a few seconds and then resume operating normally, or it might crash and restart.

Shady RAT's third step followed suit. As soon as the Trojan had installed itself on the targeted machine, it attempted to contact a command-and-control site through the target computer's Internet connection. The web addresses of these control sites were programmed into the malware. Examples were:

> http://www.swim[redacted].net/images/sleepyboo.jpg
> http://www.comto[redacted].com/Tech/Lesson15.htm
> http://www.comto[redacted].com/wak/mansher0.gif

Curiously, the addresses pointed to ordinarily used image files or HTML files, among the web's most common file formats. This tactic, Symantec explained, was designed to bypass firewalls. Most protective firewalls are configured so that .JPG, .HTM, or .GIF files can pass without problem, without arousing the program's suspicion. The Trojan's image and text files looked entirely legitimate, even if superficially inspected by a human operator. One file, for instance, was headed "C# Tutorial, Lesson 15: Drawing with Pen and Brush," pretending to be a manual for a specific piece of software. The text went on:

In this lesson I would like to introduce the Pen and the Brush objects. These objects are members of GDI+ library. GDI+ or GDI NET is a graphics library …

And so on. Yet, at closer examination, command-and-control code could be found behind the files' façade. The .HTM file, for instance, contained hidden HTML comments. Programmers and website designers can use HTML comments to make notes within HTML files. These notes will be ignored by the browser when turning the file into a visually displayed website, but are visible to anybody reading the entire HTML file, be it a human or an artificial agent. The beginning of such comments is marked with, "<!—" and their end with "—>". Shady RAT hid the coveted commands in these HTML comments. An example:

<!—{685DEC108DA731F1}—>

<!—{685DEC108DA73CF1}—>

<!—{eqNBb-OuO7WM}—>

<!—{ujQ~iY,UnQ[!,hboZWg}—>

Even if a zealous administrator opened an .HTM file in a simple text editor, which is normally used to write or modify legitimate code, these comments would be unsuspicious and harmless. Many programs that are used to design websites leave such unintelligible comments behind. But the Shady RAT Trojan would be able to decipher the cryptic comments by "parsing" them, as computer scientists say. Once parsed, the actual commands appear:

run:{URL/FILENAME}

sleep:{20160}

{IP ADDRESS}:{PORT NUMBER}

The first command, for instance, would result in an executable file being downloaded into a temporary folder on the target computer's hard drive and then executed, much like clandestinely installing a malicious app from an illegitimate app store. What the app would be able to do is not specified by the Trojan. The second command, "sleep," would tell the Trojan to lay dormant for two weeks—counted in minutes—and then awake to take some form of action. The third command is perhaps the most useful for the designers of the Shady RAT attack. It takes the attack to the next level. It does so by telling the compromised machine to open a remote connection to another computer, identified by the IP address, at a specific port.

That final step of the Shady RAT attack enables the attackers to control the target computer directly. The Trojan establishes what is called a "remote shell" with the machine that holds the desired information. A hidden remote shell is a bit like plugging in a distant screen with a separate keyboard, clandestinely, all hidden from the user who in the meantime may be working on a document in Microsoft Word or writing an email in Outlook. To install the attacker's hidden screen and keyboard, the Trojan waits for a handshake from its controller through the freshly established port connection. To identify themselves, the attackers would whisper a password to the hidden Trojan. The string characters looked somewhat like the following seemingly random characters:

"/*\n@***@*@@@>>>>*\n\r"

Once the Trojan received the password it sprang into action by copying a specific file, cmd.exe, into a folder reserved by the Microsoft operating system. The espionage software then used the newly copied file to open a remote shell, that is, the remote screen and keyboard, giving the attackers significant control over the files on the compromised machine. Below is a list of commands that the attacker may use to get to work:

gf:{FILENAME} retrieves a file from the remote server.

http:{URL}.exe retrieves a file from a remote URL, beginning with http and ending in .exe. The remote file is downloaded and executed.

pf:{FILENAME} uploads a file to the remote server.

taxi:Air Material Command sends a command from the remote server.

slp:{RESULT} sends the results of the command executed above to the remote server to report the status.[14]

These commands are quite comprehensive. The gf command, for instance, allows the attacker to infiltrate additional packets of malware, say to do a specific job that the Trojan is not equipped for in the first place. The most coveted command may be pf, which was used to exfiltrate specific files from a targeted organization to a hidden attacker, of course clandestinely.

McAfee was the first to make the attack public in a report in early August 2011.[15] The report was led by Dmitri Alperovitch, McAfee's vice president for threat research. Alperovitch's team was able to identify seventy-one organizations from the log files of one command-and-control server. Among the targets were thirteen defense contractors, six agencies that belonged to the US Federal Government, five national and international Olympic Committees, three companies in the electronics industry, three companies in the energy sector, and two think tanks, as well as the Canadian and Indian governments and the United Nations.[16] Forty-nine targets were in the United States, and the rest were in Western Europe and leading Asian countries, including Japan, South Korea, Taiwan, and India. That the Olympic Committees as well as the World Anti-Doping Agency were targeted was especially curious. Beijing hosted the Games in 2008, just when the attacks seemed to peak. Alperovitch concluded that this fact "potentially pointed a finger at a state actor behind the intrusions," especially because the Olympia-related intrusions were unlikely to result in any immediate economic benefit. Some attacks also continued for an extended period of time. McAfee reported that one major American news organization headquartered in New York City was compromised for more than twenty-one months.

McAfee called the attacks "unprecedented." Alex Gostev, chief security expert at Kaspersky Lab, one of McAfee's competitors, disputed this finding. "Until the information in the McAfee report is backed up by evidence, to talk about the biggest cyberattack in history is premature," he told *Computerworld* shortly after the attack became public.[17] Others agreed. "Is the attack described in Operation Shady RAT a truly advanced persistent threat?" asked Symantec researcher Hon Lau in a blog post. "I would contend that it isn't."[18] Whatever the operation's best description—details about the volume and the nature of the exfiltrated data remain largely unknown. It is also unclear if and how the attackers were able to take advantage of the stolen information. Unfortunately this lack of knowledge is the rule rather than the exception.

Oak Ridge National Laboratory in Tennessee is the largest research institution focusing on energy-related science and technology under the umbrella of the Department of Energy. The lab, with a workforce of more than 4,200 and approximately 3,000 guest researchers a year, is one of America's leading neutron science and nuclear energy research institutions. It houses some of the world's most powerful computers. On 7 April 2011, unknown attackers set their sights on the lab. The attack was shrewd. A spoofed email purportedly from the lab's human resource office contained a zero-day exploit, a previously unknown vulnerability, possibly in Microsoft Internet Explorer or Adobe Flash Player. The fake email was sent to 573 employees, informing them about benefit-related alterations by inviting them to follow a link for more detailed information. This trick succeeded. Department of Energy officials specified that the attacker had managed to steal approximately 1 gigabyte of data, the equivalent of a few thousand photos, or 1/64 the memory size of a standard smart phone. "When I think about how many pictures my daughter has on her iPhone, it's really not a significant amount of data," said Barbara Penland, the deputy director of communications for the Oak Ridge National Lab.[19] Thom Mason, Oak Ridge's director, suspected the attackers were after scientific data. Yet they seem to have failed to penetrate the lab's classified network. In the aftermath of the attack, Oak Ridge lab turned off Internet access, including emails, to cut off possibly ongoing exfiltrations as well as follow-on attacks.

The attack was not the lab's first. On 29 October 2007, Oak Ridge had already suffered a serious attack, along with other federal labs, including Los Alamos National Laboratory in New Mexico and California's Lawrence Livermore National Laboratory. An unknown group of hackers had sent email messages with compromised attachments to a large number of employees, with some staff members receiving seven phishing emails designed to appear legitimate. One email mentioned a scientific conference and another phishing email contained information about a Federal Trade Commission complaint. In total, the attack included 1,100 attempts to penetrate the lab. In Oak Ridge, eleven employees opened a dodgy attachment, which allowed the attackers to exfiltrate data. The data were most likely stolen from a database that contained personal information about the lab's external visitors, going back to 1990. Although the information contained sensitive personal details, such as Social Security numbers, it was probably the coveted research results or designs that the attackers were after. In Los Alamos, one of only two sites in the United States specializing in top-secret nuclear weapons research, hackers also successfully infiltrated the unclassified network and stole "a significant amount of data," a spokesman admitted.[20] DHS officials were later able to link that attack to China. The US Cyber Emergency Response Team, US-CERT, backed up that claim with a list of IP addresses registered in China that were used in the attack. Yet the details were not granular enough to link the attack to any particular agency or company. Ultimately the US was unable to attribute a wave of sophisticated attacks against some of the country's most sensitive research installations.

A comparable case was "Duqu." In early October 2011, the Laboratory of Cryptography and System Security, geekily abbreviated as CrySyS Lab, at the Budapest University of Technology and Economics discovered a new and exceptionally sophisticated malware threat which created files with the prefix "~DQ," and so the Hungarian engineers analyzing it called it Duqu.[21] The threat was identified as a remote access tool, or RAT. Duqu's mission was to gather intelligence from control systems manufacturers, probably to enable a future cyber attack against a third party using the control systems of interest. "The attackers," Symantec speculated, "are looking for information such as design documents that could help them mount a future attack on an industrial control facility."[22] Duqu was found in a number of unnamed companies in at least eight countries, predominantly in Europe.[23] The breaches seem to have been launched by targeted emails, "spear phishing" in security jargon, rather than by mass spam. In one of the first attacks, a "Mr. B. Jason" sent two emails with an attached MS Word document to the targeted company, the name of which was specifically mentioned in the subject line as well as in the email's text. The first email, sent on 17 April 2011 from a probably hijacked proxy in Seoul, Korea, was intercepted by the company's spam filter. But the second email, sent on 21 April with the same credentials, went through and the recipient opened the attachment. Duqu had a keylogger, was able to take screenshots, exfiltrate data, and exploit a Windows kernel vulnerability, a highly valuable exploit. The threat did not self-replicate, and although it was advanced it did not have the capability to act autonomously. Instead, it had to be instructed by a command-and-control server. In one case, Duqu downloaded an infostealer that was able to record keystrokes and collect system data. These data were encrypted and sent back to the command-and-control server in the form of .jpg images so as not to arouse the suspicion of network administrators. The command-and-control server could also instruct Duqu to spread locally via internal network resources.

All these attacks seemed to follow the same pattern. Duqu's authors created a separate set of attack files for every single victim, including the compromised .doc file; they used a unique control server in each case;

and the exploit was embedded in a fake font called "Dexter Regular," including a prank copyright reference to "Showtime Inc," the company that produces the popular *Dexter* sitcom about a crime scene investigator who is also a part-time serial killer.[24] Symantec and CrySyS Lab pointed out that there were "striking similarities" between Stuxnet and Duqu and surmised that the two were written by the same authors: both were modular, used a similar injection mechanism, exploited a Windows kernel vulnerability, had a digitally signed driver, were connected to the Taiwanese hardware company JMicron, shared a similar design philosophy, and used highly target-specific intelligence.[25] One component of Duqu was also nearly identical to Stuxnet.[26] But in one crucial way the two threats were very different: Duqu, unlike Stuxnet, was not code that had been weaponized. It was neither intended, designed, nor used to harm anything, only to gather information, albeit in a sophisticated way.

One of the most sophisticated cyber espionage operations to date became public in late April 2012 when Iran's oil ministry reported an attack that was initially known as Wiper. Details at the time were scarce, and the story subsided. Then, a month later, a Hungarian research group published a report on the attack that quickly led to it acquiring the nickname Flame. Competing names in the initial frenzy were "Flamer" and "Skywiper." Several parties announcing their finds on the same day created this confusion. On 28 May 2012, CrySyS Lab published a detailed 63-page report on the malware. Simultaneously, Kaspersky Lab in Russia announced news of the malware. The Iranian national CERT, the Maher Centre, had contacted well-known anti-virus vendors to alert them to the threat, dubbed by Hungarian experts to be "the most sophisticated" and "the most complex malware ever found."[27] Other experts agreed. "Overall, we can say Flame is one of the most complex threats ever discovered," Kaspersky Lab wrote.[28] *The Washington Post* also acknowledged the threat: "The virus is among the most sophisticated and subversive pieces of malware to be exposed to date."[29]

The new catch was indeed remarkable. Flame was a highly complex listening device, a bug on steroids: the worm was able to highjack a computer's microphone in order to record audio clandestinely; secretly shoot pictures with a computer's built-in camera; take screenshots of specific applications; log keyboard activity; capture network traffic; record Skype calls; extract geolocation from images; send and receive commands and data through Bluetooth; and of course exfiltrate locally stored documents to a network of command-and-control servers. Meanwhile the worm was dressed up as a legitimate Microsoft update. The 20mb-heavy file was approximately twenty times larger than Stuxnet, which made it nearly impossible to spread itself by email, for instance. Yet its handlers kept Flame on a short leash. The spying tool was highly targeted. Kaspersky Lab pointed out that it was a backdoor, a Trojan, and the malware had "worm-like features," which allowed the software's remote human handlers to give commands to replicate inside a local network and through removable drives. Kaspersky also estimated the number of infected machines to be rather small, around 1,000. Once it arrived on a targeted machine, the spying software went to work by launching an entire set of operations, including sniffing the network traffic, taking screenshots of selected "interesting" applications, such as browsers, email clients, and instant messaging services. Flame was also able to record audio conversations through a computer's built-in microphone, if there was one, and of exfiltrating the audio-files in compressed form. It could also intercept keystrokes and pull off other eavesdropping activities. Large amounts of data were then sent back, on a regular schedule, to Flame's masters through a covert and encrypted SSL channel via predefined command-and-control servers. One of Flame's most notable features was its modularity. Its handlers could install additional functionality into their spying vehicle, much like apps on an iPhone. Kaspersky Lab estimated that about twenty additional modules had been developed. Flame also contained a "suicide" functionality.[30] The lab confirmed that Stuxnet and Flame shared some design features.[31]

Flame's most impressive feature is not its multi-purpose design, but its success. The quality and the volume of intelligence that the espionage tool dispatched to its masters remain unknown, and that is highly unlikely to change. The development and possibly the deployment of Flame started as early as December 2006, logs from the command-and-control code show. The online sleuths, in other words, may have operated in the dark for as long as five years. A great deal of camouflage was necessary to accomplish this. The code also indicates that at least four programmers developed the code, and that team of four authors devised clever methods to disguise their operation. One is the control panel design. The site with the control interface looked like the early alpha version of a command-and-control panel for botnets, with vintage blue links, purple when clicked, raw table frames, no graphics, no animations. But the attackers, it seems, deliberately chose a simple-looking and unpretentious interface. They also used unsuspicious words like "data, upload, download, client, news, blog, ads, backup," not botnet, infection, or attack. "We believe this was deliberately done to deceive hosting company sys-admins who might run unexpected checks," Kaspersky Lab wrote.[32] The attackers worked hard to make their effort appear as if it was a legal content management system. Another attempt to camouflage Flame was the unusually strong encryption of the stolen data itself.

On 1 June 2012 *The New York Times* broke the news that the US government developed Stuxnet, the world's most sophisticated publicly known cyber attack to date. The US government still did not officially admit its authorship, but an FBI investigation into the leaks that led the *Times* to the story can be seen as a tacit statement of fact. Thereafter officials would occasionally comment on various aspects of government-sponsored computer attacks. Once anti-virus companies like Symantec and Kaspersky Lab discovered malware, government-made or not, patches and anti-virus measures were made available relatively quickly in order to counter the threat to their customers. Anti-virus companies, in short, could directly counter a US government-sponsored espionage program or even a covert operation. In the case of Flame, one anonymous US government official felt the need to reassure *The Washington Post*'s readership that America's cyber attack was not neutralized by countermeasures against Stuxnet and Flame, "It doesn't mean that other tools aren't in play or performing effectively," one former high-ranking American intelligence official told *The Washington Post*. "This is about preparing the battlefield for another type of covert action," he said. Stuxnet and Flame, the official added, were elements of a broader and ongoing campaign, codenamed Olympic Games, which had yet to be uncovered. "Cyber collection against the Iranian program is way further down the road than this," as *The Washington Post* quoted its anonymous source.[33] Allegedly, the joint operation involved the National Security Agency, the CIA, and most probably IDF Unit 8200. Meanwhile Iran admitted that Flame posed a new problem but did not offer many details. "The virus penetrated some fields—one of them was the oil sector," Gholam Reza Jalali, an Iranian military official in charge of cyber security, was quoted on Iranian state radio in May. "Fortunately, we detected and controlled this single incident."[34] It did not remain a single incident.

For hunters of government-sponsored espionage software, 2012 was shaping up to be the busiest year on record. The summer that year was exceptionally hot, especially in Washington, DC. On 9 August it was again Kaspersky Lab who found the newest cyber espionage platform: Gauss. The malware's capabilities were notable. Gauss was a complex cyber espionage toolkit, a veritable virtual Swiss army knife. Like Flame, this spying software had a modular design. Its designers gave the different modules the names of famous mathematicians, notably Kurt Godel, Joseph-Louis Lagrange, and Johann Carl Friedrich Gauss. The last module contained the exfiltration capability and was thus the most significant. The Russian geeks at Kaspersky therefore called their new catch Gauss.

The software's lifecycle may approximate one year. Kaspersky Lab initially discovered the new malware in the context of a large investigation initiated by the Geneva-based International Telecommunication Union. Gauss was likely written in mid-2011. Its operational deployment probably started in August and September of that year, just when Hungarian anti-virus researchers discovered Duqu, another tool for computer espionage probably created by the same entity that also designed Gauss. The command-and-control infrastructure that serviced the spying operation was shut down in July 2012.

Three of Gauss's features stand out. The first is that the espionage toolkit specialized in financial institutions, especially ones based in Lebanon. The Gauss code, which came in the file winshell.ocx, contained direct commands that were required to intercept data from specific banks in Lebanon, including the Bank of Beirut, Byblos Bank, and Fransabank.[35] Gauss attempted to find the login credentials for these institutions by searching the cookies directory, retrieving all cookie files, and carefully documenting the results in its logs. It specifically searched for cookies that contained any of the following identifiers:

> paypal; mastercard; eurocard; visa; americanexpress; bankofbeirut; eblf; blombank; byblosbank; citibank fransabank; yahoo; creditlibanais; amazon; facebook; gmail; hotmail; ebay; maktoob

These identifiers denoted global Internet companies with many users in Lebanon, including banks with significant operations in the country, such as Citibank, or purely Lebanese banks such as Banque Libano-Française, BLOM Bank, Credit Libanais, Fransabank, and Byblos Bank, as well as some Lebanese-founded institutions with international outreach. "This is the first publicly known nation-state sponsored banking Trojan," Kaspersky Lab concluded in their highly detailed 48-page report on Gauss. Gauss's geographical reach was notable but limited. Kaspersky discovered more than 2,500 infections among its customers, which means the overall number could be in the tens of thousands. That would be significantly lower than many ordinary malware infections, but much higher than the number of infections in the case of the highly targeted Duqu, Flame, and Wiper attacks. The vast majority of victims, more than 66 per cent, were found in Lebanon, almost 20 per cent in Israel, and about 13 per cent in the Palestinian Territories.

The second notable feature was its carrying load. The software used the Round Robin Domain Name Service, a technique used to handle large data loads. A Round Robin-capable name server would respond to multiple requests by handing out not the same host address, but a rotating list of different host addresses, thus avoiding congestion. Gauss's command-and-control infrastructure, therefore, was designed to handle a massive load of data sent back from its virtual spies. The authors of Gauss invested a lot of work into that structure, including several servers at the following addresses:

> *.gowin7.com
> *.secuurity.net
> *.datajunction.org
> *.bestcomputeradvisor.com
> *.dotnetadvisor.info
> *.guest-access.net[36]

These addresses were registered under fake identities, Jason-Bourne-style. Examples are: Peter Kulmann, Antala Straska, Prague (in reality a pharmacy); Gilles Renaud, Neugasse 10, Zürich (a nondescript five-storey apartment building); and Adolph Dybevek, Prinsens gate 6, Oslo (a small hotel).

The third notable feature was Gauss's mystery-features. The malware's main payload module, named Godel, had a seemingly exceptionally strong encryption. Kaspersky Lab was unable to crack the code and took the unusual step of crowdsourcing the task, "If you are a world class cryptographer or if you can help us with decrypting them, please contact us," the computer scientists wrote. Another mysterious feature is a seemingly superfluous unique custom font, "Palida Narrow." The purpose of this font is unknown. One remote possibility is that the font could serve as some form of marker for a potential target.

Gauss, in sum, has the look and feel of a state-sponsored attack. Several arguments back up this assumption. One is that Kaspersky discovered the virus when it was looking for commonalities that the software shared with Flame. The researchers found a similar architecture, similar module compositions, similar code bases, similar means of communication with command-and-control servers, and the exploitation of a specific vulnerability, the so-called .LNK vulnerability, which was already used in Stuxnet and Flame. One of Gauss's modules contains a path c:\ documents and settings\flamer\desktop\gauss_ white_1, where the "flamer" stands for the Windows username that created the product.[37] Taking all these clues together, it indeed looks as if "Gauss was created by the same 'factory' which produced Flame," as Kaspersky concluded their analysis.[38] A second reason is the software's sophistication and professional execution. And finally, and most convincingly, the target set indicates a state-sponsor. Lebanon is home to Hezbollah, an organization that is politically, criminally, and militarily a major player in the region—and, since 1999, on the US State Department's list of Foreign Terrorist Organizations. The US administration has long been concerned about Hezbollah money-laundering through Lebanon's legitimate lenders, but has so far failed to produce evidence of this. "There are a number of articles published in prestigious U.S. newspapers that claim that some of our banks are hoarding illegal cash or getting involved in terrorist funding," Makram Sader, the secretary-general of the Association of Banks in Lebanon was quoted in July 2012, "All these allegations were not substantiated by their authors."[39] Gauss could have been designed to change this.

Stuxnet, Duqu, Flame, and Gauss have one other thing in common: most likely, some of these complex malwares were clandestinely operating for years before security researchers in private companies detected them. They demonstrate a remarkable failure on the part of the anti-virus industry. Their failure is visible because their business model is developing and publishing products that mitigate such threats. Whether the world's finest signal intelligence agencies—excluding those that potentially developed the attack tools—have also failed is more difficult to say because spies don't publish what they know. But it is a fair assumption that if McAfee and Symantec miss a threat, the Bundesnachrichtendienst, the DGSE, and GCHQ could do so as well—not to speak of smaller, less well-resourced intelligence agencies. Unless, of course, these agencies themselves are the author of an attack. That, increasingly, seems to be the case.

The German government's first known use of computer espionage is the so-called Bundestrojaner. On 8 October 2011, the Chaos Computer Club caused a political uproar in Berlin. Germany's famous hacker club broke news by publishing a report that accused the federal government of using a backdoor Trojan to spy on criminal suspects inside Germany. *Bund* means federal in German, so the press started referring to the malware as *Bundestrojaner*. The software was able to take screenshots of browser windows and Skype, to record VoIP conversations, and even to download more functional modules that were yet to be defined.[40] The CCC hackers accused the federal government of "state voyeurism" and, because the Trojan's security precautions were allegedly faulty, of enabling third parties to abuse the software. In the following days several German states admitted using the spyware, although, officials insisted, under strict legal limitations. Noteworthy for spyware that was ordered by the German government is the home address of the command-and-control server: the commercial ISP Web Intellects based in Columbus, Ohio.[41]

On 7 September 2012, closer to Ohio than Berlin, Debora Plunkett, director of the information assurance directorate at the US National Security Agency, gave a lecture at the Polytechnic Institute of New York University. She spoke about defending cyberspace. "We're starting to see nation-state resources and expertise employed in what we would characterize as reckless and disruptive, destructive behaviours."[42] Plunkett, surprisingly, did not speak about the United States and its allies. Nor did she mention Stuxnet, Flame, Gauss, or the roof program Olympic Games. She spoke about America's adversaries. It is therefore important to face a stark reality: Western countries are leading the charge in cyber espionage. Stuxnet, Flame, and the Bundestrojaner are only among the best-documented cases. So it should not come as a surprise, as with many other Western tactical innovations, that less developed states are trying to catch up and develop their cyber espionage capabilities. Non-democratic states, naturally, are not limited by the same institutional, legal, and ethical constraints as liberal democracies. One case from the Middle East is especially curious.

The case in question is known as "Mahdi." As mentioned previously, 2012 proved a busy year for malware analysts, and this was especially the case for those with an interest in the Middle East. In July of that year a most curious incident became public. In Islam, the Mahdi is a messiah-like figure, a redeemer. Belief in the Mahdi is an especially important concept in Shia Islam, where the return of the Twelfth Imam is seen as the prophesized coming of the savior. And Iran is a predominantly Shia country. The malware's name comes from its dropper, which also executed a text file, mahdi.txt. The file would in turn open a Word document that contained a particular news article, published by Eli Lake from *The Daily Beast* in November 2011, "Israel's Secret Iran Attack Plan: Electronic Warfare." The article described how Israel had developed "multi-billion dollar electronic weapons" that could be deployed in the event of Israel attacking Iran's nuclear installations.[43] The Mahdi malware was not as powerful as other espionage packages that ricocheted through the region that year. But it was still remarkable.

Most remarkable of all were Mahdi's ornaments and social engineering, rather than the technology itself. For instance, the kind of social engineering the attackers used to trick their victims into opening malicious email attachments. To infiltrate victims specifically located in Israel, the Mahdi attackers sent an email that contained a PowerPoint presentation, Moses_pic1.pps, with text in English as well as Hebrew. The attackers had embedded executable code as an "activated content" in one of the slides. The presentation started by asking "Would you like to see the Moses?" in English and broken Hebrew (receiving such bilingual content is not unusual in Israel, where many immigrants from English-speaking countries—"Anglos"—may still be working on their Hebrew, hence broken Hebrew is not necessarily suspicious). The text was set against a series of tranquil and peaceful nature-themed images of snow-capped mountains, forest lakes, and tropical beaches. When the presentation had reached the slide with the embedded executable code, the text instructed the viewer—who by now may have been day-dreaming about the next holiday or spiritual experience—to "look at the four central points of the next picture | for 30 seconds … please click this file." The attackers had carefully crafted their text and anticipated that Microsoft Office would now display a pop-up window with a yellow exclamation mark, annoyingly interrupting the user's joy with the religiously themed album: "You are about to activate an inserted object that may contain viruses or otherwise be harmful to your computer. Make sure the object is from a trustworthy source. Do you want to continue?" Dozens of Israeli users wanted to continue, the attack statistics show. Once the malware was installed, it was able to perform a number of information-stealing operations: keylogging, screenshot capture, audio-recording, and data exfiltration. Mahdi included a screenshot capture functionality that was triggered by communication through Facebook, Gmail, Hotmail, and other popular platforms. Yet technically, from a programmer's point of view, the attack was simple and inelegantly designed, "No extended 0-day research efforts, no security researcher commitments or big salaries were required," commented Kaspersky Lab.[44] It seems that the attack continued for eight months.

As with almost all cases of political malware, attribution was highly difficult and incomplete. So far it has not been possible to link Mahdi to a specific actor or agency. But because the code was not particularly sophisticated, it seems highly plausible that Mahdi was an Iranian operation: in order to communicate with command-and-control servers, some of them in Canada, an Israeli security firm discovered, some of the malware's communication with its handlers contained calendar dates in Persian format as well as code with strings in Farsi, the language spoken in Iran.[45] Another indicator is Mahdi's conspicuous list of targets. The 800 victims included companies that provide critical infrastructure, financial firms, and embassies. All targets were geographically located in the wider Middle Eastern region, the vast majority in Iran, followed by Israel, Afghanistan, Saudi Arabia, and the Emirates—all of these countries are either open enemies or regional rivals of Iran (with the exception of Afghanistan, which in 2012 still hosted the armed forces of many countries Iran considers adversaries).

Mahdi was certainly not as impressive as high-powered Chinese intrusions. But cyber espionage does not necessarily have to be technically sophisticated to be successful. Israel offers two interesting cases, this time not as a high-skilled attacker switching off air-defenses or stealthily sabotaging nuclear enrichment plants—but as a victim of cyber attack. This is not despite, but because of its technological prowess. More than any other country in the region, the Jewish State is a veritable high-tech nation. By 2009, Israel had more companies listed on the tech-oriented NASDAQ index in New York than all continental European countries combined.[46] Naturally, online social networks grew rapidly in Israel, including in the armed forces, with Facebook proving to be especially popular. In early 2011, the country's Facebook penetration had grown to nearly 50 per cent of Israel's overall population. Israel was one of the most connected countries on the social network, with 71 per cent of all users being under the age of thirty-five.[47] This created a novel espionage opportunity for Israel's enemies and it was only a question of time until they would try to exploit this public, or at least semi-public, trove of information. Indeed, Hezbollah soon started collecting intelligence on online social networks. Military officers had long been wary of operational security; many were especially concerned about the spotty risk awareness of draftees and young recruits. The IDF, somewhat surprisingly, was slow in including Facebook sensibilization in its basic training. Israeli officers had good reason to be concerned. Already in September 2008, Israeli intelligence allegedly warned of Facebook-related enemy infiltrations: "Facebook is a major resource for terrorists, seeking to gather information on soldiers and IDF units," a report in the Lebanese news outlet *Ya Libnan* said, "the fear is soldiers might even unknowingly arrange to meet an internet companion who in reality is a terrorist."[48] Around that time, Hezbollah was probably already testing the waters and starting to infiltrate the Israeli Army via Facebook. One operation became public in May 2010, more than a year after it had been launched. Reut Zukerman was the cover name of a fake Facebook persona allegedly created by Hezbollah operatives. The girl's profile photo showed her lying on a sofa, smiling innocently. Hackers call unauthorized attempts to introduce networks through decision "honeypots," although usually the method is not used in the context of social networks. In Zukerman's case the honeypot was an attractive young woman, but not too salacious to be suspicious or lacking in credibility. Approximately 200 elite soldiers and reservists responded to Zukerman's friendship requests over the course of several months. Once the profile had accumulated a visible group of contacts on Facebook, newcomers assumed that Reut would be just another Special Forces soldier herself. "Zukerman" allegedly succeeded in gaining the trust of several soldiers who volunteered information about the names of other service personnel, along with explanations of jargon, detailed descriptions of military bases, and even codes. Only after one full year did one of Zukerman's "friends" become suspicious and alert the IDF's responsible unit.[49]

In July 2010, one of the Israel Defense Force's most serious security breaches became known. Soldiers serving at one of the country's most highly classified military bases opened a Facebook group. Veterans of the base could upload photos and videos of their shared time in the IDF.

The group boasted a motto, in Hebrew, "There are things hidden from us, which we will never know or understand." The group had grown to 265 members, all approved by an administrator. But the administrators apparently did a sloppy job. A journalist from the Israeli daily *Yedioth Aharonot* got access to the group, did some research, and wrote a story. "Guys, we were privileged to get to be in this fantastic place," one veteran wrote, "Keep in touch and protect the secret."[50] The group members posted pictures of themselves on the base. Yet, according to *Yedioth*, the material made available by the group did not contain any compromising information. Some of the group's members had repeatedly warned on the page's wall not to upload classified or sensitive information.

One feature that appears as a common trait in almost all high-profile cyber espionage cases is the use of some form of social engineering, or spear-phishing. The use of emails or websites that trick users into unwittingly installing malware highlights the human dimension of cyber espionage. This human dimension is more important, at closer examination, than commonly assumed. Two of the most high-profile examples on record illustrate this significance of human sources for computer espionage: the first is a Chinese operation, the second an American one.

A recent row between an American and a Chinese maker of wind turbines is instructive. AMSC, an American green energy company formerly known as American Superconductor Corp., based in Devens, Massachusetts, sought $1.2bn in damages, thus making the case the largest intellectual property dispute between the US and China on record. Sinovel, China's biggest manufacturer of such turbines, is known for building the country's first offshore wind farm. Sinovel used to be the AMSC's largest customer, accounting for about 70 per cent of the American company's revenue. But on 5 April, the US company informed its shareholders that Sinovel was refusing delivery of its products and had cancelled contracts during the previous month.[51] "We first thought that this was an inventory issue, and we were understanding," Jason Fredette, AMSC's vice president of communications and marketing told *IEEE Spectrum*. "Then in June we discovered this IP theft, and that changed things quite a bit."[52] The coveted design that the Chinese company was after was a new software package that enabled so-called "low-voltage ride through," a way of allowing the wind turbines to maintain operations during a grid outage. AMSC reportedly gave Sinovel a sample for testing purposes, but the brand-new software had an expiry date, just as some commercial software suites for users require a purchase after thirty days or so. So when an employee in China discovered a turbine operating with "cracked" software beyond its expiry date, AMSC became suspicious. Somebody from inside the firm must have helped the Chinese to remove the expiry date, the company reckoned. The Massachusetts-based firm started an investigation. Only a limited number of AMSC's employees had access to the "low-voltage ride through" software in question, and even fewer people had traveled to China. The firm quickly identified one of its staff based in Austria, Dejan Karabasevic. At the time of the leak this 38-year-old Serbian was working as a manager at a Klagenfurt-based subsidiary of American Superconductor, Windtec Solutions. The suspect confessed while waiting for his trial in an Austrian prison. On 23 September, the engineer was sentenced to one year in jail and two years of probation. The Klagenfurt district court also ordered Karabasevic to pay $270,000 in damages to his former American employer. As it turned out during the trial, Karabasevic had used a thumb drive to exfiltrate "large amounts of data" from his work laptop at Windtec in April 2011, the Austrian judge Christian Leibheuser-Karl reported, including the entire source code of a crucial program in the most recent version. He then allegedly sent the relevant code via his Gmail account to his sources in Sinovel. This source code enabled the Chinese company to modify the control and supervisory program. Thanks to the rogue engineer's help, the Chinese were able to copy and modify the software at will, thus circumventing the purchase of new software versions as well as new licences. The Austrian prosecutors estimated that Karabasevic had received €15,000 from Sinovel for his services.[53] Florian Kremslehner, an Austrian lawyer representing American Superconductor, revealed that his client had evidence that Sinovel had lured its valuable spy by offering him an apartment, a five-year contract that would have doubled his AMSC salary, and "all the human contact" he desired, the attorney said, "in particular, female co-workers."[54] The affair was economically highly damaging for American Superconductor. The company's yearly revenue dropped by almost 90 per cent; its stock plunged from $40 to $4; it cut 30 per cent of its workforce, around 150 jobs; and it reported a net loss of $37.7 million in the first quarter after the Sinovel affair.[55]

A second instructive example is offered by the lead-up phase to Operation Olympic Games. Even the Stuxnet saga, the only potent cyber weapon ever deployed, demonstrates the continued significance of human agents in getting coveted, actionable intelligence. The "holy grail," in the words of one of the attack's architects, was getting a piece of espionage software into the control system at Natanz. The designers of what was to become the Stuxnet worm needed fine-grained data from inside the Iranian plant to develop their weaponized code.[56] The problem was that the control system was air gapped, as it should be. But the American intelligence operatives had a list of people who were physically visiting the plant to work on its computer equipment, therefore traveling across the air gap. The list included scientists as well as maintenance engineers. Anybody could carry the payload into the targeted plant, even without knowing it. "We had to find an unwitting person on the Iranian side of the house who could jump the gap," one planner later told Sanger.[57] The list of possible carriers involved Siemens engineers, who were helping their Iranian colleagues in maintaining the programmable logic controllers. The work of engineers would often involve updating or modifying bits of the program that ran on the programmable logic controllers, but because the controllers don't have a keyboard and screen, the work had to be done on the engineers' laptops. And the laptops needed to be connected directly to the PLCs to modify their software. Siemens was reportedly helping the Iranians to maintain their systems every few weeks. Siemens, it should be noted, had been dealing with Iran for nearly one-and-a-half centuries. In 1859, the company's founder Werner von Siemens emphasized the importance of business in Iran in a letter to his brother Carl in Saint Petersburg. In 1870 Siemens completed the construction of the 11,000-kilometer Indo-European telegraph line, linking London to Calcutta via Tehran.[58] Some 140 years later, Siemens engineers were again carrying a novel piece of IT equipment into Iran, but this time without their knowledge: "Siemens had no idea they were a carrier," one US official told Sanger. "It turns out there is always an idiot around who doesn't think much about the thumb drive in their hand."[59] American intelligence agencies apparently did not infiltrate Siemens, as they sought to avoid damaging their relationship with Germany's Bundesnachrichtendienst, the country's foreign intelligence service. But Israel was allegedly not held back by such considerations. Another version of events is that Siemens engineers willingly helped infiltrate the malware into Natanz. One recent book on the history of the Mossad, *Spies Against Armageddon*, claims that the Bundesnachrichtendienst, an agency traditionally friendly to Israel out of a habit of trying to right past wrongs against the Jewish people during the Holocaust, "arranged the cooperation of Siemens."[60] Executives at Siemens may have "felt pangs of conscience," the Israeli-American authors suspected, or they may have simply reacted to public pressure. Ultimately the Iranians became suspicious of the German engineers and ended the visits to Natanz.[61] But by then it was too late.

The precise details of Stuxnet's penetration technique remain shrouded in mystery. Yet some details and facts have been established. We may not know who ultimately bridged the air gap and made sure the worm could start its harmful work. But it now seems highly likely that a human carrier helped jump that gap, at least at some stage during the reconnaissance or the attack itself. An earlier assumption was that Stuxnet had a highly aggressive initial infection strategy hardwired into its software, in order to maximize the likelihood of spreading to one of the laptops used to program the Siemens PLCs.[62] It should be noted that the two possibilities do not necessarily stand in contradiction, as the attack was a protracted campaign that had to jump the air gap more than once.

The evolution of the Internet is widely seen as a game-changer for intelligence agencies. Appropriate historical comparisons are difficult to make.[63] But in terms of significance, the Internet probably surpasses the invention of electrical telegraphy in the 1830s. The net's wider importance for human communication may be comparable to Johannes Gutenberg's invention of the printing press in the 1440s, a time that predates the existence of the modern state with its specialized intelligence agencies. The more precise meaning of this possibly game-changing development will remain uncertain for years to come. Isolating three trends may help clarify the picture.

The first unprecedented change is an explosion of data. Individuals, companies, non-commercial groups, and of course states produce a fast-growing volume of data in the form of digital imagery, videos, voice data, emails, instant messages, text, metadata, and much more besides. The digital footprint of almost any individual in a developed country is constantly getting deeper and bigger, and so are the digital fingerprints that all sorts of transactions are leaving behind in log-files and metadata. The same applies to companies and public administrations. More data is produced at any given moment than at any time in the past. Vast quantities of this information are instantly classified. Yet, perhaps counterintuitively, the ratio of information that is actually secret is shrinking and becoming better protected, argues Nigel Inkster, a former British intelligence official now working at the International Institute for Strategic Studies.[64] Non-classified data is growing faster than classified data. The ongoing rise of social media epitomizes this trend: social media generate gigantic amounts of data; this data is half-public, depending on the privacy settings, thus creating potentially collectable intelligence.

The second novel change is the rise of the attribution problem. Acts of espionage and even acts of political violence that cannot be attributed to a perpetrator are of course not new, but their number and significance certainly is. In September 2010, Jonathan Evans, the director-general of MI5, Britain's domestic intelligence service, gave a speech to the Worshipful Company of Security Professionals, a younger livery company (an old institution related to medieval guilds), in London. Evans highlighted the emerging risks: "Using cyberspace, especially the Internet, as a vector for espionage has lowered the barriers to entry and has also made attribution of attacks more difficult, reducing the political risks of spying," he said.[65] More actors were spying, it was easier to hide for them, and the risk they were taking was lower. As a result of falling costs and rising opportunities, he argued, the likelihood that a firm or government agency is the target of state espionage was higher than ever before. The range and volume of espionage that can be accomplished without attribution has probably never been so great. The same applies to the amount of goods that can be [pilfered clandestinely].

The third trend partly follows from the first two: the blending of economic and political espionage. In late 2007, Evans sent a confidential letter to the top executives of 300 large companies in the United Kingdom, including banks, financial services firms, accountants, and law firms. Evans warned that they were under attack from "Chinese state organizations."[66] This was the first time that the British government had directly accused the Chinese government of cyber espionage. The summary of the letter on the website of the UK's Centre for the Protection of the National Infrastructure warned that the People's Liberation Army would target British firms doing business with China in an effort to steal confidential information that may be commercially valuable. The foreign intruders had specifically targeted Shell Oil and Rolls Royce, a leading producer of high-tech engineered jet engines. Evans's letter allegedly included a list of known "signatures" that could be used to identify Chinese Trojans, as well as a rundown of URLs that had been used in the past to stage targeted attacks. Economic espionage is more than just a subset of this problem. Especially in highly developed knowledge societies—the West, in short—the most profitable and the biggest companies have integrated global supply chains with many exposures to the Internet. One agency in Washington is in charge of integrating the defense against foreign spies across various government agencies, the Office of the National Counterintelligence Executive, abbreviated as NCIX. In October 2011, the outfit published a report on foreign spying operations against US economic secrets in cyberspace. "Cyber tools have enhanced the economic espionage threat," the report states, "and the Intelligence Community judges the use of such tools is already a larger threat than more traditional espionage methods."[67] The report clearly stated that Chinese actors were the world's most active and persistent aggressors, noting an "onslaught" of computer intrusions against the private sector—yet even the intelligence agency in charge of detecting such intrusions noted that it was unable to confirm who within China was responsible.

These trends create a number of novel challenges for intelligence agencies, especially those agencies or subdivisions traditionally focused on signal intelligence, SIGINT. The first challenge is selection: identifying and exploiting the most relevant sources for the most relevant information. This challenge is a consequence of big data. The problem is best illustrated by modifying the old quip of the drunk looking for the car keys underneath the streetlight, because that's where the light is. Big data means the drunk is now searching for the car keys in a sprawling and brightly lit field of streetlights, stretching out in all directions as far as the eye can see. Finding the keys there is a problem in itself. But the selection problem is that *the key may still be in the dark*, beyond that field of streetlights. Just because a signal intelligence agency has a lot of data, this doesn't necessarily mean it has the right data.

The second challenge is interpretation and analysis (i.e. finding the keys within that field of streetlights). Big data means that turning data into intelligence has become harder, and turning that intelligence into "actionable" intelligence even more so. Pure cyber espionage—that is, remote infiltration of a system, remote reconnaissance, and remote exfiltration of data—comes with a number of problems built in. A lack of insider knowledge almost always means that putting data and information into context is far harder. The story of Tanaka's head baker epitomizes this problem. If a company is set to steal and replicate an entire industrial process, a lot of tacit knowledge is required to replicate that process, not just explicit knowledge stored in data. Data can be downloaded, but not experience and skills and hunches, all of which are crucial in order to understand complex processes as well as complex decisions. Access to insiders may be necessary to put a deluge of information into context. Big data, in short, also means that intelligence agencies can collect far more data than they can sensibly analyze.

The third challenge is reorienting and reconnecting human intelligence. The specter of cyber espionage, especially from the point of view of the attacked, is threatening to drive a wedge between SIGINT and HUMINT, with the former receiving lots of funds, even in times of scarce budgets, and the latter receiving queries about its continued relevance. "[H]uman spies are no longer the whole game," observed Brenner, formerly at the NSA, "If someone can steal secrets electronically from your office from Shanghai or Moscow, perhaps they don't need a human spy."[68] Yet seeing a cleavage between the two forms of intelligence would be mistaken. Stuxnet and the Sinovel case, two of the most high-profile cyber espionage operations, highlight the crucial relevance of human operatives within cyber espionage operations. As Evans noted to the Worshipful Company of Security Professionals, "Cyber espionage can be facilitated by, and facilitate, traditional human spying."[69] The two prime challenges induced by the explosion of data and the attribution problem—selection and interpretation—may be dealt with only through old-fashioned HUMINT work, albeit sometimes technically upgraded, and not merely by "pure" cyber espionage and data-crunching. One crucial job of intelligence agents is to recruit and maintain a relationship of trust with informants, for instance Iranian scientists working on the nuclear enrichment program clandestinely passing on information to the CIA. The recruitment and maintenance of informants is a delicate task that requires granular knowledge of an individual's personality and history, and establishing a personal relationship between the handler and the informant. It has become possible to establish and maintain such relationships online, although such online-only recruitment presents significant challenges to intelligence agencies. Making sure that a person on Skype, Facebook, or email is a bona fide member of a specific group or profession is more difficult than in a face-to-face conversation and interrogation.[70] Human intelligence is still needed, and tacit knowledge makes it clear why this is the case. Neither the value of tacit knowledge nor the value of personal trust and face-to-face connections has diminished in the twenty-first century.

The fourth challenge for secretive intelligence agencies is openness: not openly available data, but the need to be open and transparent to succeed. On 12 October 2010, the head of the Government Communications Headquarters (GCHQ), the UK's equivalent to the National Security Agency, gave a noteworthy speech. The speech by Iain Lobban was noteworthy for the fact alone that it was the first-ever major address by an acting head of the secretive agency, known as the "doughnut" in England because of its ring-shaped headquarters building near Cheltenham, a large spa town in Gloucestershire, two hours west of London. Lobban indeed made a few important points in the speech. Perhaps the most crucial one was that he highlighted an opportunity that the United Kingdom could seize if only the government, telecommunication companies, hardware and software vendors, as well as service providers, would "come together:"

> It's an opportunity to develop a holistic approach to Cyber Security that makes UK networks intrinsically resilient in the face of cyber threats. And that will lead to a competitive advantage for the UK. We can give enterprises the confidence that by basing themselves here they gain the advantages of access to a modern Internet infrastructure while reducing their risks.[71]

It is no longer enough that the government's own networks are safe. Securing a country's interest in cyberspace requires securing a segment of the entire domain that goes far beyond just the public sector within it. But such a holistic approach to cyber security, and the intelligence agency–private sector cooperation needed for that approach, comes with built-in difficulties. Giving enterprises confidence before they even come to the UK implies some form of international marketing to highlight the security benefits of Britain as a new home for financial firms and high-tech entrepreneurs. But GCHQ was formed in 1919 as the Government Code and Cypher School and is known for inventing public key cryptography, a tool to keep information secret. This long-fostered secretive culture may now turn from virtue to vice. Only by being significantly and aggressively more open will intelligence agencies be able to meet their new responsibilities, especially those concerning the economic dimension of that responsibility.

This fourth challenge leads to a fifth one that is even more fundamental. The Internet made it far more difficult to draw the line between domestic and foreign intelligence. The predominant administrative division of labor in the intelligence community is predicated on a clear line between internal and external affairs, as is the legal foundation of espionage. That line, which was never entirely clear, has become brittle and murky. The attribution problem means that an agency that intercepts an email of grave concern, for instance, may find it impossible to locate the sender and the receiver, therefore making it impossible to identify a specific piece of intelligence as foreign or domestic. But the intelligence may still be highly valuable. In 1978, US President Jimmy Carter signed the so-called Foreign Intelligence Surveillance Act (FISA) into law. Introduced by Senator Ted Kennedy, the act was designed to improve congressional oversight of the government's surveillance activities. The backdrop of the new law was President Richard Nixon's abuse of federal intelligence agencies to spy on opposition political groups in America. FISA, as a consequence, imposed severe limits on the use of intelligence agencies inside the United States, including intercepting communication between foreigners on American soil.

In sum, intelligence agencies engaged in some form of cyber espionage are facing down an ugly catch-22: on the one hand, taking cyber espionage seriously means unprecedented openness vis-à-vis new constituencies as well as unprecedented and borderline-legal surveillance at home. This means change: changing the culture as well as the administrative and possibly legal setup of what intelligence agencies used to be in the past. Such reforms could amount to a veritable redefinition of the very role of intelligence agencies. On the other hand, taking cyber espionage seriously means reintroducing and strengthening the human element, in order to penetrate hard targets, big data, and the wicked attribution problem. But by recruiting, placing, and maintaining human intelligence sources, an agency may effectively move an operation *outside* the realm of cyber espionage narrowly defined, thus removing the "cyber" prefix from espionage.

6

SUBVERSION

The previous chapters discussed two general types of cyber attack, namely sabotage and espionage. The third remaining offensive activity is subversion. Subversion was one of the most complex and intellectually challenging political phenomena long before the arrival of modern tele-communication. But the Internet and the commoditization of telecom-munication are changing the nature of subversion, making it even more complex. As a consequence, this chapter, more than the two previous chapters, is only able to scratch the surface of a much deeper subject. Remarkably, that subject has received comparatively little recent scho-larly attention. But by focusing on subversion, and not on insurgency or terrorism, the following paragraphs open fresh perspectives on past examples that help to understand the likely lifespan and endurance of resistance movements in a networked present and an even more net-worked future.

The first dozen years of the twenty-first century have seen an explo-sion in protest and political violence. The most extreme and cataclysmic expression of this trend was al-Qaeda's attack on New York's World Trade Center. One decade later, and only across the street in Zuccotti Park, yet in many ways on the opposite end of the spectrum, rose the Occupy Wall Street movement. The panoply of subversive movements in-between includes Arab youth triggering uprisings against despised despots, the alter-globalization movement, animal rights activists, anonymous hacktivists, and assorted social media-enabled protest movements in Russia, China, Iran, and elsewhere. At first glance these phenomena have little in common: some are seen as a righteous force for progress and overdue change—others as an expression of perfidy, barbarism, and regression.

Yet at second glance these diverse examples have at least two common characteristics to all observers, regardless of their allegiances. The first is that they all share the goal of undermining the authority of an existing order. Activists in any of these examples may not share one vision of what the despised existing order should be replaced by, but they share the belief that the establishment should be forced to change its ways, if not its constitutional setup. Whether extreme or mainstream, whether peaceful or violent, whether legal or criminal, whether progressive or regressive, these movements were all *subversive*. The second common characteristic is that all these movements or groups benefited to a certain degree from new communication technologies. Taking action seems to have been enabled, at least initially, by the newfound ability to send and receive information, often interactively and often personal, on platforms that were no longer controlled by the very establishment the activists were up against, like their country's mainstream media, state-run or not. Whether radical or conventional, whether non-violent or militant, whether legitimate or outcast, these movements all had a virtual trait.[1] This chapter proceeds from the assumption that new subversive movements in a networked twenty-first-century context merit a general discussion: cyberspace is changing the nature of subversion, both to the benefit and to the chagrin of activists and militants.

Subversion is an old idea that arose in Europe's own democratic revolutions at the turn of the nineteenth century. Its virtual dimension was added only 200 years later, with the emergence of the interactive Internet at the turn of the twenty-first century. The concept is time-tested, nimble, and remarkably fruitful: subversion is not necessarily focused on violence and counter-force, and may therefore overcome the inadequate terminology of victory and defeat. Once subversion is conceptually fleshed out, a number of illuminating questions become visible: how is it possible to distinguish between regenerative and more radical subversion? When is subversion likely to become violent? And under what conditions is subversion likely to lose momentum, peter out, and disappear again?

SUBVERSION

This chapter argues that networked computers and the commoditization of consumer electronics have affected subversion in one overarching way: the early phases of subversively undermining established authority and collective trust require less violence than they did before. Launching a subversive "start-up" has therefore become easier—but technology has a darker flipside for those attempting to undermine established powers. Turning this subversive start-up into a successful insurgent or revolutionary "enterprise" has become more difficult. Technology, in short, has lowered the entry costs but raised the threshold for success.

Pointing out three conceptual strengths of subversion plus three hypotheses will outline the argument. The first strength is that the notion of subversion is much older and better established than its more narrow-minded recent rivals. The second strength is that subversion takes the debate beyond a counter-productive focus on violence. The concept's third strength is that it is able to grasp the phenomenon of limited goals and motivations. From these rather uncontroversial insights follow three more provocative hypotheses, each of which will be illustrated with one or more examples of recent subversive movements that were influenced by networked communication technology to some degree. The first hypothesis is that new technologies have enabled a proliferation of subversive causes and ideas, leading to a larger supply of subversive ideas, and to a more diversified landscape of subversive entrepreneurs and start-ups: *subversion, in short, has become more cause-driven.* The second hypothesis holds that new technologies have made it easier to join a subversive cause, and they have also made it easier to stop subversive activity again: *subversion, consequently, is seeing higher levels of membership-mobility.* The third hypothesis is that technology is enabling new forms of global and participant-driven organization—and that has made it more difficult for subversive movements to establish organizational discipline and trust, features that are enabled by what legal theorists call an internal coercive order: *Internet-driven subversion, therefore, is characterized by lower levels of organizational control.* Each of these three changes comes with advantages as well as disadvantages for subversives. The balance sheet, and whether the bottom line is red or black, may depend on the political environment of the subversive activity, whether it takes place in the context of a liberal democracy or under authoritarian rule.

A brief word of caution on methodology is necessary here: the examples used to illustrate this chapter's argument—such as the anti-globalization movement, Anonymous, or online organizations that helped spark the 2011 Egyptian Revolution—are far more complex subjects than the discussion of single instances of malicious programs in previous chapters. They are multi-layered social and political phenomena that were, to a certain extent, enabled or influenced by technological innovations. And studying social phenomena is often harder than studying technology. What follows are therefore mere illustrations and examples to demonstrate very specific points, not full-blown case studies.

Subversion is the deliberate attempt to undermine the trustworthiness, the integrity, and the constitution of an established authority or order. The ultimate goal of subversion may be overthrowing a society's established government. But subversive activity often has more limited causes, such as undermining and eroding an organization's or even a person's authority. The modus operandi of subversive activity is eroding *social* bonds, beliefs, and trust in state and other collective entities. The means used in subversion may not always include overt violence. One common tool of subversive activity is media work, such as writing pamphlets and literature, and producing art and film. Naturally, the rise of social media and Web 2.0 has greatly facilitated the subversive tactics of public outreach. Influencing the loyalties and the trust of individuals and uncommitted bystanders provides the vehicle for subversion to take place, not influencing technical systems. *Human minds are the targets, not machines.*

Subversion, as a concept, is much older than insurgency or terrorism. Yet for many observers and some contemporary historians it misleadingly conveys a mid-twentieth-century feel. Indeed, the term arose—again—in the 1950s and 1960s, when the cold war between the Soviet Union and the United States resulted in global proxy conflicts where both sides employed all means at their disposal to undermine the influence of the other ideological bloc. Subversion was one of those means, applied by one state clandestinely against the established order in another state. But historically, the heyday of subversion was much earlier (Figure 1).

The concept of subversion came to be used more widely in the English language around the time of the French Revolution of 1789 and the crushed Irish Rebellion of 1798. Many words alter their meaning over the course of time. But subversion did not significantly change its meaning. "To make a revolution is to subvert the ancient state of our

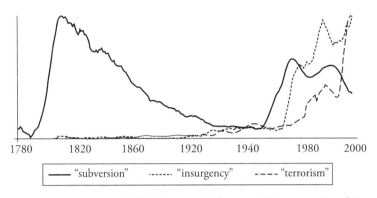

Figure 1: *Semantic rise and fall of the terms "subversion," "insurgency," and "terrorism." Source Google Ngram Viewer.*[2]

country," wrote the Irish statesman and orator Edmund Burke in his famous conservative manifesto, *Reflections on the Revolution in France* (1790). And he added that "no common reasons are called for to justify so violent a proceeding."[3] It is noteworthy to point out that, for Burke, subversion included violent action. The term, like sabotage and espionage, was imported into the English language via the French. It was already in widespread use before Paris descended into insurrection, mutiny and then civil war in the 1780s. In earlier sources, to subvert was to overthrow, to overturn, and to corrupt, said one authoritative dictionary of the English language of 1768.[4] A thesaurus of 1806 gave the synonyms: overthrow, destruction, ruin, end.[5] (The term "insurgency" was not in common English use at the time and does not appear in historic dictionaries.) A book about George III, who reigned in Britain in turbulent times from 1760 to 1820, has several fleeting remarks about attempts at subversion: of the government, of the state, of the constitution, and of the "established faith."[6] Military jargon had a similar understanding. One military dictionary of 1810 compiled by Charles James, a major in the Royal Artillery Drivers, described subversion as "a state of total disorder and indiscipline; generally produced by a neglect of small faults at the beginning, and a gradual introduction of every sort of military insubordination."[7]

Over the course of the next century, subversion boomed. Europe's *anciens régimes* would be unsettled and its populations uprooted again and again by rival political ideologies, expressing themselves in agitation,

117

violence, and revolution. By the turn of the century the geopolitical balance of power slowly began to shift to the New World, as America's economy bloomed and expanded rapidly. The United States grew into a capitalist giant thanks in part to the hard labor of European immigrants who filled its factories and mines. Many of these workers had experienced oppression under Europe's kings and czars, and they brought with them radical and utopian ideologies from Italy, Russia, Germany, and France. Not without justification, America's political establishment feared the specter of subversion. "The time of the great social revolutions has arrived," wrote Theodore Roosevelt in 1895. That year the future president served as police commissioner in New York City, "We are all peering into the future to try to forecast the action of the great dumb forces set in operation by the stupendous industrial revolution," he wrote.[8] One year earlier, activists representing one of those dumb forces—anarchism—had assassinated the president of France. Several heads of state would die at the hands of anarchists over the next six years, including Roosevelt's predecessor as America's president, William McKinley, who was killed in 1901. A little more than a century after McKinley's assassination, it was the stupendous information revolution that was again setting in operation great forces that toppled heads of states and removed *anciens regimes*, this time across the Middle East. And we are again peering into the future to try to forecast the course of action of these subversive forces.

Subversion is not just older than insurgency. It is important to note that subversion is a broader concept than insurgency. The most prominent aspect is that subversion goes beyond violence, that the concept has not merely a military meaning, but also a political and philosophical one. To date, military writers and security scholars neglect this aspect. But for this very reason the security literature is a helpful point of departure. One useful author on subversion was Frank Kitson, a well-known British general who had seen action in the Kenyan Mau Mau Uprising, the Malayan Emergency, and in Northern Ireland. Kitson defined subversion in a narrow and rather linear way as "all illegal measures short of the use of armed force,"[9] essentially as non-violent political crime. A subversive campaign of non-violence, Kitson argued, may fall into one of three classes: it may be intended as a stand-alone instrument, without ever becoming violent; it may be intended to be used in conjunction with full-scale insurgency, for instance to divert limited government assets away from another, more violent battle; or subversive action may be intended as a phase in a larger progression towards a more intensive violent insurrection.[10] Kitson aptly recognized that subversion is much broader than insurgency, but like great military writers before him who highlighted political aspects of war, he had precious little to say about these broader political aspects, let alone the social and cultural aspects.[11] By defining subversion as illegal yet non-violent, the British general maneuvered himself into conceptually murky territory that is difficult to reconcile with an open and democratic political order, as will become evident shortly.

Kitson's narrow take on subversion may be contrasted, for maximum effect, with the views of one of his contemporaries, Johannes Agnoli (both were born in the mid-1920s). Agnoli was a Marxist professor at Freie Universität Berlin and one of the intellectual forebears of the 1968 student revolt. In a final lecture series before retirement in 1991, Agnoli grandly attempted to draw a positive theory and history of subversion, from "paradise" to the French Revolution.[12] He depicted Eve as the mother of subversion. It was Eve, derived from Adam's rib, which was in turn derived from God, who heard the voice of reason and subverted the two layers of hierarchy that had created her. Not God and not Man, but the subversive Eve, for the first time, made the step from the unconscious to the conscious, from *mythos* to *logos*, from object to subject.[13] The strongly left-leaning intellectual professor in Berlin was unabashedly in favor of subverting the West German government and society in the 1970s. Yet dismissing Agnoli's ideas and his impressive analysis would be just as naïve as some of his radical students probably were. One of the professor's prime questions was the nature of subversion, of "the thing itself," as he called it with awe. Should subversion be understood as action, as praxis? Or should it be understood as reflection, as thinking about something, about "the conditions that aren't," as he quoted from Bertold Brecht's refrain in the 1928 play *Dreigroschenoper*?[14] "The utopic is always blended into the subversive," he wrote.[15] He understood utopia as a hope toward a better life, as a dream. If there was no utopia, Agnoli argued, then the human side of society would disappear. By that he meant a humanity that wouldn't limit itself to pity and merciful philanthropy, but a humanity that is fighting for its freedom and its happiness. "Those who declare the end of utopia while criminalizing the subversive," Agnoli wrote, "want to prevent the possibility of progress."[16]

Refusing such progress and innovation would be "pissing thought,"[17] the Berlin professor deadpanned in reference to Hegel. The German idealist philosopher once compared the creation of new consciousness (*Bewußtsein*) and novel thought with siring new life—and staying within the boundaries of a used framework with "pissing."[18] Even after only superficially comparing Kitson's and Agnoli's ideas, it is easy to see how subversion as a broad and overarching political idea appeals more to those in favor of change, perhaps even radical change, than to those in favor of keeping the social order as it is or as it has been. For Agnoli, Kitson's book must have oozed the smell of stale urine.

A third aspect is that subversion usually has more limited goals than insurgency. Insurgency and revolution are only the most extreme forms of subversive activity. And insurgents and revolutionaries, by implication, have the goal of overthrowing the government and putting in place a revolutionary regime. Subversives, by contrast, tend to have more limited causes, such as undermining and eroding an organization's or even a person's authority. The modus operandi of subversive activity is eroding *social* bonds, beliefs, and trust in a government, a company, or other collective entities. The means used in subversion may not always include overt violence. The vehicle of subversion is always influencing the worldviews and loyalties of individuals and uncommitted bystanders, the way they interpret relationships of authority and power vis-à-vis their own political, social, and economic situation. The purpose of subversion is to make resistance more likely, be it non-violent or violent. If violence is used, decision-makers are the prime targets, not technical systems. In other words: even when violence, sabotage, or arson is explicitly targeted at technical installations or property, not people, it is the mind and the cost–benefit calculations of politicians, owners, managers, or consumers that is the actual target of such attacks.

A subversive movement may fail to progress and mature into a full-fledged insurgent group not for lack of strength, but for lack of intention, even when some more extreme members and cells resort to systematic violence. Activists may simply not want to make revolution. Indeed, historical examples of regime change or revolution through non-violent subversion alone are extraordinarily rare.[19] Again it is useful to consider Kitson, who aptly pointed out that the goal of subversion may either be overthrowing an established economic or governmental order—or "to force them to do things they do not want to do."[20] The first objective is revolutionary and existential; the second objective is evolutionary and pragmatic. Here one of the main defining features of subversion becomes visible. The objective of insurgency is always to overthrow an existing order, nothing less. The objective of a subversive movement is attempting to change an organization's behavior, but not attempting to overthrow an existing order. Subversion, in short, can be limited to forcing those in power to do things they do not want to do, rather than to force them out. Yet radical activists may well resort to systematic violence. Subversion can therefore take two principal forms: it may be intended as a non-violent prelude to insurrection and revolution, or it may evolve into a campaign with a non-revolutionary dynamic, be it violent or non-violent.[21]

A good example of this logic of limited ambitions is the Earth Liberation Front (ELF), a well-established and influential subversive movement originally based mainly in Britain and the United States, but with some activists scattered across the globe. The ELF illustrates that even an amorphous group without leadership and hierarchy can limit its goals as well as its tactics, in this case to violence against inanimate objects.

The Earth Liberation Front was launched in 1992 in Brighton, England, as an offshoot of the larger movement "Earth First!" The ELF had its most active phase in the mid-2000s. The elves, as its members affectionately referred to themselves, engaged in *ecotage*, a pun on sabotage. The movement initially benefited from academic participation, with book authors and scholars mobilizing for the elves' cause.[22] The movement—dubbed "eco-terrorism" by its critics—had a clear ideology and a powerful cause: defending the planet and stopping the exploitation and destruction of the natural environment. The destruction of the environment, the ELF's propaganda reasoned, was driven by the pursuit of monetary gain, by corporations and by the governments that allow these corporations to continue. In principle, this cause spoke to a very large constituency in many countries. The ELF's amorphous organizational form reflected its potentially broad appeal. The movement relied on a leaderless resistance model with "no discernable organizational structure," one of the most detailed academic studies of the "elves" pointed out.[23] The activists' website says it is an "international, underground movement consisting of autonomous groups of people." The radical green activists formed a cell structure, based on a shared ideology, but not much more. Activists remained largely unknown to each other. Instead of relying on clear lines of command and internal discipline, the movement relied on members "who understand the organization's goals and orientation to take action on their own initiative."[24] The organization operated with "no central leadership, no hierarchy, no membership databases, but a rather strict adherence to a set of very basic guidelines."[25] These rules were three in number. The first was to educate the public on the "atrocities" committed against the environment and all the species that cohabitate in it. This amounted to a built-in reminder not to forget to market the cause. The second rule concerned the use of violence and specific targets, "to inflict maximum economic damage" on all those who profit from environmental destruction.

The third guideline was especially noteworthy: to take "all necessary precautions against harming any animal—human or non-human."[26] Taking these rules seriously means limiting the form of activism to economic damage, not damage in life. The elves are known to have staged attacks in more than a dozen countries. Violent attacks have targeted developers, logging companies, those engaged in genetic engineering research, ski resorts, and even SUV dealerships. The amount of property damage caused by the radical environmentalists is remarkable.[27] In the five-year period between 1996 and 2001, one of the movement's cells, called "The Family," inflicted damages as high as $80 million against federal land and animal management sites, meat-packing plants, lumber facilities, and car dealerships. The cell's most high-profile "direct actions" were a $12-million arson at the Vail Ski Resort in Colorado in 1998 and the sabotage of a high-tension power line near Bend, Oregon, in the following year. Since 1997, the Earth Liberation Front claims to have inflicted damage totaling well over $150 million worldwide. Yet, "in the history of the ELF internationally no one has been injured from the group's actions and that is not a coincidence," as the group's Frequently Asked Questions point out.[28] The elves took care to walk a fine but clearly demarcated line: labs, research facilities, and company infrastructure were legitimate targets, while workers and managers were not: "we want a lot of people watching, not a lot of people dead."[29]

The ELF, like many subversive movements that gravitate towards violence, is a highly diverse and fractured movement. This effect is enhanced by the movement's non-hierarchical setup as well as by an absence of consensual decision-making, in contrast to Earth First! There are, therefore, more radical streaks within the movement that embraced revolutionary rhetoric, albeit without attempting to turn the revolutio-nary vision into reality.[30] By and large, the ELF seems to be subversive and to have embraced violence against property—but at the same time the movement is limited; it is subversive but not revolutionary, and its violence carefully avoids targeting human beings. Radical environmen-talism and the ELF predate the broad use of the Internet, and in contrast to other subversive movements it was not enabled by new technologies. But new technologies drastically enhanced one feature that the elves also grappled with: diverse causes.

The more technologically sophisticated a subversive movement and its targeted constituencies, the more cause-driven it is likely to become. One of the key drivers behind this dynamic is collective emotion. The concept of "cyber war" is inept and imprecise. But other classic concepts of the study of war retain their relevance and pertinence for the study of cyber offenses. Clausewitz, and many other strategic thinkers, consis-tently highlighted the role of passions and emotions in conflict, be it regular or irregular conflict. "The intensity of action," Clausewitz obser-ved, "is a function of the motive's strength that is driving the action." That motive may be a rational calculation or it may be emotional indi-gnation (*Gemütserregung*), he added. "If power is meant to be great, the latter can hardly be missing."[31] Subversion, like insurgency, is driven by strong motives that mobilize supporters, volunteers, and activists and, if violence comes into play, justify why fighters and insurgents would take up arms and possibly kill civilians. Another revered military thinker, David Galula, described the driving force behind an insurgent group as the cause. An insurgency's treasure would be a "monopoly of a dynamic cause," wrote the French expert of counterrevolutionary war in the 1960s.[32] But fifty years later, the demise of grand ideologies[33] and the rise of highly networked movements have altered the logic of dynamic causes. Rather than grand narratives, it is highly specific issues that are likely to mobilize a critical mass of enraged activists, if only temporarily. This dynamic has a flipside: the monopoly over a dynamic cause is replaced by a dynamic market of causes. Individuals and small groups may join a movement for their own individual reasons. These individual causes may have a strong emotional draw, but that benefit comes at the cost of coordination, coherence, and unity.

Perhaps the most insightful example of cause-driven subversion is the rise and decline of the anti-globalization movement, a left-leaning international protest movement that climaxed at the turn of the twenty-first century. Globalization became a widely used buzzword in the early 1990s. For many, globalization was equivalent to *economic* globalization. And economic globalization soon stood for the increasing liberalization of goods and services, unfettered capitalism, the power of multinational corporations, and regimes of global governance put in place to perpetuate a system that seemed unjust and oppressive to many. The globalization critics identified the World Trade Organization, the International Monetary Fund, and the World Bank as their main targets, along with a much-hated multilateral agreement on investment, the MAI. The anti-globalization movement understood itself as a counter-ideology. Globalization from above, as some activists saw it, needed to be resisted by globalization from below.

Initially, the movement was driven by the excitement of large, international protest events. One of the most visible founding events, the Carnival Against Capital, was held in Cologne, Germany, on 18 June 1999, and is therefore known as "J18". Simultaneous events in the City of London and Oregon helped galvanize international media attention. The international day of protest had the rallying cry, "Our resistance is as transnational as capital."[34] Perhaps the most memorable event in the short history of the anti-globalization movement was a march on Seattle in November and December 1999. The magnet for the protest was a World Trade Organization ministerial conference. Approximately 50,000 people took to the streets of downtown Seattle, a mid-size city of 600,000. On the morning of a cold and rainy Tuesday, 30 November, the "Battle of Seattle" began to unfold. The large number of demonstrators caught the city's security agencies off-guard and effectively shut down the conference by blocking the Seattle Convention Center. The police resorted to tear gas, rubber bullets, and mass arrests. "N30," as the November day is known among protesters, became symbolic for the anti-globalization movement and helped mobilize follow-on events.

Two things leaped to the eye. The first was the movement's diversity. N30 did not just catch the authorities off-guard; it also caught those with a subversive agenda off-guard. The diversity of this early twenty-first-century phenomenon surprised even the organizers. At the time Carl Pope was the executive director of the Sierra Club, America's oldest grassroots environmental organization founded in 1892. "From my perspective, and I came out of the '60s, Seattle was the first time when you saw multi-generation, multi-class, and multi-issue in the streets together," Pope told *Time* magazine shortly after Seattle.[35] The banner of "anti-globalization" seemingly united a motley crew of activists: environmentalists of various shades, animal rights activists, union members, human rights advocates, anarchists of different stripes, even participants from the White supremacist scene. More than 600 groups, out of a total 15,000 participants, converged on Washington, D.C. in April 2000 in an event known as A16. The groups ranged from Greenpeace, one of the most established groups, to the Third Position, a curious mix of anarchist left and right positions and one of the more violent outfits.[36] The combination of such a sundry set of small groups into a larger movement resulted in a swirl of media attention and political responses. This visibility, in turn, created an impression of power that far exceeded what any single group could accomplish. CSIS, the Canadian intelligence service, summed up this dynamic in a report published shortly after Seattle:

> The melding of the various groups into one large body implies power, and attracts attention and publicity, which, in turn, draws more and more participants. Many groups and individuals take part largely because of the ensuing attention and publicity, almost in the manner of self-generating growth.[37]

Some groups united under the anti-globalization umbrella frequently changed their names. Also, individual activists may have been members of more than one group or changed membership as a group stopped operating for one reason or the other. It was not the mode of organization that matters most, but the underlying psychological forces of activism, "Of more importance are the causes and motivations per se," the Canadian intelligence analysts observed. The activists' positive visions and ideals included fairer trade, more organic products, improved labor conditions in developing countries, corporate social responsibility, advancements of human rights, green energy, sustainable development, global justice, gay rights, feminism, and more.

But this diversity had a thorny side-effect: it diluted the movement. More causes meant less content. The result was empty slogans. "Another world is possible" was the motto of Porto Alegre, Brazil, where the first World Social Forum was held in late January 2001. For a few years, the meetings became counter-events to the World Economic Forum in Davos, Switzerland, which the critics saw as the embodiment of global capitalism. In Porto Alegre, various committees approved a so-called charter of principles later in 2001. The meeting, the charter said, was a place for:

> groups and movements of civil society that are opposed to neo-liberalism and to domination of the world by capital and any form of imperialism, and are committed to building a planetary society directed towards fruitful relationships among Mankind and between it and the Earth.[38]

This statement was so general and broad as to be nearly meaningless. But its authors had little choice. The principles expressed in the document needed to be all-inclusive in order to offer a roof to anybody who self-identified with what had become a global network of protest. Building a planetary society and organizing for fruitful relationships among mankind and the earth seemed to do the trick. This leads to the second noteworthy feature.

The rise of the popular anti-globalization network curiously coincided with the rise of another popular global network: the Internet. Many activists, young and with experimental lifestyles, were early technology adopters. Naturally, they suspected a correlation between the new technologies and the new ideas they embraced so passionately. One example is Evan Henshaw-Plath, founder of the then-popular site http://protest.net. Shortly after Christmas 2001, Henshaw-Plath gave an interview to a graduate student. He commented on the relationship between the web and the movement, and mused that the former had enabled the latter:

> The anti-globalization movement could not exist without the Internet. This is not to say that we wouldn't be struggling over similar issues but the movement that we have now wouldn't exist. We wouldn't be making the connections and coalitions. We couldn't organize such massive coalitions with almost non-existent overhead if we didn't have email mailing lists and websites. I think the tactics of having very large broad protests with indymedia centers, conference spaces, counter conferences, legal protests, illegal protests, and direct action wouldn't be possible without the net.[39]

Henshaw-Plath probably overstated the point. The anti-globalization movement could probably exist without the Internet. The question was *how* the new media affected political activism. That question, how the global Internet impacted on the anti-globalization movement, naturally became a sexy topic for sociologists and political scientists, many of whom at least sympathized with the protesters.[40] One assumption was that the new media facilitated participation, "Political action is made easier, faster and more universal by the developing technologies," one widely read article argued in 2002. New information technologies would "lower the costs and obstacles of organizing collective action significantly."[41] By following simple yet detailed guidelines, the article continued, "all supporters can easily become real participants."[42] The dotcom bubble, it seemed, had not burst in academia, where enthusiasm for the positive and possibly revolutionary impact of new information technologies refused to go away.[43] The Internet, many sociologists argued, enabled a collective identity, effective mobilization of participants, and the ability to network the organizations into a larger movement that would be more reactive as a result. Until the early 1990s, big hierarchical groups had a "fundamental" advantage, another prominent article argued in 2006. But by then, a decade later, the comparative advantage had shifted. "In the Internet age, the transaction costs of communicating to large audiences, of networking, and of working transnationally have diminished," wrote one World Bank-based researcher about the anti-globalization movement, "while the advantages of nimbleness—of being able to respond swiftly to events as they unfold— have grown."[44] As entry costs and organizational costs are lowered, new entrants, groups outside the establishment of public institutions, such as parties, labor organizations, or unions, would benefit most in relative terms. By 2006, Twitter was founded and Facebook had opened to the public. The web continued to inspire entrepreneurs, politicians, academics, and activists. Social media had lowered the cost of organizing collective action, thus drastically increasing the number of people who would actively contribute to society and politics, and not just passively consume information as "couch potatoes," a prominent web evangelist, Clay Shirky, argued in 2010.[45] But by then the anti-globalization movement had again outpaced sociological scholarship: the movement, despite its "fundamental advantage," had quietly disappeared from the planetary stage. By the end of the 2000s, a decade after the Battle of Seattle, the fighters for global justice had scattered—this did not happen despite the rise of the Internet, but at least partly *because of the rise of the Internet*. To understand why, another subtle change of twenty-first-century subversion has to be considered.

These considerations about a proliferation of small causes lead to the second hypothesis: the more a subversive movement relies on multiple causes, new technologies, and networked communications, the more likely it is that this movement will be characterized by high membership mobility. At closer examination, several factors that go beyond the attractiveness of a dynamic cause increase the number and the frequency of members joining a new movement: the ease of finding out about the movement and its cause; the opportunity to participate at low costs; and the benefits of participation. One overarching factor, by contrast, is likely to determine whether participants terminate their subversive activity, independent of success or failure: the costs of ending the participation and leaving the "movement." Of course other considerations influence an individual's decision to continue supporting a subversive cause, for instance whether the movement is making progress, whether it has achieved any results, whether participation pays off in one way or the other, or whether there are other competing movements or better ways to make a difference. But all these motivations are contingent on the costs of leaving. In some cases, the increased ease of temporarily joining a movement and leaving that movement again represents a hard challenge to the leaders and organizers of subversive action.

An insightful example of high membership mobility is Anonymous, a loose and largely leaderless movement of activists that became visible to the larger public in 2008. The movement's activities initially took place only online. These activities could be legal or illegal, for instance hacking into protected computer networks. But Anonymous's activities remained entirely non-violent, in contrast to its brick-and-mortar predecessors like the ELF or the anti-globalization movement. Supporters concealed their identities and rallied around self-defined causes, often promoting free speech, agitating against censorship and government oppression. The movement's motto was frequently posted at the end of announcements: *We are Anonymous. We are Legion. We do not forgive. We do not forget. Expect us.* By late 2010, Anonymous had become to protest what Wikipedia was for encyclopedias and Linux for software; an improved, open, and crowd-produced alternative: nimble and effective to the point of appearing dangerous to the establishment. That, at least, is how enthusiastic sympathizers and frightened critics alike saw the phenomenon. By mid-2011, Anonymous seemed to have peaked. A closer look at this curious movement exposes three tender spots that are of general interest for the study of subversive social movements.

The first feature is the movement's internal fissures and contradictions. Anonymous has, in simplified terms, two main streaks that reflect the movement's lopsided rise: crude entertainment and political activism. Anonymous initially rose from the raunchy online message board 4chan, an online platform and image board with forced anonymity visited by more than 20 million unique visitors a month. The original activists were in it for the laughs, the "lulz." Lulz is a concept related to *Schadenfreude*, derived from a plural of "lol," which stands for laugh-out-loud.[46] An example was Anonymous's "YouTube porn day," a concerted prankster raid on 20 May 2009 where hundreds of pornographic videos were defiantly uploaded to the popular video-sharing site to retaliate against Google's removal of music videos.[47] In a video titled "Jonas Brother Live On Stage," a viewer commented: "I'm 12 years old and what is this?" The phrase, quoted in a BBC story, went on to become an Internet meme. Such trolling didn't need to have any social or political dimension. It could just be crude and mean and entertaining. For instance "doxing" an innocent victim by hacking or tricking him or her and then posting embarrassing private pictures, ideally of body parts, on /b/, 4chan's most popular and unmoderated forum, or on the victim's Facebook wall, for family and friends to see.[48]

On the other side of that internal divide are those who are genuinely driven by a political cause. Those who disagree with the ethics of this or that prank are called "moralfags" on /b/. This slur is also applied to politically motivated activism. One of the early major campaigns became known as "Project Chanology." The op's name was a portmanteau of 4chan and the name of the target, the Church of Scientology. Chanology was triggered by Scientology's attempt to get YouTube to remove a weird promotional video with Tom Cruise that had allegedly been leaked and edited. Anonymous initially reacted with DDoS attacks on Scientology's website, but it soon expanded the campaign. The Internet collective launched the operation publicly with its own YouTube video on 21 January 2008.[49] The high point of the Anonymous campaign was the wave of demonstrations that took place in front of the sect's main centers worldwide. The protesters wore the now-famous Guy Fawkes masks, adopted from the film *V for Vendetta*. The global turnout on 10 February 2008 may have been as high as 8,000 protesters. The campaign was widely covered in the international press. "*Oh fuck*," one famous photo of a group of anti-Scientology protesters read, "The Internet is here." Scientology noticed that the Internet was here in unexpected ways: by receiving large numbers of unpaid pizzas, black faxes to

cartridges, unwanted taxis, and prank calls. Some of the
ns had a shallow political dimension, as the YouTube-porn
, and some of the political activism has retained an amu-
ie Chanology shows. This mix was a recipe for success, and
temporarily bridged the internal divide among the "Anons."

The second feature is the movement's low internal visibility. In late
November 2010, the crowd on 4chan's /b/ board was again jolted into
action. After WikiLeaks published secret US diplomatic cables, PayPal
and other financial firms announced that they would block payments to
the whistleblowing start-up. Anonymous staged a few high-profile
DDoS attacks in defense of Julian Assange's outfit, most notably against
PayPal, Visa, and Postfinance, a leading Swiss bank. Operation Payback,
as it was known, received wide attention in the international press and
Anonymous's channels on Internet Relay Chat, better known by its
acronym IRC, were brimming with new members. A number of follow-
on operations, most notably the hacking of HBGary Federal, further
increased the group's visibility. Policy-makers began to be concerned
about the dangerous hacker collective. Scholars and PhD students started dissecting the phenomenon. Books were published.[50] But this high
public visibility of Anonymous contrasted sharply with a low internal
visibility for those who decided to participate in its activities. A multi-
tude of platforms, IRC channels, changing pseudonyms, and simultaneous communication in high volumes made understanding what was
going on a challenge. Anonymous activists, naturally, remain anonymous—also amongst each other. This lack of visibility means that participants may not know how many people join an operation, why they
join an operation, and most importantly who they really are. This situation, combined with the knowledge that many hacks and DDoS attacks
were illegal, ultimately created distrust, paranoia, and fragility.

The third feature is Anonymous's myth-making. Many part-time
participants in Anonymous's operations share a core tenet: the belief in
the power of the collective, the "hive mind" or just "the hive." This
vision of the collective is an old and appealing one. Anonymous's participants see themselves as a veritable popular force, as the masses of the
web, a powerful sum of elements that would be weaker individually.
Plus anonymity seemed to be the ultimate form of egalitarianism: everybody could be anybody, without hierarchy, without titles or degrees.
The epitome of the hive was a voluntary Denial of Service Attack, with

thousands of individuals joining a Twitter-coordinated collective attack against unsuspecting targets. To stimulate the hive mind, the virtual "weapons" would have fancy names like Warbot, Russkill, Good Bye v3.0, or—to name an initially popular tool—the Low Orbit Ion Cannon, the LOIC.[51] The problem was: hive-distributed denial of service attacks were far less effective than many assumed. The collective DDoS attack on PayPal.com on 8 December 2010 illustrates this. On that day about 4,500 participants who had downloaded the LOIC and set it on the "hive option" joined the collective to take down the payment service provider who had been critical of WikiLeaks. But when Twitter and 4chan exploded with excited posts of "*FIRE FIRE FIRE FIRE*," nothing happened. Only when one botnet operator joined the attack by commandeering more than 30,000 zombie computers to contribute did PayPal's website go down. The legitimate owners of these many thousands of hijacked computers did of course not know that the temporary slowdown of their Internet connection meant they were participating in an attack on PayPal.[52] The Anonymous hive, likewise, did not know that one single botnet operator outgunned them nearly ten-to-one. Remarkably, a tiny elite of Anonymous hackers did not want to discourage the collective by mentioning the botnets. The myth of the hive may be misleading, but it is also very powerful. It kept morale high—but it also ensured that there was fluctuation among the participants. "What sets Anonymous apart is its fluid membership and organic political evolution," wrote Gabriella Coleman, an anthropologist who has tracked the Anonymous phenomenon for many years. The movement has neither a strategy nor structures in place that could set a strategy. It is tactically driven. "Anonymous has no consistent philosophy or political program," Coleman observed.[53] This observation leads to the final thesis.

The third hypothesis follows from the preceding theoretical and empirical observations on subversion: the more a subversive movement relies on new technologies and networked communications, the more difficult it will be to establish an internal coercive order. An internal coercive order must not always express itself in actual acts of punishment, as the chapter on violence explored in some detail. But the knowledge of such an enforced order is what endows rules and guidelines of behavior with authority—it is this internal order that differentiates a movement from a group. Enforced orders also enable strategic decisions by preventing random membership mobility and thus facilitating a coherent purpose that may overcome a movement's cause-driven character.

For any subversive movement, there are two principal sources of cohesion, an internal coercive order or external coercion. An extreme example of the former, internal enforcement, is a drug cartel or a mafia organization: even if a disillusioned member decides to leave his or her group by cooperating with law enforcement, they would still have to fear the group's punishment—that punishment is an expression of the group's ability to maintain an internal coercive order. The other source of cohesion, paradoxically, is the strength of the established system that a subversive movement is up against. But as soon as the despised coercive order collapses, the frail unity of a web-enabled movement is likely to collapse as well. Online subversion may facilitate the goal of collectively undermining trust in an established order, but it may also obstruct the broader aim of collectively establishing trust in the new order that is to be put in its place.

Powerful examples can be found in the way the Arab Spring of 2011 was triggered. Initially the Arab youth movements that shattered the established order in Tunisia, Egypt, Libya, Yemen, and elsewhere had a strong web presence on social media platforms. One example from Egypt, the second country to revolt against its old regime, is instructive. Wael Ghonim, an Egyptian Google marketing executive who was based in Dubai at the time, offered an inside view of one of the Facebook groups that helped trigger the revolution of 25 January 2011 in an autobiographical book, *Revolution 2.0*.[54] Ghonim had been the administrator of Kullena Khaled Said, a Facebook group that formed spontaneously in order to protest against the fatal beating of a young Egyptian man at the hands of the secret police. In the early subversive stages of what would later become a revolution, Internet forums, but mostly Facebook and to a lesser extent Twitter, helped coordinate small activities, such as a human chain along the corniche in Alexandria and "silent stands" of protestors, dressed in black. The social network offered a platform for planning as well as after-action-deliberation. Some posts later received thousands of "likes" and comments, and hundreds of thousands read the messages.[55] But most importantly, Facebook helped middle-class Egyptians understand that they were not alone in their frustration, and that there was a real potential to stage protests that were too large for the government to suppress by force. The majority of Egyptian Facebook users joined the online protest under their real names, by becoming a "member" of a specific Facebook group, by "liking" that group's status update, or by writing a short comment—such small expressions of solidarity were not enough to jolt the security forces into action (if they even noticed).

But such small expressions of solidarity were enough to begin undermining the trust that many if not most Egyptians had in the efficiency of the secret police, the confidence they had in the efficiency of the state's coercive order—or, put inversely, it increased the prospective protesters' confidence in the uprising. The Facebook coordination combined a potent mix of anonymity and real names: the moderators of various Facebook groups that helped spark the unrest remained anonymous, trying to evade the prying eyes of the state's security forces, but the mass of those who "liked" the posts and commented were not anonymous. Real names lent a reality and urgency to the phenomenon that would have been difficult to achieve anonymously. On 25 January, protesters had planned to take to the streets and to Tahrir Square for the first time in very large numbers. Going to that preannounced demonstration meant taking considerable personal risk. The authoritarian regime would not stand idly by, and had mobilized large numbers of security forces. The hope of the Facebook-organized protest movement was to overwhelm the police and thugs hired by the regime with even larger numbers of peaceful protesters. Individuals, if they turned out in numbers that were large enough, would be protected by the sheer mass of the demonstration.

But the step from online to offline protest had momentous consequences. Once the initial spark started a larger political movement, street protests gained a revolutionary dynamic that could not be stopped, neither by Hosni Mubarak's clumsy shutdown of the Internet in Egypt nor by the brutality of the state's security forces. This remarkably fast initial mass-mobilization seemed possible only through online social networks by savvy individuals like Ghonim. But until the very last moment on 25 January, even Ghonim and the other organizers did not know if their work would create the turnout they had hoped for: "We could not believe our eyes," he wrote afterwards, recalling his surprised arrival at the main protest site. "I began tweeting like a madman on my personal account, urging everyone to come out and join the protest."[56] But by then it was probably already too late for tweets: once the uprising had manifested itself in the street, the significance of social media instantly diminished. Facebook proved highly efficient in undermining the trust in the state's monopoly of force and the regime's ability to crush the protests; but the web had little to offer after that was accomplished. Building trust in new political institutions is an entirely different matter.

This chapter has argued that subversion is a useful concept to understand the potential and limits of activism in cyberspace—it is an old idea that manages to overcome the debate's focus on violent methods and opens the comparison to resistance movements with limited, non-revolutionary goals. These shifts in perspective help to understand how new technologies are changing subversive activism.[57] Three hypotheses were introduced to capture that change: that subversion has become more cause-driven; that subversion is characterized by higher levels of membership-mobility; and that subversive movements find it more difficult to exert organizational control by erecting an internal enforced order. If these conclusions are accurate, cynics may conclude, then "cyber subversion" does not represent a formidable and perhaps even *existential* challenge to modern, liberal democracies. Such a conclusion would be naïve and short-sighted. But the real challenge will come as a surprise to many: the challenge is not effectively stamping out subversion; the challenge is finding the right balance that maintains the fragile and hard-to-achieve degree of healthy subversion that characterizes the most successful liberal democracies and the most successful economies.

Subversion, in contrast to what some security scholars seem to think, is not principally illegal and it is not even principally illegitimate—only the most extreme forms of subversion are. The above examples were such moderate forms, and they were deliberately chosen for that reason. Understanding subversion's extreme form requires understanding its moderate relatives first. Ideas and activities acquire subversive character not through inciting violence while remaining non-violent, but when these activities undermine and erode established authority. This thought immediately leads to a conclusion that is as surprising as it may be discomforting for most students of political violence: subversion may not just remain entirely non-violent; it may remain entirely within the boundaries of the law, especially in free and open democracies. In sharp contrast to Kitson's ideas, neither non-violence nor illegality can successfully delineate subversive activity in its earliest stages. More in line with Agnoli's ideas, subversive thought is not necessarily radical or militant, but it is almost always political and often embraces progress. Put differently, democracies are political systems designed to accommo-

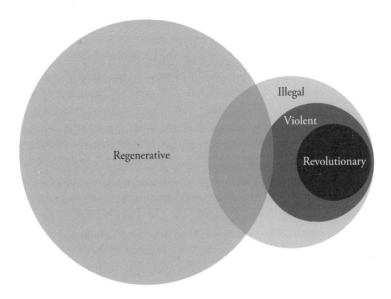

Figure 2: schematic graph of four types of subversion.

date a certain amount of subversive activity—if warranted even by changing its legal and possibly its constitutional foundation. Subversion therefore spans the philosophical and the practical; the legal and the illegal; the non-violent and the violent; and the non-revolutionary and the revolutionary. Most importantly, it can be regenerative or it can be degenerative.

In any democratic political system, some degree of subversive activity is a necessary precondition of a free, open, and critical polity. The side effect must not be undesirable let alone destructive; subversion may be a constructive social force that is highly desirable from a systemic point of view. Productively challenging established authority helps bring about a dynamic, adaptive, and innovative culture—in business, scholarship, and politics. Some of the demands of students and protesters in the 1960s and 1970s, such as the end of racial discrimination, or later the promotion of gay rights, were subversive at the time in the United States and Western Europe, but were broadly accepted across the political spectrum a few decades later. It is a mainstay of capitalism that even established market leaders should be constantly challenged to stay innovative and drive competition. As soon as a firmly established authority, be it political or economic, is shielded from all criticism and challenges, it is likely to become stale, inert, and complacent.

This raises a more elementary issue: the question of when subversion flips. When and how subversion flips from the regenerative and legitimate expression and the articulation of dissent to regression, illegality, and violence—or indeed the other way round. In any democratic state, the boundary between what is considered legal and what is considered illegal is always the outcome of ongoing political debates that shape a state's legislative measures and its laws. The line between regenerative and degenerative subversion is forever blurred and the subject of fierce disputes on both ends of any society's political and cultural spectrum. Here time is of the essence. Subversive movements, for instance the anti-globalization movement or the "Occupy" phenomenon, may appear limited, isolated, extreme, or inconsequential, especially to conservative observers in the context of their time. But perspectives and interpretations may change slowly and imperceptibly over time. The conclusion is that it is difficult to assess subversion as it happens; some historical shifts are hard to spot in real time.[58] Yet one historical trend is clear: in liberal democracies, subversion has been successfully legalized and institutionalized.[59] Three examples serve to make this point.

Subversion has been institutionalized in academia. Scientific progress itself relies on periodically overthrowing established knowledge in scientific revolutions, so-called "paradigm shifts," as the historian of science Thomas Kuhn famously outlined.[60] In some disciplines scholarly practice did not remain implicitly subversive, but turned explicit. As postmodernism rose to prominence in the 1980s and 1990s, it became possible for scholars who crafted subversive theories to make a career in the establishment of philosophy, sociology, and adjacent disciplines, and, rather ironically, to become part of an increasingly dominant order in their own right. By the early 2000s, for instance, the language of subversion had become so common in cultural studies that scholars began avoiding verbs like "undermine," "erode," and "deconstruct" because in the wider field of cultural studies these phrases had been overused and had become stale.[61] Writing too subversively could narrow a funding proposal's chances for success—not because the proposed ideas were running the risk of being too radical, but of being too bland.

Subversion has also been institutionalized in literature and art. In a much-noted 1981 study, *Fantasy: The Literature of Subversion*, Rosemary

Jackson highlighted the critical and subversive potential of fantastic literature. The fantastic, as Jackson saw it, may trace the unsaid and the unseen of a society's cultural and political established order, that which has been silenced, concealed, and covered. Telling a story within the bounds of the rational and the accepted would imply using the language of the dominant order, thus accepting its norms and contributing to keeping the "dark areas" covered by the dominant discourse. Literature and art, not just of the fantastic kind, often playfully explore the limits of the established. Irene Rima Makaryk's *Encyclopedia of Contemporary Literary Theory* has a two-page entry for *Subversion*. The encyclopedia understands subversion as an articulation, as the "'becoming visible' of any repressed, forbidden, or oppositional interpretation of the social order."[62] Cultural critics and literary scholars are fond of quoting the controversial German philosopher and philologist Friedrich Nietzsche, whose writings inspired a great deal of critical philosophical and political thought in the twentieth century. "So what is truth?" asked Nietzsche, and then responds forcefully,

> A moving army of metaphors, metonymies and anthropomorphisms, in short a summa of human relationships that were poetically and rhetorically exaggerated, transposed, and beautified until, after long and repeated use, a community considers them as solid, canonical, and binding. Truths are illusions whose illusionary nature has been forgotten; metaphors that have been used up and have lost their imprint; coins that have lost their image and that are now appear as mere metal, no longer as coins.[63]

For Paul De Man, a founding figure in literary theory, Nietzsche's passage stands for "the necessary subversion of truth."[64]

Perhaps most importantly, subversion is institutionalized in liberal constitutional orders. An impressive example is the well-known right to resistance enshrined in some liberal constitutions. In 1968, Germany added article 20, paragraph 4, to its basic law, or *Grundgesetz*. The clause states that the Federal Republic of Germany is a democratic and social state, that all power is ultimately in the hands of the people, and that the constitutional legal coercive order, the executive branch, and law enforcement are bound by the law. The basic law then adds, "All Germans have the right to resist anybody who attempts to remove this order, if no other courses of action are available."[65] This right to resistance was designed as a safeguard against an abuse of power at the hands of the government and its law-enforcement agencies. The law is informed by the idea that, during a state of exception (*Notstand*), the State itself may undermine the constitutional order. The king can do wrong. In times of perceived constitutional peril, governments with an authoritarian bent react with crackdowns, censorship, or emergency laws to mounting dissent. Authoritarian regimes see the rise of Internet-fueled subversion as such a dangerous trend that it needs to be met with aggressive countermeasures. For liberal democracies, the problem is far more delicate: they need to find out how to rebalance the right to resistance and civil liberties with national security. By overshooting the target in a new and confusing digital environment, liberal states may inadvertently push previously legitimate civic action into the realm of illegal subversion. "The restoration of the old order constitutes a permanent risk," Johannes Agnoli told his students in Berlin on 31 October 1989, just days before the Berlin Wall fell. The old Marxist closed his lecture that Tuesday by warning of unknown innovations that would again and again tempt those in power: therefore "the theoretical and practical work of subversion will never be finished."[66]

7

ATTRIBUTION

There is perhaps no better example of the retreat of violence through cyber attacks than the attribution problem. To understand why, some background is needed. Conflict, like so many other human interactions, occurs online where possible. The resulting changes, this book has argued, are mostly overestimated in their breadth and depth and in their overall significance. But that does not mean that no fundamentals of human conflict are being altered. Nearly all political cyber attacks on the empirical record—whether they were done for purposes of espionage, sabotage, or subversion—have one feature in common, as the cases discussed in this book illustrate. That feature of digital conflict represents a fundamental, and in many ways disturbing, change when compared to political confrontations in earlier, analogue times, be they violent or non-violent: that change is the attribution problem.

Mike McConnell was director of the National Security Agency from 1992 to 1996 and later George W. Bush's director of National Intelligence until 2009. About a year later, in February 2010, he gave an interview to *The Washington Post*. Admiral McConnell portrayed the lack of traceability as a grave problem for US foreign policy and demanded far-reaching action. It is worth quoting America's former top-spy at length:

> We need to develop an early-warning system to monitor cyberspace, identify intrusions and locate the source of attacks with a trail of evidence that can support diplomatic, military and legal options—and we must be able

to do this in milliseconds. More specifically, we need to reengineer the Internet to make attribution, geolocation, intelligence analysis and impact assessment—who did it, from where, why and what was the result—more manageable.[1]

Two-and-a-half years later, on 11 October 2012, Leon Panetta gave a much-noted speech to business leaders at the Intrepid Sea, Air and Space Museum. The venue had a powerful subtext: the museum is on a decommissioned *Essex*-class aircraft carrier, the USS *Intrepid*, today floating off a pier in the Hudson River in New York City. The Second World War-tested *Intrepid* sports a number of high-powered military airplanes on deck, most prominently an early model of a SR-71 "Blackbird," an advanced strategic spy plane that holds several speed and high-altitude records. That Thursday in New York, The US Secretary of Defense also a former director of the CIA, was uniquely well placed and well qualified to talk about a novel threat facing the nation, cyber attack. "The department," Panetta continued, "has made significant advances in solving a problem that makes deterring cyber adversaries more complex: the difficulty of identifying the origins of an attack." This statement was a historic first. Technicians and computer scientists say that a clever attacker can successfully avoid identification. Indeed, the US government itself had just done so with several high-profile attacks under the code-name Olympic Games. But the secretary's speech that day painted a very different picture:

> Over the last two years, the department has made significant investments in forensics to address this problem of attribution, and we are seeing returns on those investments. Potential aggressors should be aware that the United States has the capacity to locate them and hold them accountable for actions that harm America or its interests.[2]

The secretary's rhetoric included a measure of bluff and bluster, but how much is difficult to gauge. Assessing the potential countermeasures that McConnell and Panetta ominously referred to first requires understanding the problem at hand. That problem is simple: under what conditions can a cyber attack be attributed to an agent? Are there any trends and possible changes that may affect the attribution problem by making it easier or more difficult to solve? The answer to this simple question is complicated and surprising.

This chapter argues that the attribution problem, at its core, is a political problem more than it is a technical problem. "Reengineering" the

Internet, as McConnell suggested, is not only unrealistic, it would not even solve the problem at hand.[3] There is no purely technical solution to the conundrum of attribution, and this is highly unlikely to change. The attribution problem has a territorial dimension, and therefore turns into a political problem. In the vast majority of cases of international political cyber attacks, especially when they are professionally executed, the attribution problem therefore cannot be solved—unless the political stakes are high enough. This leads to a counterintuitive insight: *the attribution problem is a function of an attack's severity.* The following pages make clear why.

The argument will be established in four quick steps, each of which is illustrated by at least one representative example. This chapter first puts the attribution problem in the appropriate context; it then distinguishes three layers of the attribution problem; the difficulties of attribution under near-optimal conditions will then be discussed; and finally the offender's perspective on the attribution problem will be considered.

The attribution problem is not new in itself. Punishing an offender, or threatening to do so, requires identifying that offender. The problem is well known in criminal justice. Once a criminal offense has been committed, the prosecution has to find a suspect, possibly arrest her, establish acceptable criminal evidence, and ultimately sentence the criminal to be punished. The attribution problem is less well explored in international relations, where conventional state-on-state offenses mostly left little doubt about the attacker's identity. Even in the case of surprise attacks, the prized questions were usually when and from where the attack was coming, not from whom. Military history knows no major battles where the enemies did not reveal themselves. In the context of the conventional use of armed force, the attribution problem arises in two principal situations. One is the use of covert operations. The United States, for instance, tried to hide its hand in the support of the Afghan mujahedeen in the 1980s. Iran has been trying to conceal its support for Hezbollah. Examples of covert operations abound, especially in the context of proxy conflicts where third parties intervene. The other principal situation is political violence and terrorism. Individual attacks cannot always be easily and immediately attributed to one specific militant group or actor when no group claims credit in a credible way. Two prominent examples are the 1988 attack on Pan Am Flight 103 (the Lockerbie bombing) and the 1995 Oklahoma City bombing, where

Timothy McVeigh tried to hide his role. Yet in the vast majority of cases perpetrators do claim credit, especially when the attack was a lethal and spectacular one.[4] Both the history of covert operations and the history of terrorism know attacks where no enemies revealed themselves, and where none could be clearly identified in hindsight. Yet such cases are rare.[5] When hard weapons are used, non-attribution is the exception, not the rule—when malicious software is used, non-attribution is the rule, not the exception. This important contrast makes clear that cyber attacks are especially well suited for two activities that have always tended towards the shadows, crime and espionage.

The so-called GhostNet incident ideally illustrates the attribution problem in the context of a complex cyber espionage operation. In 2008, the Dalai Lama suspected that his staff was being spied on. The spiritual leader had to flee Tibet in 1959. For the past half-century he has lived and worked in exile in India. The Dalai Lama has often crossed the Chinese government, diplomatically as well as with wider publicity campaigns. In the 1990s, the spiritual leader started to make use of the web to publish talks and speeches and later to reach out to potential supporters. But over time, the web also offered his enemies a way to strike back. Early in 2008, the Tibetan leader's office invited two experts to help examine their computers in Dharamsala in a thorough forensic investigation. Two researchers came, Greg Walton from the Citizen Lab, a group of information security researchers at the Munk Center for International Studies at the University of Toronto in Canada, and Shishir Nagaraja, a computer scientist of Indian origin working with the University of Cambridge. They found that the holy Tibetan leader was indeed under attack. Ron Deibert, head of the Citizen Lab, who broke the story in March 2009, called it GhostNet. GhostNet was indeed a sophisticated international spying operation, probably of Chinese origin. In less than two years, the shadowy network had infected 1,295 host computers in embassies, international organizations, news media, and NGOs in 103 countries, and ministries of foreign affairs were also affected, including the foreign offices of Iran, Bangladesh, Latvia, Indonesia, the Philippines, Brunei, Barbados, and Bhutan. The Dalai Lama's offices in India, Brussels, London, and New York were also infected with the clandestine spying software. The cyber espionage operation uncovered by the visiting academics turned out to be the largest of its kind ever uncovered, at least in terms of the countries affected by the threat. The malware was able to take full control of infected computers, including searching and downloading documents, logging keystrokes, and even covertly activating PC cameras and microphones and capturing the recorded information.[6]

The attack had two vectors. Like many targeted attacks, it employed social engineering, in the form of "spear phishing," to lure unsuspecting victims to open email attachments. One email, for instance, sent on 25 July 2008, pretended to come from campaigns@freetibet.org and allegedly contained the translation of a "freedom movement ID book" in the form of an attached .DOC file. If the user opened the attachment, the malicious file would exploit a vulnerability in Microsoft Word and install the espionage malware on the user's computer.[7] Some malicious emails allegedly came from monks or other Tibetan co-workers, thus making them more trustworthy. Even worse, the attackers also stole some emails in transit and replaced legitimate attachments with infected files.[8] The other way attackers would gain entry into a targeted system was by getting the user to visit a website that contained malware which was then downloaded. Infected computers would routinely get in touch with a command-and-control server and possibly receive instructions for the next step, such as installing a remote access tool.

Technically, the operation relied mainly on backdoors, more precisely a Remote Access Trojan (RAT), especially a modified version of a tool called Poison Ivy or Gh0st RAT (spelled with a zero, not the letter "o"), hence the name GhostNet. Once the Gh0st RAT was installed on a targeted machine, the infected computer would periodically try to connect to a specific IP address, and as soon as the attackers had fired up the remote access Trojan on the infected machine they would be able to use a wide range of commands, including using the file manager, taking screen shots, logging keystrokes, using the computer's webcam, and the built-in microphone. The attackers were also able to execute programs on infected machines. This was supposed to happen clandestinely. But one monk reportedly happened to look at his screen when Outlook Express fired up on its own and started sending emails to his contacts with toxic documents attached.[9]

Such remote administration tools are openly available on the Internet, maintained as openly available backdoors by loosely organized hackers. One such hacker group, Wolfexp, even made videos available in Chinese on how to use their tool to take over targeted machines remotely, complete with grainy screenshots of unsuspecting web users to illustrate the potency of their spying program.[10] This means that the tools to execute GhostNet were openly available as well as relatively easy to use. The social engineering part of the attack was sophisticated, but the operation, in contrast to more tailored and more complex attacks such as Stuxnet or Flame, most likely did not require the intelligence, the resources, or the skills that only a nation-state could muster. This raises the question of attribution. The highly detailed Canadian report pointed out that the targets reflected China's security priorities, especially Tibet and Taiwan. And the IP addresses that were used to launch the attack were located on Hainan, an island in the South China Sea with a population of about 8 million people and home to a large signals intelligence base, just west of Lingshui Air Base. One of the main tasks of this intelligence base is monitoring satellite communication. Lingshui is one of Asia's most important intelligence bases and it reportedly houses more than 1,000 intelligence analysts working for the PLA's much larger Third Technical Department based near Beijing. Deibert's team was careful not to point the finger directly at the Chinese government because the uncovered evidence was inconclusive: "we do not know the motivation or the identity of the attacker(s)," the highly detailed and thorough Canadian report said.[11] The authors of the much shorter University of Cambridge report were less careful in their wording: "it was a targeted surveillance attack designed to collect actionable intelligence for use by the police and security services of a repressive state, with potentially fatal consequences," they wrote.[12] Despite all this technical evidence, it remains unclear if the Chinese government, intelligence agencies, or the military were directly responsible for the operation. China's government denied the accusations through its embassy in London.

Attribution, in the context of computer attacks, has several layers. The first layer is technical. The Internet is a so-called packet-switched network. A packet is a slice of a larger piece of information, for instance an email, a website, a Word document, or a piece of malware.[13] Finding malicious packets or malicious functionality is a forensic problem. The forensic goal, in starkly simplified terms, is to trace malicious activity to an IP address. The second layer is social. The difficulty is connecting a machine to a human user. If an individual used an open WiFi network, stole a computer including its Internet connection, or never left any traces that personally and geographically would identify the user's identity, the second layer is very hard, if not impossible, to penetrate. The third layer is political. If the Internet was confined to a territory where one entity has a monopoly of force, the attribution problem could be solved much more easily.[14] Suppose online fraud at a London bank was committed from a specific IP address, say 80.4.248.191, on 5 September at 21:09. Scotland Yard would then be able, through a simple WHOIS lookup, to trace the IP address to a postal address registered in Bartley Wood Business Park in Hampshire in the United Kingdom, the registered address of Virgin Media Ltd, one of Britain's leading ISPs.[15] The London police authorities could request, and possibly subpoena, Virgin Media to reveal information from its log files to identify which of the ISP's individual customers had used that particular address on 5 September at quarter past nine. Virgin is required by English law to keep this data. The police could then simply knock at the suspect's door and confiscate his computer. But reality often works differently.[16] The lookup of a fraudulent transaction on 5 September at 21:09 may lead to 217.66.19.45, with an unidentified host and an unidentified owner in the Russian Federation. The London police could then request authorities in Russia to investigate—if the Russian authorities cooperate, if they identify the ISP correctly, and if the ISP provides the log files, they may find the relevant traffic was encrypted and routed through yet another country that may or may not cooperate. And so on. Already this oversimplified example shows that what appears to be a technological problem soon morphs into a political one, creating conditions that require foreign authorities to cooperate swiftly before logs are lost, if ISPs keep log files at all, which they may not be legally required or willing to do. Needless to say, in the case of political cyber attacks, especially economic espionage, some foreign political authorities may have no interest in cooperating at all. The more clearly an attack is of a purely for-profit criminal nature, the less political the attribution problem will become, and continued investigation will depend more on the criminal justice system of a particular country.

But even in real-life criminal cases, the technical picture is far more complex. Richard Clayton of Cambridge University prepared one of the most detailed and comprehensive studies on attribution, although he rarely used the term in the report. His analysis focuses on "traceability" on the Internet. Anonymity is present when traceability fails, in Clayton's words.[17] The computer scientist discussed traceability in four simplified steps: determining the IP address that is to be traced; establishing the Internet Service Provider, which could be an independent non-commercial entity like a government or university; identifying the user account in the ISP's records; and finally connecting the actual identity of the responsible individual that operated a specific account at a specific time. On each step along the way of traceability, there can be obstacles that are impossible to overcome. As the Internet became more complex and dynamic at the turn of the millennium, the possibilities for obscuring traceability increased, even on a purely technical level. Clayton concluded that the future will bring even more uncertainty. "Quite clearly there will be many more examples of traceability problems to understand, explain and perhaps even fix." In addition, the presently used techniques are already less reliable than often assumed. "Far too many of the systems that underpin traceability are far less accurate than anyone really imagines," Clayton wrote, adding a warning:

> There is a real risk of significant miscarriages of justice should traceability start being seen as "evidence" rather than "intelligence" and it is vital to educate Law Enforcement and Governments on the limitations of traceability—whilst still accepting that a great deal of the time it is perfectly possible to work out "who did that" and smash down the right door.[18]

Looking at a simple historical case where these technical complexities do not apply brings the basic features of attribution into relief. Even in the best-documented court cases where a criminal made mistakes, motivations are known, and detailed supporting evidence is available, attribution may still not be a certainty. This is ideally illustrated by the Burleson case, the very first felony conviction for the malicious use of software in American history. It played out in 1985, and it did not involve any remote network intrusion. The software systems at the time were much simpler—the malware in question was developed for an IBM System/38, a server platform at least as big as two washing machines, which was commercially available as early as 1979. The machine had a working memory of 1MB, 1,000 times less than the working memory of a 2012 iPhone. From a purely technical point of view, the case was therefore vastly simplified.

On the morning of 21 September 1985, a programmer came into the offices of the Fort Worth, Texas, offices of the United Services Planning Association and its subsidiary, the Independent Research Agency for Life Insurance. The company and its 450 agents sold insurance to US military personnel.[19] The programmer had come to run tests on a new bonus system. As he tried to run simulations on the payroll file, the results repeatedly came up with zeros. It turned out that 168,000 commissions' payroll records had been deleted. The monthly volume of those payrolls averaged $2 million. A log file from 21 September 1985 showed that a terminal had been fired up at 03:03 in the morning. Somebody had physically broken into the offices and caused the damage. The subsequent forensic investigation found that a sequence of malicious scripts had been implanted into the IBM system three weeks before that break-in. A forensic analysis found that an employee with privileged access had rigged the system over Labor Day, 2 September 1985. That employee allegedly wrote a number of scripts that would be clandestinely inserted into a legitimate program that ran a routine every day. One of the malware's modules, ARF-1, checked the timestamp every time the legitimate program was running. When the date matched, ARF-1 triggered a series of other scripts that then resulted in overwriting the commissions' payroll records. Among forensic experts, the case is also known as one of the first documented "logic bombs."[20]

The main suspect was Donald Gene Burleson, known as a quarrelsome and unpleasant colleague. The forty-year-old programmer had been fired just two days before the break-in. So Burleson had the motive and the means to commit the crime. Yet there were other suspects. The evidence in the monumental trial was not conclusive, and the jurors were in doubt and ready to acquit the defendant. Then, however, Burleson made the mistake of trying to come up with an alibi, which blew up in his face. After the jury returned to the courtroom with the guilty verdict, one juror reportedly told another, "If Burleson had just said he couldn't remember where he was that day, I would have voted for him. The state really didn't prove anything. But why did he have to lie?"[21] The trial concluded on 19 September 1988. It was the first case in American history in which the defendant was charged with the malicious destruction of files. "As far as I know, it's the first case of this type in the nation," explained Tarrant County Assistant District Attorney Davis McCown at the time. "We've had people stealing through computers, but not this."[22] McCown had spent almost three years on the case. In the end, Burleson did not have to go to prison; he received seven years on probation and had to pay $11,800 in restitution to the USPA. Burleson was convicted not under a federal law, but under the Texas Penal Code, section 33.03, act of 14 June 1985.

Another, vastly different malware incident complements the Burleson case, and enables an insightful comparison between a well-documented domestic case and a well-documented international case. On 12 January 2010, Google disclosed in a post on its corporate blog that it had become the subject of a sophisticated cyber attack. "In mid-December, we detected a highly sophisticated and targeted attack on our corporate infrastructure originating from China that resulted in the theft of intellectual property from Google," the company announced.[23] Initially Google engineers had suspected an individual security incident, albeit an especially sophisticated one. But during an investigation they discovered that the attack was "something quite different." Google announced that two email accounts of Chinese human rights activists had been hacked, not by stealing the login credentials from the user, but by penetrating Google itself. It also became evident that intellectual property was stolen.

The hack followed a by now familiar pattern. First a specific Google employee would be identified. Then that user would receive an email from a trusted source with a link. When the unsuspecting employee followed that link, he or she would be directed to a website hosted in Taiwan. This site contained malicious JavaScript code. If the Google employee was using Internet Explorer, the site would exploit a zero-day vulnerability to inject the payload in the form of a binary file disguised as an image. Next the malicious code would open a backdoor and set up a hidden communication to command-and-control servers in Taiwan. Only then did the attackers play their trump card. The Aurora hackers had devised a method to gain access to Google's software configuration management system (SCM), in this case an installation of Perforce, a platform widely used by large software developing companies. Vulnerabilities in such source code management systems were not widely known at the time, but are relatively easy to exploit.[24] Gaining clandestine access to a company's source code is the holy grail of cyber attacks: it would give the intruder the power not just to pilfer proprietary programming code, but to make changes to the source code, for instance to install a secret peephole that would be passed on to trusting customers of Google or Adobe products. Aurora had the look and feel of a sophisticated bank shot across Mountain View to pocket dissidents at home. Yet the attack could also have an economic motivation.

Its sophistication and the suspected mixed motivation made the attack highly unusual. The attacker's motivation for the intrusion into the systems of the Californian search giant seemed to combine international economic espionage as well as domestic political surveillance of activists. That pattern was not limited to one target, Google. What became known as Operation Aurora targeted at least thirty-four leading US companies from various sectors, among them Yahoo!, Symantec, Adobe, Northrop Grumman, and Dow Chemical.[25] (There are not that many Chinese dissidents who happen to have email accounts with Northrop Grumman or Dow Chemical, it should be noted.) Aurora, unusually, was a multi-purpose attack. It exploited a previously unknown vulnerability in Microsoft's Internet Explorer. Once inside an organization, the attackers used another clever technique, called man-in-the-mailbox—a pun on man-in-the-middle attacks—where an attacker would send emails that allegedly came from trusted colleagues, thus tricking others into opening attachments.

Attempts to attribute Operation Aurora yielded unexpectedly detailed results. The National Security Agency participated in a detailed investigation. The origin of the attack was traced to two Chinese schools that train computer scientists. One was Shanghai Jiaotong University, which runs one of China's top computer science programs. Students at Jiaotong had recently won a well-known computer science competition, the so-called Battle of the Brains, sponsored by IBM since 1997, surpassing 103 of the world's top universities, including US institutions such as Stanford University. *The New York Times* interviewed academics on Jiaotong's faculty. "I'm not surprised. Actually students hacking into foreign Web sites is quite normal," one professor said anonymously (ironically he also didn't want to be attributed for fear of reprisal from the school). He then offered two scenarios:

> I believe there's two kinds of situations. One is it's a completely individual act of wrongdoing, done by one or two geek students in the school who are just keen on experimenting with their hacking skills learned from the school, since the sources in the school and network are so limited. Or it could be that one of the university's IP addresses was hijacked by others, which frequently happens.[26]

The other school was Lanxiang Vocational School in East China, which was established with military support. The head of Lanxiang's computer science department doubted the school's involvement, and argued, plausibly, that the Aurora attacks were too sophisticated for Lanxiang's students:

I think it's impossible for our students to hack Google or other US companies because they are just high school graduates and not at an advanced level. Also, because our school adopts close management, outsiders cannot easily come into our school.[27]

Even five weeks after Google made the attack public, the *Times*, and much of the world, could only guess and assume that Aurora had been a Chinese state-sponsored attack. Most likely the attack had only been routed through the schools' servers, which are often badly protected, in order to deflect attention from the actual attacker. Behind closed doors however, the US government already had more information about the attack, just ten days after the story broke. On 22 January, a political officer in the US embassy had a confidential conversation with Chen Jieren, the editor of a Communist Youth League website. That editor was also the nephew of He Guoqiang, a Politburo Standing Committee member and thus a senior and well-placed government official. Chen revealed that the attack was coordinated by the State Council Information Office and overseen by two other Politburo members, Li Changchun and Zhou Yongkang.[28] Information about the attack appeared to be closely held by them, and only after Google made the announcement on its blog was the operation discussed more widely in the party. It therefore remained unclear if China's president, Hu Jintao, as well as Prime Minister Wen Jiabao, had been aware of the attack against Google. What also remained vague was the attack's motivation. Chen insisted that the operation was "one hundred percent" political and designed exclusively to spy on Chinese dissidents. But the former CEO of Google China told the US embassy that Li Changchun, one of the attack's masterminds, was actively supporting the country's main search company Baidu against Google, its biggest competitor. Verisign, a leading Internet security company that also runs two of the web's thirteen root servers, has detailed knowledge of China's online activities. In an unpublished 2011 report, Verisign considered it "probable" that "state agencies" from the People's Republic of China were behind Aurora. Operation Aurora, it should be noted, is one of the best-attributed political cyber attacks on record—and the group behind Aurora has been continuing its operations for years, mostly against targets in the defense, shipping, aeronautics, and energy sectors, but also against NGOs and human rights organizations. No other hacking group has used more zero-day exploits than this group, dubbed the "Elderwood Project" by Symantec, approximately eight between 2009 and 2012.[29]

A third example offers a Tom Clancy-style story of solving the attribution problem: active defense, which in this case meant hacking back. The case is known as "Georbot." Georbot began unfolding in Georgia in early 2011. The country's troublesome relationship with Russia had expressed itself in military confrontations as well as in hacking attacks before, most recently in 2008. Then, nearly three years later in March 2011, a suspicious file on the computer of a government official came to the attention of the Georgian CERT. "Dr.WEB," a Russian anti-virus scanner, had flagged up the allegedly corrupted file. Georgian computer experts soon discovered that unknown hackers had infected between 300 and 400 computers across six government agencies. The machines formed a Georgia-focused botnet, hence the case's nickname. The intruders were obviously looking for political information: the malware was primed to search for obvious keywords in Microsoft Word and PDF documents, almost in a naïve way, for instance for "USA," "Russia," "NATO," or "CIA."[30] When a document met the search criteria, it was copied to command-and-control servers from which the attackers would move the document to their own computers, and then delete the dropped file on the interim server. The intrusion evolved over time and the attackers added functionalities. They were able to clandestinely exfiltrate screenshots and recorded audio material—but for once the trick backfired. The case took an odd turn when the Georgian government cut off the command-and-control servers. The hackers didn't stop, but changed their methods. They knew they had been discovered, so they presumably decided to increase the stealthiness of their spying operation. The attackers did so by using a PDF vulnerability that was not publicly known at the time.[31] As usual, the intruders would trick unsuspecting users into opening a compromised email attachment to penetrate a network. But the address they used, admin@president.gov.ge, was suspicious. When the Georgian CERT started digging into the details, the found circumstantial information that possibly implicated Russian intelligence agencies. The spam service that was used to send the fake emails, legalcrf.in, lead to a name, cover company, and street address in Moscow: Artur Jafuniaev, WSDomains, Lubianka 13, 346713 Moscow—the street address of the Russian Ministry of Internal Affairs, which is next to the Federal Security Service of the Russian Federation, FSB. The Georgians decided to take action and set up a honeypot, not just for research purposes, but to hack back. The Georgian experts offered the attacker an appropriately named target document that was itself infected. The CERT's highly technical report described the operation in broken English:

> We have Infected our PC from Lab, then gave Cyber Attacker Fake ZIP Archive with his own virus inside and the name "Georgian-Nato Agreement."[32]

The Russian hackers indeed stole the fake Georgian-Nato Agreement, opened it, and unknowingly executed the document's embedded payload. This allowed the Georgians to maintain control of the hacker's PC for at least ten minutes. That was enough time for the Georgian government team to dig into their victim's computer. They were able to obtain one document, written in Russian, that detailed further plans to attack more targets. Most remarkably, though, the Georgian CERT managed to switch on the hacker's own webcam and film a short video of him: "We had maintained control over his PC," the official report stated in raw English, "then captured got video of him, personally. We have captured process of creating new malicious modules." Their target presumably noticed the ruse after a short while and switched off access. But it was too late. The Georgian government's official report, highly unusually, contained two photos of the unknown Russian hacker. It shows a skinny, mustachioed man with dark hair, perhaps in his 30s, hunched over the screen, typing, while sitting in a neon-lit residential apartment with a trashy interior design. Yet his name and affiliation ultimately remained unclear: the Georgian CERT could hardly count on the on-the-ground support of Moscow law enforcement authorities to verify their suspicions.

The Georbot incident is probably the only detailed example of a successful case of active attribution on the public domain. But perhaps its most unusual feature is the fact that the Georgian government made the information public. Most intelligence agencies and their governments are highly reluctant to publicize such operations, for that could reveal vulnerabilities, tactics, skills, and create potential political blowback. Yet, if a small and technologically limited agency like Georgia's Ministry of Justice can pull of an active attribution operation in a legally grey area, then the assumption is reasonable that mighty and highly specialized intelligence agencies of the world's most technologically sophisticated powers can achieve a much higher degree of attribution. But by no means does this mean that Leon Panetta's cocky general statement about solving the attribution problem can be taken at face value.

ATTRIBUTION

One crucial limitation of attribution comes to the fore if intelligence is distinguished from the narrower concept of evidence. In criminal justice as well as in some scientific disciplines, the standards of evidence are clearly defined. In the legal systems of the United Kingdom as well as the United States, the highest threshold of proof is "beyond reasonable doubt," a long-used term in criminal justice. Proof is beyond reasonable doubt if the available evidence (or the absence thereof) logically implies the incriminating facts, based on reason and common sense. This criterion must be met in any criminal trial if the defendant is to be pronounced guilty—if it is not met, the judge or jury will acquit the defendant. Lower standards of proof are possible in civil litigation, for instance "preponderance of the evidence," which means that one side has more evidence in its favor than the other side. In intelligence collection and analysis, the standards of proof are less clearly defined—and they are necessarily lower than "beyond reasonable doubt." Most intelligence collection takes place in hostile and less permissive environments than the hands-on, on-the-ground collection of forensic evidence on a crime scene, particularly in the case of intelligence on ongoing computer breaches. It is therefore unrealistic and unreasonable to hold intelligence to the same standards of proof as the evidence produced in criminal trials. The following story vividly illustrates this problem.

In 2004 Jack Wang was an ambitious young man in his early 20s with a keen interest in military affairs and a notable nascent skill in hacking. He was also a Chinese patriot. On 16 January that year, Wang attended an online question-and-answer session hosted by the PLA Daily's China Military Online, at chinamil.com.cn. The forum offers its users the option of a profile picture. Wang chose a glossy picture of air force-style insignia that depict a golden star adorned with hammer and sickle sitting on golden eagle wings, with the caption "junior pilot." The guest on the forum was Zhang Zhaozhong, a military theorist and now retired rear admiral. That Friday he took part in a hosted event, "Outlook 2004," to discuss China's international strategic situation. At the time Zhang was a professor at the PLA's National Defense University in Beijing. One of his books, *Network Warfare*, was popular among students. Casually seated in a civilian black turtleneck in front of a large screen, Zhang responded to the questions that were coming in from his online audience. Jack Wang, the would-be pilot, was logged in as UglyGorilla. He asked a rather prescient question:

Professor Zhang, I read your book *Network Warfare* and was deeply impressed by the views and arguments in the book. It is said that the US military has set up a dedicated network force referred to as a "cyber army." Does China have a similar force? Does China have cyber troops?[33]

Wang soon had the answer. That same year, it turned out, he would join the growing ranks of China's cyber troops by becoming a member of PLA Unit 61398, henceforth using that same pseudonym in many of his hacking sprees. The infamous unit was part of the PLA's cyber command, situated in the General Staff Department (GSD), specifically the 3rd Department, 2nd Bureau, which operates under the Military Unit Cover Designator 61398. Just ten months after his online Q&A session with the professor, on 25 October, Wang registered hugesoft.org, a URL that over the next nine years would continuously be used to facilitate sophisticated computer spying operations against western and especially American targets. Wang was one of hundreds if not thousands of military spies busily pilfering secrets from abroad. He often signed his work with a clearly notable autograph in the code, in the self-assured style of an artist signing his painting: "v1.0 No Doubt to Hack You, Writed by UglyGorilla, 06/29/2007 [sic]."[34]

By 2007, Unit 61398 had grown so much that the PLA constructed a large but nondescript twelve-story office building off Datong Road, in Gaoqiaozhen, in Shanghai's Pudong New Area. Pudong on its own is a sprawling metropolis of 5 million, twice the population and twice the area of Chicago, with a world-famous skyline. Over a period of seven years, Jack Wang's group worked on brazen intrusions against at least 141 organizations in twenty different industries, including the Coca-Cola hack mentioned earlier. On average, the Chinese army hackers maintained access to their victims' computer networks for almost one year at a time, 356 days to be precise. The longest breach continued for four years and ten months. Unit 61398 drained gigantic amounts of data from its victims, in the case of one unidentified organization 6.5 terabytes over a ten-month period. The group used at least 937 command-and-control servers that were hosted on 849 distinct IP addresses, with the majority registered in China. When Wang's group attacked a target, they almost never connected directly from Shanghai but instead "hopped" through various nodes to cover their traces. The unit's vast and growing espionage campaign created its own administrative and logistical challenges. In 2009, China Telecom even had to provide a dedicated high-speed fiber-optic line to the new building.

ATTRIBUTION

This remarkably detailed story is based on intelligence, not evidence that would meet the beyond-reasonable-doubt test. Most of these details were revealed in a seventy-four-page report, simply titled APT1, published on 19 February 2013 by Mandiant, an American security firm that has investigated hundreds of security breaches at organizations worldwide. The study is the most significant, publicly available document that attributes major espionage operations to a Chinese entity. Mandiant's path-breaking report focused on one specific group, APT1, shorthand for Advanced Persistent Threat 1, alternatively known as Comment Crew or Comment Group. The report—and Jack Wang's story as recounted here—made several major links that were based on estimations of various degrees of certainty. The first link was that it bundled 141 attacks and attributed them to APT1. This connection could reasonably be made with a high degree of certainty on the basis of digital forensic evidence, for instance the attack methodology, the type of software used, or specific tools and techniques that have not been used by others.

A second link concerned the mission of Unit 61398. The difference between passive intelligence gathering and active computer network attack is subtle but important. The source that Mandiant cited in its report merely *estimated* that Unit 61398 is in the business of intelligence gathering, not necessarily computer network attack.[35] Consequently, the fact that China Telecom upgraded the unit's fiber-optic infrastructure does not inevitably imply that it was used to support a larger volume of high-profile attacks. The installation could merely reflect that the company is a legitimate contractor for the PLA, and possibly that the new data link was used for passive intelligence gathering, either of domestic or international nature.

But the report's most explosive claim rested on a third link: that APT1 is PLA Unit 61398. The proof for this third link is far more difficult. It relied on circumstantial evidence. The first piece of intelligence was that one of the "personas" that the report described, similar to the story of UglyGorilla above, identified himself as a local of Shanghai's Pudong New Area. The second piece of intelligence was that the IP addresses used by APT1 originated partly in Pudong, "Although they control systems in dozens of countries, their attacks originate from four large networks in Shanghai—two of which are allocated directly to the Pudong New Area," the report found. Unit 61398 is also in Pudong. Therefore, Mandiant's computer security specialists concluded, the two were identical, "Given the mission, resourcing, and location of PLA Unit 61398, we conclude that PLA Unit 61398 is APT1."[36] But conspicuously the report did not mention that Pudong is not a small neighborhood ("right outside of Unit 61398's gates")[37] but in fact a vast city landscape twice the size of Chicago.[38]

The lack of caution and nuance in the report's black-and-white conclusion unfortunately undermined its credibility more than it bolstered its important case. Since at least the 1960s intelligence analysts were conscious of their *estimative* language. Major intelligence failures in the wake of the Iraq invasion of 2003 have made the intelligence communities in the UK and the US far more cautious in their assessments and more nuanced in their language used to convey the quality and certainty of the available intelligence to their political masters.[39] In the intelligence profession, this communication problem has long been known as Words of Estimative Probability.[40] Computer security companies should heed the spies' insights. Nevertheless the Mandiant study cannot be dismissed out of hand, as the Chinese government tried to in its official response. The standards of proof that can be achieved in an intelligence operation without human sources on the ground, let along without support by local law enforcement agencies, are bound to be lower than ideal—but estimates that are "probable" or "almost certain," to use two of the highest gradations of intelligence, may still be sufficient to take meaningful political action, even action with serious consequences.

The brief consideration of four rather different yet highly instructive cases—Burleson, Aurora, Georbot, and the Mandiant report allows two important generalizations: one is that the attribution problem is almost never perfectly solved—attributing identity without an agent claiming credit or confessing nearly always entails a call of judgment. That is the case even in a highly simplified scenario like the Burleson incident and the subsequent trial. It is also the case in a complex and international high-stakes attack like Operation Aurora. Another generalization: to achieve even imperfect attribution, supplemental non-technical evidence, or at least intelligence, is required. And that evidence has to come from human sources or witnesses. In the context of a state-sponsored attack, one added difficulty arises in identifying the agency and the level of leadership that ultimately has the responsibility for an operation. Again a short comparison with conventional military operations is instructive. In the case of the conventional use of force, both the responsible agencies and the levels of authorization are historically well established, although in specific cases there may be significant uncertainty. For cyber attacks, the situation is again reversed. Uncertainty and a lack of orientation are the norm, not the exception.

Yet it is crucial to note that these four relatively well-documented cases are the exception, not the rule. In the majority of cases of cyber espionage, the attribution problem has the unpleasant effect that even the most fundamental insights remain clouded in mystery, including the specific motivation of the attack. Two short examples illustrate this shortfall. The first example is a series of attacks uncovered about a year after Aurora, in February 2011. In an operation that became known as as "Night Dragon," unknown intruders attacked a number of global energy and petrochemical companies along with individuals and business executives in Kazakhstan, Taiwan, Greece, and the United States.[41] When it was discovered, the attack had already been underway for more than a year, since November 2009. The intruders started this hack by going after the companies' external web servers, using attack tools such as SQL-injection or remote administration tools that were readily available on illicit forums online, for instance on http://rootkit. net.cn. Once inside, the online spies used a variety of techniques to hop from machine to machine on a company's internal network. The intrusions appeared to have been staged by a small group of attackers, perhaps of a dozen or fewer people. The records show that the attack took place during regular office hours, between 9 a.m. and 5 p.m. Beijing time during the workweek, indicating that it was the work of professionals, not hackers. "These were company worker bees, not freestyle hackers," said Dmitri Alperovitch, then at McAfee.[42] Yet such details are not evidence—at best, they are shoddy intelligence. Stewart Baker, a former assistant secretary at the Department of Homeland Security, pointed out how difficult it is to draw clear conclusions. The intrusion of oil and gas companies, he said, "could well be [the] Chinese government, but I can't say the government would even have to be aware of it." Baker then speculated that the intruders' motivation may well have been economical, not political. "The most valuable intelligence in the commercial world may be what oil exploration companies have found and not found," he told the *Financial Times*.[43] McAfee, who broke the news on the attack, was appropriately careful to warn that attribution was difficult: "*Important*: McAfee has no direct evidence to name the originators of these attacks but rather has provided circumstantial evidence."[44]

A second example happened about a year later. In May 2012, an attempted attack on American natural gas pipelines was discovered. The Department of Homeland Security, in charge of protecting the country's critical infrastructure, made it publicly known that the attacks were ongoing. The department's Industrial Control Systems Cyber Emergency Response Team said that its experts had identified a live campaign of intrusions. The ICS-CERT, as the response team is known, had contacted natural gas and oil pipeline operators in order to help them recognize the attacks. Attackers had used a tried and tested method to trick employees at those companies into opening infected attachments or clicking on infected links. In quite sophisticated spear-phishing attacks, the attackers had managed to send fake emails purportedly from colleagues. The attacks did not target the actual control systems, and did not cause any damage to the pipelines. Yet the wider purpose of the attacks remained unclear. The operators voiced their concern through an industry group. "These intrusions are reconnaissance," said Cathy Landry from the Interstate Natural Gas Association of America, "But we don't know if they are trying to get into the pipeline control system, or into company information."[45]

To appreciate the true significance of the attribution problem, the other perspective has to be considered in turn. The other perspective is the perspective of the attacker. The targeted party nearly always has an interest in attributing violent action to its agent—but the situation is more complex for the offender. An offensive actor may have one of four interests in attributing a cyber attack: avoiding attribution; message attribution; full attribution; or false attribution. The four will be briefly considered in turn.

The first and often very likely scenario is that an attacker attempts to *avoid attribution*: in the vast majority of cases of cyber espionage, spies simply want to avoid all attribution. All cases discussed above under espionage have this trait in common. Avoiding attribution is also likely to be in the interest of professional saboteurs, where the act of sabotage itself—Stuxnet is the prime example—carries its own implicit message that does not need to be explicitly explained to the target.

This may be different in the second scenario, *message attribution*. If an attacker or a group of attackers wants to use a cyber attack, for instance a Denial of Service Attack, as a vehicle to make a political statement, then this statement almost always requires some sort of explanation.

ATTRIBUTION

Military as well as militant action, generally speaking, requires an explanation. The perpetrators of a terrorist bombing, for instance, usually follow up with a communiqué that explains the rationale of the offense. Something similar applies in the case of some cyber attacks. The Shamoon incident, the hacking attack against Saudi Aramco on 15 August 2012, illustrates the messaging requirement. A new entity, The Cutting Sword of Justice, successfully claimed credit for the attack. On the same day that the attack became public, a user by the default name of "A Guest" published a communiqué by simply posting it to Pastebin, an Internet platform used to publicize text anonymously by copying-and-pasting it there. The message contained information that had not been in the public domain at this point in time: the number of compromised computers as well as the precise kill time of the malware. Both were later confirmed separately by Saudi Aramco and Symantec. These confirmed facts in turn established the credibility of the anonymously posted communiqué, thus attaching a political message to the mysterious attack. The attackers, in other words, succeeded in four ways: infiltrating the target, engaging the target, attaching a message to the attack, and at the same time remaining anonymous. The attackers thus divorced the main cost of attribution from the main benefit: suffering consequences as a result of making an identifiable political statement.

The third and perhaps the most interesting scenario *is correct attribution.* The attribution problem has a flipside for potential authors of offensive malware. Equipping an attack with an anonymous message is easy, but it may not be in the interest of the attacker if the stakes are high. An act of war, including a potential although unlikely act of cyber war, is an act of physical force to compel an actor to change their behavior. The notion that a powerful state actor would try to coerce another actor anonymously is highly unrealistic. The exception is covert operations in a proxy conflict or sabotaging machines in a covert operation of a mostly tactical nature. If the political stakes in a one-on-one confrontation are high enough, the offender will have an interest in taking credit for an attack—or, more likely, the attribution issue will retreat into the background in the heat of crisis.

A fourth scenario *is false attribution.* Martin Libicki, a cyber security analyst at the Rand Corporation in Washington, DC, pointed to the problematic incentive structure of cyber attacks that could be designed to get one state to "retaliate," mistakenly, against another state or possibly non-state actor, "the more serious the threat of retaliation, the greater the incentive for false-flag operations on the part of the presumed attacker's enemies."[46] Verisign's Eli Jellenc described the problem of "false-flags" as the mimicry problem and surmised that it could be even more serious than the attribution problem conventionally understood.[47] But deliberate false attribution remains highly speculative. The only empirical examples of false attribution are command-and-control servers routed through various third countries. An unusual form of false attribution is what may be called a false-credit ruse: falsely claiming a cyber attack where none had happened. Perhaps the only example is al-Qaeda's inept and ridiculous claim to have caused the 2003 power blackout, as the Egyptian newspaper *Dar al Hayat* reported.[48]

Several factors are likely to facilitate attribution. Firstly, it is helpful if the intruders make mistakes and unknowingly leave forensic evidence behind. Mahdi, discussed in an earlier chapter, is an example of a rather unprofessional execution. But some professional attackers may maintain the highest standards of operational security and not make mistakes. Secondly, knowing the motivation of a particular attack may limit the number of suspects, especially in political cyber attacks. GhostNet or Gauss are examples where the design and the target set of the attack point to a limited number of suspects (China and the United States, respectively). Thirdly, supporting evidence may be available, such as wiretaps or leaks of internal communication that shows a cyber attack was planned and authorized by a specific leader or manager, as in the Aurora follow-up of the US embassy in Beijing.[49] Fourthly, some attacks require a high degree of specialized and hard-to-get intelligence, for instance process knowledge about the control system installation in large oil refineries. The more specialized, the more expensive, and the more hard-to-get the intelligence required for such a strike, the smaller the circle of organizations able to acquire that intelligence. Finally, the most sophisticated military-grade cyber attacks are likely to be embedded in a broader campaign of covert or overt operations, as Stuxnet demonstrated. If cyber attacks merely precede or accompany conventional strikes, then the attribution problem steps into the background.

This analysis leads to a conclusion that is both sobering and comforting at the same time: *the attribution problem is a function of an attack's severity*. Attributing political cyber attacks, if executed professionally and if unsupported by supplemental intelligence, is very hard if not impossible. Even if an attack can be traced to a particular state, and even if that state's motivation to attack seems clear, the attribution problem's technical, social, and political architecture gives the accused state sufficient deniability. The Aurora attack demonstrated such a scenario for the Chinese. Stuxnet demonstrated it for the United States and Israel. But because the attribution problem is a political problem, there is room for maneuver. Both Aurora and Stuxnet were high-profile attacks. But the sophistication and the impact of a cyber attack could be significantly higher, which leads to an important insight: the more damaging and the more violent an attack, the higher the political stakes. And the higher the political stakes, the more pressure the targeted country will be able to bring to bear on the country of the suspected origin to cooperate in a forensic investigation. Consider an Operation Aurora scenario on steroids: a highly sophisticated attack, but one that includes a trailblazing campaign of cyber attacks against US critical infrastructure, for instance a number of targeted Stuxnet-class intrusions into nuclear power plants resulting in damage to the reactors' cooling mechanisms and possibly radioactive incidents that cause casualties and fatalities. Further consider that—as with the Aurora attacks—nobody took credit for the attack but its destructive design and the high-grade intelligence that enabled it limited the number of possible perpetrators; within weeks the NSA would be able to trace the origin to Chinese IP addresses at two educational establishments with links to the military. Such an attack may be extraordinarily unlikely, perhaps unfeasible—yet it is helpful to consider how a "cyber 9/11" would affect the attribution problem. The political situation in the wake of such an event would be extraordinary, and military retaliation would be a real option. In such a situation, two changes would be likely: first, the standards of attribution would be lowered, not to the unreasonable but to the realistic. These standards as well as the transparency of the evidence are already lower than in an American court trial, perhaps comparable with the far murkier intelligence that regularly supports covert operations and drone strikes in far-flung places. The second change would be that the burden of proof would shift to the suspect. If Chinese authorities denied their authorship without aggressively cooperating with US investigators, providing detailed log-files and all available forensic evidence that can lead the investigation a step closer to the perpetrators, either inside or outside China, then such a refusal of cooperation may be understood as a tacit admission of authorship; *we won't tell you who did it* would simply translate into *we did it*. The attribution problem, in short, would most likely be resolved within a reasonable time frame in such an extreme situation. If cyber war takes place, the attribution problem will likely be solved. This is the argument's comforting part. The sobering part is that this statement can be flipped on its head and turned into a weighty question: if cyber war will not take place, can the attribution problem ever be solved? The answer, as this chapter argued, entirely depends on the standards of proof that policy makers and the public are willing to accept as a sufficient basis for political action. Attribution is always a call of judgment.

8

BEYOND CYBER WAR

Before moving on to conclusions, one subject needs to be moved out of the way. That subject has permeated this analysis—and it is a subject that pervades, if not distorts, many other publications on cyber security: analogies.

Analogies, similes, and metaphors have enabled and shaped the discussion of computers for many decades. As engineers developed new technologies, they needed new words to describe what they and their technology were doing. *Storage* and *packets* and *firewalls* are all spatial analogies that refer to something humans could intuitively relate to. Hard disks were a repository for lots of data, old and new, so referring to them as storage devices must have seemed intuitive. Small pieces of information, bundled between a header and footer with an address on it, naturally could be called a packet. Calling software that prevented unauthorized access a firewall just made sense. Pointing out that cyberspace itself is a spatial metaphor may be obvious. Less obvious is the fact that it was not an engineer who coined the term, but William Gibson, a novelist. Gibson first used the word in his 1982 science fiction story *Burning Chrome.*[1] He later popularized it in the 1984 novel *Neuromancer.* It is worth quoting the paragraph that introduced the word to the book's readers. The segment describes the fictional thoughts of Henry Dorsett Case, a low-level drug dealer in the dystopian underworld of Chiba City, Japan:

A year here and he [Case] still dreamed of cyberspace hope fading nightly. All the speed he took, all the turns he'd taken and the corners he'd cut in Night City, and still he'd see the matrix in his sleep, bright lattices of logic unfolding across the colorless void ... The Sprawl was a long strange way home over the Pacific now, and he was no console man, no cyberspace cowboy. Just another hustler, trying to make it through.[2]

Cyberspace, for Gibson, was meant to evoke a digital virtual world of computer networks that users would be able to "jack" into through consoles. Cyberspace, Gibson later explained, was an "effective buzzword ... evocative and essentially meaningless." The writer imagined the word as a suggestive term, one that had "no real semantic meaning."[3] But probably not even the resourceful Gibson could have imagined a more spectacular rise of his evocative yet meaningless expression. To this day, this creative lack of semantic clarity remains a potent source of agility that helped the analogy jump out from the pages of an obscure sci-fi novel and "jack" cyberspace into the political reality of international relations and national security.

Yet analogies should be used with caution and skill, especially in the conceptual minefield that is cyber security. Analogies can be triply instructive. Firstly, a metaphor can make it easier to understand a problem—analogies are *didactic devices* (saying that cyber security is a conceptual minefield, as the opening sentence of this paragraph just did, makes one thing obvious: be careful, something can go wrong if you don't pay attention to detail). Secondly, the comparisons that metaphors force upon us can highlight areas of importance and connections that might otherwise have been missed—analogies are *inspirational and creative devices* (if cyber security is a conceptual minefield, then perhaps we can come up with a way to better find the "mines?"). Finally, and most importantly, at some point a metaphor will begin to fail, and at this point of conceptual failure we may learn the most important things about the subject at hand, how it differs from the familiar, how it is unique—analogies are also *testing devices*.[4] This triple approach to evaluating the utility of metaphors is simple in concept but difficult in practice. Perhaps especially in the context of cyber security—a field which encompasses the technological knowledge of various subdisciplines of computer science as well as social science, political science, legal studies, and even history—each step on this three-bar ladder of abstraction by analogy requires progressively more specialized expertise.

Taking the first step is easy. Even laypersons may use analogies as *didactic devices*. Going to the second step is not too difficult. Using analogies as *creative devices* requires some working knowledge of a field but not special training. But using analogies as *testing devices* requires expertise and skill. Recognizing a complex analogy's point of failure and taking advantage of the additional insights afforded by the conceptual limitations of a given metaphor takes expert knowledge, perhaps even knowledge from across unrelated disciplines and subdisciplines. In practice, therefore, analogies often begin to fail without their users noticing the defect. The short-sighted and flawed use of metaphors is especially prevalent in the cyber security debate, particularly, it seems, among experts in military affairs both in uniform and outside uniform. Talking about cyber war or cyber weapons, for instance, is *didactically* useful: the audience instantly has an idea of what cyber security could be about; it inspires *creativity*: perhaps evoking thoughts of "flying" or "maneuvering" in cyberspace, not unlike Henry Dorsett Case jacking in. But too often analogies are used without understanding or communicating their point of failure (if cyber security is a conceptual minefield, then stepping on one of the dangerous devices causes harm that cannot instantly be recognized). The line between using such comparisons as self-deception devices and testing devices, in other words, can be a subtle one.

A perfect illustration of this problem is the much-vaunted war in the ostensible fifth domain. "Warfare has entered the fifth domain: cyberspace," *The Economist* intoned in July 2010.[5] Indeed, referring to cyber conflict as warfare in the fifth domain has become a standard expression in the debate. This author was taken aback in a closed-door meeting in the Department of War Studies at King's College London in early 2012 when a senior lawyer for the International Committee of the Red Cross referred to cyber war and wondered whether the ICRC needed to work toward adapting the law of armed conflict to that new "fifth domain." Five points will help clear the view. First: the expression of war in the fifth domain has its origin as a US Air Force lobbying gimmick. The Air Force had already been in charge of air and space, so cyberspace came naturally. In December 2005 the US Air Force expanded its mission accordingly. That alone is not a strong argument against the term's utility, but it should be clear where the expression comes from, and what the original intention was: claiming a larger piece of a defense budget that would start to shrink at some point in the future. Second: ultimately, code-triggered violence will express itself in the other domains. Violence in cyberspace is always indirect, as chapter two discussed at length. By definition, violence that actually harms a human being cannot express itself in a fifth domain. Third, if warfare in the fifth domain, as consequently would be necessary, referred only to damaging, stealing, or deleting information stored in computer networks, rather than to affecting something that is not part of that domain in the first place, then the very notion of war would be diluted into a metaphor, as in the "war" on obesity. Fourth, cyberspace is not a separate domain of military activity. Instead the use of computer networks permeates all other domains of military conflict, land, sea, air, and space. To an extent, that has always been the case for the other domains as well. But in the case of IT security an institutional division of labor is far more difficult to implement, especially in a military context: the air force doesn't have tanks, the army has no frigates, but everybody has computer-run command-and-control networks. Finally, cyberspace is not even space. Cyberspace is a now-common metaphor to describe the widening reaches of the Internet. "Firewall" and "surfing" the web are other well-established and widely accepted spatial metaphors. Saying the air force "flies" in cyberspace is like the army training troops to "scale" firewalls or the navy developing new "torpedoes" to hit some of those surfing the web. In fact the very idea of "flying, fighting, and winning … in cyberspace," enshrined in the US Air Force's mission statement, is so ill-fitting that some serious observers can only find it faintly ridiculous—an organization that wields some of the world's most terrifying and precise weapons should know better. The debate on national security and defense would be well served if debating war was cut back to the time-tested four domains. After all there is no cyber attack, not even the over-cited Stuxnet, which unequivocally represents an act of war on its own. No cyber offense has ever caused the loss of human life. No cyber offense has ever injured a person. No cyber attack has ever seriously damaged a building.

Once the distraction of the "fifth domain of warfare" is moved out of the way, five fundamental and largely novel conclusions become visible.

The first and main conclusion, and this book's core argument, is that the rise of cyber offenses represents an attack on violence itself. Almost all cyber attacks on record are non-violent. Those cyber attacks that actually do have the potential to inflict physical violence on machines or humans can do so only indirectly, as chapter two argued in detail: so far, violence administered through cyberspace is less physical, less emotional, less symbolic, and less instrumental than more conventional uses of political violence. This applies in all three main areas where political cyber attacks appear: *sabotage operations* may be violent or, in the majority of cases on record, non-violent. The higher the technical development and the dependency of a society, the higher the potential for both violent and non-violent cyber sabotage. This has double significance: it is easier to distinguish between violence and non-violence, and it is more likely that saboteurs choose non-violence over violence. *Espionage operations* seem to be making less use of personnel trained in the management of violence than in the pre-Internet age. To an extent, experts in the use of code are replacing experts in the use of force, though only in relative terms and at a price. Finally, *subversion* has changed. The early phases of subversively undermining an established authority require less violence than before, but turning a budding subversive movement into a revolutionary success has become more difficult. Technology seems to have lowered the entry costs while raising the costs of success. Yet cyber attacks of all strands, even in their predominantly non-violent ways, may achieve a goal that previously required some form of political violence: to undermine the collective social trust in specific institutions, systems, organizations, or individuals. And cyber attacks, whether executed by a state or by non-state groups, may undermine social trust, paradoxically, in a more direct way than political violence: through a non-violent shortcut.

The second conclusion concerns the balance between defense and offense in the context of cyber attacks. Most conventional weapons may be used defensively and offensively. But the information age, the argument goes, has "offence-dominant attributes."[6] A 2011 Pentagon report on cyberspace still stressed "the advantage currently enjoyed by the offense in cyberwarfare."[7] Cyber attack, proponents of the offense-dominance school argue, increases the attacker's opportunities and the amount of damage to be done while decreasing the risks (sending special code is easier than sending Special Forces).[8] The attribution problem unquestionably plays into the hands of the offense, not the defense. Hence expect more sabotage and more saboteurs.

But adherents of the offense-dominance ideology should reconsider their arguments, for three different reasons: one is that when it comes to cyber weapons, the offense has to deal with a set of costs and difficulties that the defense does not have to deal with. One implicit assumption of the offense-dominance school is that cyberspace favors the weak. But cyber attack may also favor strong and rich countries in unexpected ways: the Idaho National Laboratory, for instance, has many of the mainstream industrial control systems installed on range, in order to test them, find vulnerabilities, and build stronger defensive systems. But the same testing environment is also a tremendous offensive asset. By the time engineers have understood how to fix something, they also know how to break it. In addition to this, some installations are highly expensive to simulate and to install in a testing environment, for instance the control systems used in complex and highly bespoke refineries. At the same time only very few systems are used in refineries. This means that only a country that has this capability may be in a position to attack that capability elsewhere—this could limit the number of potential attackers.[9] Cyber sabotage with serious destructive potential is therefore possibly even more labor intensive than the brick-and-mortar kind, even if the required resources are dwarfed by the price of complex conventional weapon systems.[10] Vulnerabilities have to be identified before they can be exploited; complex industrial systems need to be understood first; and a sophisticated attack vehicle may be so fine-tuned to one specific target configuration that a generic use may become impracticable—consider a highly sophisticated rocket that can only be fired against one single building and at nothing else, and it can only be fired once the attacker knows precisely what's inside that building. The target set of a cyber weapon is therefore more limited than commonly assumed—the reverse is true for robust defenses.

Another reason is that, when it comes to cyber weapons, the offense has a shorter half-life than the defense.[11] Clandestine attacks may have an unexpectedly long life-cycle, as Stuxnet and especially Flame illustrated. But weaponized code that is designed to maximize damage, not stealth, is likely to be more visible. If an act of cyber war was carried out to cause significant damage to property and people, then that attack would be highly visible by definition. As a result it is highly likely that the malicious code would be found and analyzed, probably even publicly by anti-virus companies and the software vendors that provide the attacked product. The exploits that enabled the attack would then most likely be patched and appropriate protections put in place. Yet political crises may stretch out for many weeks, months, or even years. Updated defenses would make it very difficult for the aggressor to repeat an attack. But any threat relies on the offender's *credibility* to attack, or to repeat a successful attack. If a potent cyber weapon is launched successfully once, it is questionable if an attack, or even a salvo, could be repeated in order to achieve a political goal. The problem of repetition reduces the coercive utility of destructive cyber attacks.

The final factor favoring the defense is the market. One concern is that sophisticated malicious actors could resort to asymmetric methods, such as employing the services of criminal groups, rousing patriotic hackers, and potentially redeploying generic elements of known attack tools. Worse, more complex malware is likely to be structured in a modular fashion. Modular design could open up new business models for malware developers. In the car industry, for instance,[12] modularity translates into the possibility of a more sophisticated division of labor. Competitors can work simultaneously on different parts of a more complex system. Modules could be sold on underground markets. But even if this analysis is correct, emerging vulnerability markets pose a limited risk: the highly specific target information and programming design needed for potent weapons is unlikely to be traded generically. To go back to the imperfect analogy of chapter four: paintball pistols will continue to be commercially available, not intelligence devouring preprogrammed warheads of virtual, one-shot smart missiles. At the same time the market on the defensive side is bullish: the competition between various computer security companies has heated up, red-teaming is steadily improving, active defense is emerging, and very slowly but notably consumers are becoming more security aware.

Once the arguments are added up, it appears that cyberspace does not favor the offense, but actually has advantages for the defense in stock. What follows may be a new trend: the level of sophistication required to find an opportunity and to stage a successful cyber sabotage operation is rising. The better the protective and defensive setup of complex systems, the more sophistication, the more resources, the more skills, the more specificity in design, and the more organization is required from the attacker. Only very few sophisticated strategic actors may be able to pull off large-scale sustained computer sabotage operations. A thorough conceptual analysis and a detailed examination of the empirical record corroborates one central hypothesis: developing and deploying potentially destructive cyber weapons against hardened targets will require significant resources, hard-to-get and highly specific target intelligence, and time to design, test, prepare, launch, execute, maintain, and assess an attack. Successfully attacking the most highly secured targets would probably require the resources or the support of a state actor; terrorists are unlikely culprits of an equally unlikely cyber-9/11.

The third conclusion is about the ethics of cyber attacks. If cyber attacks *reduce* the amount of violence inherent in conflict, rather than increase it, then this analysis opens a fresh viewpoint on some important ethical questions. Some observers have suggested creating an agreement like the Geneva Conventions to limit the use of weaponized code.[13] Often such demands reach back to comparisons to the Cold War and nuclear weapons. For example: Brent Scowcroft, a cold warrior who served presidents Gerald Ford and George H.W. Bush, addressed a group of experts and students at Georgetown University in March 2011. The Cold War and cyber security are "eerily similar," said Scowcroft, arguing that the US–Soviet arms control treaties should serve as a blueprint for tackling cyber security challenges. "We came to realize nuclear weapons could destroy the world and cyber can destroy our society if it's not controlled," a nouning Snowcroft told his Georgetown audience.[14] Many views along similar lines could be added, and several academic articles have attempted to extract useful Cold War parallels.[15] Naturally, avoiding the "destruction of our society" at all costs appears as the ethically correct choice. Many observers naturally fall back into well-established patterns of thought: striving for an international treaty to stop the impending "cyber arms race" or trying to apply *jus ad bellum* to acts of war that have not taken place.[16] But lazy and loose comparisons cannot replace sober and serious analysis—nuclear analogies are almost always flawed, unhelpful, and technically misguided.[17]

Once cyber attacks are broken down into their three strains, sounder ethical considerations become possible. *Subversion* is the most critical activity. It is probably impossible to find much common ground on this question between the United States and the European Union on the one hand and the authoritarian political regimes in Russia or China on the other—and it would be ethically unacceptable to make compromises. Russia and China have famously suggested finding such a compromise in the form of an "International code of conduct for information security," laid out in a letter to the United Nations Secretary-General on 12

September 2011. One of the core tenets of this suggested code was "respect for sovereignty" online in order to "combat" criminal and terrorist activities that use the Internet. The goal: curbing the dissemination of information that incites extremism, secessionism, and "disturbance." Unnerved by the web-driven Arab revolutions, China and Russia wanted to set the international stage for better counter-subversion at home, as became evident during the World Conference on International Telecommunications (WCIT) in Dubai, United Arab Emirates, in early December 2012.

Yet for liberal democracies, the most normatively crucial question is a very different one. The question is not how to curb subversion, but how to maintain the right forms of subversion that enable democratic as well as entrepreneurial self-renewal: how should a free and open liberal democracy draw and renegotiate the line between regenerative subversion, which is enshrined in the constitution of truly free countries, and illegal subversive activities? This fine line has evolved over hundreds of years in liberal democracies, along with the tacit understanding that at rare but important junctures illegal activity can be legitimate activity. This line will have to be carefully reconsidered under the pressure of new technologies that may be used to extend control as well as to protest and escape control. The real risk for liberal democracies is not that these technologies empower individuals more than the state; the long-term risk is that technology empowers the state more than individuals, thus threatening to upset a carefully calibrated balance of power between citizens and the governments they elect to serve them.

The *ethics of sabotage* look very different. Weaponized code, or cyber attacks more generally, may achieve goals that previously would have required the use of conventional force. This analysis has also argued that the most sophisticated cyber attacks are highly targeted, and that cyber weapons are unlikely to cause collateral damage in the same way as conventional weapons. Therefore, from an ethical point of view, the use of computer attack in many situations is clearly preferable to the use of conventional weapons: a cyber attack may be less violent, less traumatizing, and more limited. Sabotage through weaponized code, in short, is likely to be more ethical than an airstrike, a missile attack, or a Special Forces raid. Something comparable applies to the *ethics of cyber espionage*. Again the use of computer attack as a tool of statecraft has to be compared with its alternatives, not with taking no action at all. Juxtaposing the alternatives is useful: intelligence may be gained by infiltrating computer systems and intercepting digital signals—or intelligence may be acquired by infiltrating human spies into hostile territory at personal risk, possibly armed, or by interrogating suspects under harsh conditions. Depending on the case and its context, computer espionage may be the ethically safer choice. The major problems are not ethical, but operational. This leads to the next conclusion.

The fourth conclusion is the most sobering one—it concerns the starkly limiting subtext of stand-alone cyber attacks.[18] A state-sponsored cyber attack on another state sends a message in the subtext. The best-known and most successful example is Stuxnet. An assessment of this technically impressive operation has to be put into the larger strategic context: it was designed to slow and delay Iran's nuclear enrichment program, and undermine the Iranian government's trust in its ability to develop a nuclear weapon. Yet, firstly, it long remained unclear and controversial how successful the designers of Stuxnet were in this respect—it was probably clearer for the Iranians themselves. What is clear for outsiders, though, is that Stuxnet did not succeed in stopping Iran or denting the regime's determination to develop a nuclear weapons capability. Several countries, secondly, pursued a number of policies vis-à-vis Iran in order to prevent the Islamic Republic from acquiring nuclear weapons. The instruments range from diplomacy, negotiations and sanctions of various sorts to covert operations, the assassination of nuclear scientists (and others), military threats, and ultimately to air strikes against key Iranian installations. Cyber attacks are only one instrument among many. Focusing on cyber attacks with questionable efficiency, and possibly with an AC/DC soundtrack, therefore runs the risk of sending a counterproductive message to the Iranians in the subtext: *we're alert and technically sophisticated, but we're not really serious about attacking you if you cross a red line.* A stand-alone cyber attack, especially done clandestinely and in a fashion that makes it impossible or nearly impossible to identify the attacker *in situ*, can be executed from a safe distance. Such an attack does not put the lives of service personnel at risk—therefore the political stakes are by definition lower than in a conventional operation. It is useful to remember the Cold War-logic of the trip-wire here. Throughout the Cold War, substantial numbers of American ground forces were stationed in West Germany and elsewhere to make a credible statement to the Soviet Union in the subtext: *we're alert and technically sophisticated, and we're really serious about attacking you if you cross a red line.*[19] The White House credibly demonstrated its seriousness by putting the lives of American citizens on the line. Cyber attacks could yield very valuable intelligence, no doubt. But from a political vantage point their coercive utility is far more questionable. Based on the empirical record and on a technical analysis, the political instrumentality of cyber attacks has been starkly limited and is likely to remain starkly limited. Paradoxically this effect is enhanced by the wide gulf between hype and reality, as those at the receiving end of cyber sabotage hear a lot of noise but feel (comparatively) little pain. Put simply, cyber sabotage attacks are likely to be less efficient than commonly assumed.

The final conclusion is about the reaction, about countermeasures to cyber attacks. Senator John McCain commented on the failed Cybersecurity Act of 2012 over the summer that year. The prominent national security leader had voted against the proposed bill: "As I have said time and time again, the threat we face in the cyber domain is among the most significant and challenging threats of twenty-first-century warfare." Early in 2013 the Pentagon announced that it would boost the staff of its Cyber Command from 900 to 4,900 people, mostly focused on the offense. The use of such martial symbolism points to a larger problem: the militarization of cyber security.[20] William Lynn, the Pentagon's number two until October 2011, responded to critics by pointing out that the Department of Defense would not "militarize" cyberspace. "Indeed," Lynn wrote, "establishing robust cyberdefenses no more militarizes cyberspace than having a navy militarizes the ocean."[21] There is one major problem with such statements.

The US government, as well as many other governments, has so far failed to establish robust cyberdefenses. Robust defenses against *sabotage* mean hardening computer systems, especially the systems that are moving stuff around, from chemicals to trains—but the actual security standards of the systems that run the world's industrial and critical infrastructure continued to be staggeringly low in 2013. Robust defenses against *espionage* mean avoiding large-scale exfiltration of sensitive data from companies and public agencies—but Western intelligence agencies are only beginning to understand counter-espionage and the right use of human informants in a digitized threat environment. Robust defenses against *subversion* finally mean maintaining social stability by strengthening the Internet's openness and the citizen participation in political process—the best insurance against degenerative subversion is allowing and even protecting regenerative subversion. If militarizing cyberspace means establishing robust cyber defenses, then cyberspace has not been "militarized." What has been militarized is the debate about cyberspace. One result is that the quality of this debate dropped, or, more accurately, never rose to the level that information societies in the twenty-first century deserve. This book has argued that this remarkable double-standard is not merely a coincidence. What appears as harmless hypocrisy masks a knotty causal relationship: loose talk of cyber war overhypes the offenses and blunts the defenses.

In the 1950s and 1960s, when Giraudoux's play was translated into English, the world faced another problem that many thought was inevitable: nuclear exchange. Herman Kahn, Bill Kaufmann, and Albert Wohlstetter were told that nuclear war could not be discussed publicly, as Richard Clarke pointed out in his alarmist book, *Cyber War*. He rightly concluded that, as with nuclear security, there should be more public discussion on cyber security because so much of the work has been stamped secret. This criticism is justified and powerful: too often countries as well as companies do not share enough data on vulnerabilities as well as capabilities. Of course there are limits to transparency when national security and corporate revenue is at stake. But democratic countries deserve a public debate on cyber security that is far better informed than the status quo. Open systems, no matter whether we are talking about a computer's operating system or a society's political system, are more stable and run more securely. The stakes are too high to just muddle through.

The Pearl Harbor comparison and the Hiroshima analogy point to another limitation: unlike the nuclear theorists of the 1950s, cyber war theorists of the 2010s have never experienced the actual use of a deadly cyber weapon, let alone a devastating one like "Little Boy." There was no and there is no Hiroshima of cyber war. Based on a careful evaluation of the empirical record, based on technical detail and trends, and based on the conceptual analysis presented here, a future cyber-Hiroshima must be considered highly unlikely. It is about time for the debate to leave the realm of myth and fairytale—to a degree, serious experts have already moved on, and the political debate in several countries is beginning to follow their lead. Cassandra, it is true, was right at the end and had the last word in the famous Greek myth. But then, did the Trojan War really take place?

NOTES

PREFACE

1. Dillon Beresford, "Exploiting Siemens Simatic S7 PLCs," a paper prepared for Black Hat USA+2011, 8 July 2011, http://bitly.com/OtcuJx+

THE ARGUMENT

1. Jean Giraudoux, *Tiger at the Gates (La guerre de Troie n'aura pas lieu)*, translated by Christopher Fry, New York: Oxford University Press, 1955.
2. John Arquilla and David Ronfeldt, "Cyberwar is Coming!" *Comparative Strategy*, vol. 12, 2 (1993), pp. 141–65.
3. William J. Lynn, "Defending a New Domain," *Foreign Affairs*, vol. 89, 5 (2010), pp. 97–108, p. 101.
4. Richard A. Clarke and Robert K. Knake, *Cyber War*, New York: Ecco, 2010, p. 261.
5. Lisa Daniel, "Panetta: Intelligence Community Needs to Predict Uprisings," American Forces Press Service, 11 Feb. 2011.
6. Paul Taylor, "Former US Spy Chief Warns on Cybersecurity," *Financial Times*, 2 Dec. 2012.
7. Michael Joseph Gross, "A Declaration of Cyber-War," *Vanity Fair*, Apr. 2011.
8. Several critical contributions have helped improve the debate since 2010. Among the most important are the security technologist Bruce Schneier, Obama's former cybersecurity coordinator Howard Schmidt, and the scholar Sean Lawson, see: Bruce Schneier, "The Threat of Cyberwar Has Been Grossly Exaggerated," Schneier on Security, 7 July 2010; Ryan Singel, "White House Cyber Czar: 'There Is No Cyberwar'," *Wired*, 4 Mar. 2010; Sean Lawson, "Beyond Cyber Doom," Working Paper, Washington, DC: George Mason University, Jan. 2011.

1. WHAT IS CYBER WAR?

1. Carl von Clausewitz, *Vom Kriege*, Berlin: Ullstein, 1832 (1980), p. 27.
2. One of the most creative and important theoreticians of deterrence, Jack Gibbs, once pointed out that fear and the threat of force are integral ingredients of deterrence, "Unless threat and fear are stressed, deterrence is a hodgepodge notion." Jack P. Gibbs, "Deterrence Theory and Research," in Gary Melton, Laura Nader, and Richard A. Dienstbier (eds), *Law as a Behavioral Instrument*, Lincoln: University of Nebraska Press, 1986, p. 87.
3. Thomas Mahnken, in a useful conceptual appraisal of cyber war, also uses Clausewitz's definition of war as violent, political, and "interactive," and argues that the basic nature of war was not fundamentally altered by the advent of nuclear weapons or by cyber attack. Thomas G. Mahnken, "Cyber War and Cyber Warfare," in Kristin Lord and Travis Sharp (eds), *America's Cyber Future: Security and Prosperity in the Information Age*, vol. 2, pp. 53–62, Washington, DC: CNAS, 2011.
4. Clausewitz, *Vom Kriege*, p. 29.
5. "[Der Gegner] gibt mir das Gesetz, wie ich es ihm gebe," ibid., p. 30.
6. Ibid., p. 35.
7. In *Vom Kriege* Clausewitz uses similar phrases a few times. This quote is a translation of the heading of Book 1, Chapter 24, "Der Krieg ist einer bloße Fortsetzung der Politik mit anderen Mitteln," ibid., p. 44.
8. For a sophisticated critique of this argument, see John Stone, "Cyber War Will Take Place!," *Journal of Strategic Studies*, vol. 36, 1 (Feb. 2013).
9. This is not a statement about the different levels of war: connecting between the political, strategic, operational, and tactical levels always remains a challenge.
10. This problem has also been extensively discussed among legal scholars. For an excellent recent overview, see Matthew C. Waxman, "Cyber-Attacks and the Use of Force," *The Yale Journal of International Law*, vol. 36 (2011), pp. 421–59.
11. For a particularly vividly told scenario, see the opening scene of Richard A. Clarke and Robert K. Knake, *Cyber War*, New York: Ecco, 2010.
12. See, for instance, Yoram Dinstein, "Computer Network Attacks and Self-Defense," *International Legal Studies*, vol. 76 (2002), p. 103.
13. For more on this argument, see Waxman, "Cyber-Attacks and the Use of Force," p. 436.
14. Michael V. Hayden, "The Future of Things 'Cyber'," *Strategic Studies Quarterly*, vol. 5, 1 (2011), pp. 3–7.
15. Thomas C. Reed, *At the Abyss*, New York: Random House, 2004, pp. 268–9.
16. Clarke and Knake, *Cyber War*, p. 93.

17. Anatoly Medetsky, "KGB Veteran Denies CIA Caused '82 Blast," *The Moscow Times*, 18 Mar. 2004.
18. Nikolai Brusnitsin, *Openness and Espionage*, Moscow: Military Pub. House, USSR Ministry of Defense, 1990, pp. 28–9. I would like to thank Mike Warner for pointing out this source to me.
19. I would like to thank Richard Chirgwin for pointing out and explaining this part of technological history to me.
20. Richard Chirgwin, email exchange with the author, 23 Mar. 2012.
21. Eneken Tikk, Kadri Kaska, and Liis Vihul, *International Cyber Incidents*, Tallinn: CCDCOE, 2010, p. 17.
22. These disruptions were the worst of the entire "cyber war," according to ibid., p. 20.
23. "Estonia Has No Evidence of Kremlin Involvement in Cyber Attacks," Ria Novosti, 6 Sep. 2007. It should also be noted that Russian activists and even a State Duma deputy (although perhaps jokingly) have claimed to be behind the attacks, see Gadi Evron, "Authoritatively, Who Was Behind the Estonian Attacks?" Darkreading, 17 Mar. 2009. See also, Gadi Evron, "Battling Botnets and Online Mobs," *Science & Technology*, Winter/Spring 2008, pp. 121–8.
24. Tim Espiner, "Estonia's Cyberattacks: Lessons Learned, a Year On," ZDNet UK, 1 May 2008.
25. Andrei Zlobin and Kseniya Boletskaya, "Elektronnaya bomba," *Vedomosti*, 28 May 2007, http://bitly.com/g1M9Si+
26. Ron Deibert, Rafal Rohozinski, and Masashi Crete-Nishihata, "Cyclones in Cyberspace: Information Shaping and Denial in the 2008 Russia-Georgia War," *Security Dialogue*, vol. 43, 1 (2012), pp. 3–24.
27. The intensity of the attacks was high, with traffic reaching 211.66 Mbps on average, peaking at 814.33 Mbps, see Jose Nazario, "Georgia DDoS Attacks—A Quick Summary of Observations," Security to the Core (Arbor Networks), 12 Aug. 2008.
28. Eneken Tikk, Kadri Kaska, Kristel Rünnimeri, Mari Kert, Anna-Maria Talihärm, and Liis Vihul, *Cyber Attacks Against Georgia*, Tallinn: CCDCOE, 2008, p. 12. Jeffrey Carr, a cyber security expert, published a report which concluded that Russia's Foreign Military Intelligence Agency (GRU) and Federal Security Service (FSB) probably helped coordinate the attacks, rather than independent patriotic hackers. Yet, to date, this has neither been proven nor admitted.

2. VIOLENCE

1. Sun Tzu, *The Art of War*, translated by Samuel B Griffith, Oxford: Oxford University Press, 1963, p. 141.

2. Jürgen Kraus, "Selbstreproduktion bei Programmen," Dortmund: Universität Dortmund, 1980, p. 160.

3. John Roberts, "Exclusive: Drones Vulnerable to Terrorist Hijacking, Researchers Say," Fox News, 25 June 2012.

4. Scott Peterson and Payam Faramarzi, "Exclusive: Iran Hijacked US Drone, Says Iranian Engineer," Christian Science Monitor, 15 Dec. 2011.

5. Catherine Herridge, "US Data in Iranian Hands After Downed Drone?" Fox News, 10 Feb. 2012.

6. So reads the opening paragraph of Chapter 13, "Of the natural condition of mankind, as concerning the felicity, and misery," Thomas Hobbes, *Leviathan*, London: Penguin, 1651 (1996), p. 86.

7. Ibid., Chapter 13, paragraph 9.

8. Hobbes did not use the word monopolize; Max Weber introduced the expression to describe a well-established idea. Max Weber, *Politik als Beruf*, Berlin: Duncker & Humblot, 1968 (1919).

9. See for instance John Austin, *The Province of Jurisprudence Determined*, Plaistow: Curwen Press, 1832 (1954), Hans Kelsen, *Pure Theory of Law* (Second Edition), Berkeley: University of California Press, 1984, Alessandro Passerin d'Entrèves, *The Notion of the State*, Oxford: Oxford University Press, 1967.

10. Sofsky's work, despite its quality, is not sufficiently referenced. Wolfgang Sofsky, *Traktat über die Gewalt*, Frankfurt am Main: Fischer, 1996

11. Heinrich Popitz, *Phänomene der Macht*, Tübingen: Mohr Siebeck, 2004, p. 68, also p. 24; Sofsky, *Traktat über die Gewalt*, p. 31.

12. Sofsky, *Traktat über die Gewalt*, p. 82.

13. Ibid., p. 19.

14. For a superb analysis of the similarities between early airpower enthusiasts and proponents of cyberpower, and for stunning quotes from that debate, see David Betz and Tim Stevens, *Cyberspace and the State*, Adelphi Series, London: IISS/Routledge, 2011, "Airpower Redux," pp. 82–8.

15. See for instance Lamia Joreige's video installation documenting the trauma caused by the 2006 Israeli air campaign, "Objects of War No. 4," 2006, *Tate Modern*, Reference T13250, purchased 2011.

16. On 5 Dec. 2005 the US Air Force expanded its mission accordingly. See mission statement, as of 9 Aug. 2012, http://www.airforce.com/learn-about/our-mission. Also, Sebastian M. II Convertino, Lou Anne DeMattei, and Tammy M. Knierim, "Flying and Fighting in Cyberspace," *Air War College Maxwell Paper*, 40 (2007), Michael Wynne, "Flying and Fighting in Cyberspace," *Air & Space Power Journal* (2007), pp. 5–9.

17. For a more detailed critique of the "fifth domain" see the concluding chapter of this book.

18. A patrol may have several functions next to displaying force, including gathering intelligence and maintaining readiness and morale.

19. For a more specific discussion on the notion of cyber attack, see the following chapter on cyber weapons.

20. See for instance J. David Lewis and Andrew J. Weigert, "Social Atomism, Holism, and Trust," *The Sociological Quarterly*, vol. 26, 4 (1985), pp. 455–71, p. 455, "In a word, society is possible only through *trust* in its members, institutions, and forms." For an insightful study of trust in the context of computer security, see Bruce Schneier, *Liars and Outliers*, Indianapolis, IN: Wiley, 2012.

21. For an influential yet exceedingly narrow view of trust, see Russell Hardin, *Trust and Trustworthiness*, New York: Russell Sage Foundation, 2002.

22. See J. David Lewis and Andrew J. Weigert, "Trust as a Social Reality," *Social Forces*, vol. 63, 4 (1985), pp. 967–85, p. 986.

23. Under conditions of civil war, even trust within families is likely to erode. See Stathis Kalyvas, *The Logic of Violence in Civil War*, Cambridge: Cambridge University Press, 2006, p. 178, 226. For a radically different (and implausible) argument, namely that anarchy, and not government, generates cohesion and trust, see Ernest Gellner, "Trust, Cohesion, and the Social Order," in Diego Gambetta (ed.), *Trust: Making and Breaking Cooperative Relations*, London: Wiley-Blackwell, 1990, pp. 142–57.

24. One of the foundational classic texts is Kelsen, *Pure Theory of Law* (Second Edition), especially Chapter 1.

25. Passerin d'Entrèves, *The Notion of the State*, p. 2.

26. Hobbes, *Leviathan*, second paragraph, Chapter 17, in context, "And Covenants, without the Sword, are but Words, and of no strength to secure a man at all. Therefore notwithstanding the Lawes of Nature, … if there be no Power erected, or not great enough for our security; every man will and may lawfully rely on his own strength and art, for caution against all other men."

27. Ibid., opening line of Chapter 30.

28. John Locke, *Two Treatises of Government*, Cambridge: Cambridge University Press, 1689 (1988), §171, "An essay concerning the true original extent and end of civil government," see also §136, "To this end it is that men give up all their natural power to the society they enter into, and the community put the legislative power into such hands as they think fit, with this trust, that they shall be governed by declared laws, or else their peace, quiet, and property will still be at the same uncertainty as it was in the state of Nature."

29. See Hannah Arendt's discussion of Passerin d'Entrèves's contribution, Hannah Arendt, *On Violence*, New York: Harcourt, Brace, Jovanovich, 1970, p. 37.

30. Walter Benjamin, "Critique of Violence," in *Reflections*, New York: Schocken Books, 1978, p. 277.

31. Ibid., p. 278.

32. Ibid., p. 284.

33. The invasion of Iraq in the spring of 2003 offers one of the most illustrative case studies. For a detailed analysis, see Thomas Rid, *War and Media Operations: The U.S. Military and the Press from Vietnam to Iraq*, London: Routledge, 2007.

34. One example is the Westboro Baptist Church, an extreme independent group known for anti-gay militancy, picketing funerals of American soldiers, and desecrating the US flag. See http://en.wikipedia.org/wiki/Westboro_Baptist_Church

35. On this day, to be more precise, the first fraudulent certificate was issued. The attack may have started even earlier. See J.R. Prins, *DigiNotar Certificate Authority Breach 'Operation Black Tulip'*, Delft: Fox-IT, 2011, p. 8.

36. The fake Google certificate is archived at Pastebin, "Gmail.com SSL MITM ATTACK BY Iranian Government," 27 Aug. 2011, http://bitly.com/qGTf0a+

37. Jochem Binst, "DigiNotar Reports Security Incident," Vasco Press Release, 30 Aug. 2011, http://bitly.com/vasco-diginotar+; see also Prins, *Op Black Tulip*, p. 5.

38. Seth Schoen and Eva Galperin, "Iranian Man-in-the-Middle Attack Against Google Demonstrates Dangerous Weakness of Certificate Authorities," Electronic Frontier Foundation, 29 Aug. 2011.

39. "Is This MITM Attack to Gmail's SSL?" Google Product Forums, http://bitly.com/alibo-mitm+

40. Schoen and Galperin, "Iranian Man-in-the-Middle Attack Against Google Demonstrates Dangerous Weakness of Certificate Authorities."

41. Heather Adkins, "An Updated on Attempted Man-in-the-Middle Attacks," Google Online Security Blog, 29 Aug. 2011. See also Prins, *Op Black Tulip*.

42. Charles Arthur, "Rogue Web Certificate Could Have Been Used to Attack Iran Dissidents," *The Guardian*, 30 Aug. 2011.

43. Prins, *Op Black Tulip*, p. 8, also p. 13.

44. See especially the alleged hacker's 7 Sep. 2011 post on Pastebin, http://pastebin.com/u/ComodoHacker

45. Somini Sengupta, "Hacker Rattles Security Circles," *The New York Times*, 11 Sep. 2011.

46. Comodo Hacker, "Striking Back …," Pastebin, 5 Sep. 2011, http://pastebin.com/1AxH30em

47. Mikko Hypponen, "DigiNotar Hacked by Black.Spook and Iranian Hackers," F-Secure, 30 Aug. 2011.

48. Ibid.
49. Ian Traynor, "Russia Accused of Unleashing Cyberwar to Disable Estonia," *The Guardian*, 6 Sep. 2007.
50. Tim Espiner, "Estonia's Cyberattacks: Lessons Learned, a Year On," ZDNet UK, 1 May 2008.
51. "Statement by the Foreign Minister Urmas Paet," *Eesti Päevaleht*, 1 May 2007, http://bitly.com/QoC9FE+
52. Andrei Zlobin and Kseniya Boletskaya, "Elektronnaya bomba," *Vedomosti*, 28 May 2007, http://bitly.com/g1M9Si+
53. Joshua Davis, "Hackers Take Down the Most Wired Country in Europe," *Wired*, 21 Aug. 2007.
54. Ralph Peters, "Washington Ignores Cyberattack Threats, Putting Us All at Peril," *Wired*, 23 Aug. 2007.
55. For a more detailed description, see the next chapter.
56. David Sanger, *Confront and Conceal*, New York: Crown, 2012, p. 199.
57. Ibid.
58. Ibid., p. 200.
59. Mikko Hypponen, "Emails from Iran," F-Secure, 23 July 2012.
60. Ibid., see also Ladane Nasseri, "Iran Nuclear Plants Hit By Virus Playing AC/DC, Website Says," Bloomberg News, 25 July 2012.
61. "Iran Denies its Nuclear Computer Systems Hit by New Virus," *Haaretz* (DPA), 1 Aug. 2012.
62. See Dexter Filkins, *The Forever War*, New York: Knopf, 2008, p. 3.

3. CYBER WEAPONS

1. Ellen Nakashima, "U.S. Cyberweapons had Been Considered to Disrupt Gaddafi's Air Defenses," *The Washington Post*, 18 Oct. 2011.
2. William J. Lynn, "The Pentagon's Cyberstrategy, One Year Later," *Foreign Affairs*, 28 (Sep. 2011).
3. Department of Defense, "Defense Strategic Guidance," Washington, D.C., Jan. 2012, p. 4.
4. JP 1–02, as amended through 15 Sep. 2011, p. 365.
5. Thomas Rid, "Cyber War Will Not Take Place," *Journal of Strategic Studies*, vol. 35, 1 (2012).
6. Department of Defense, "Cyberspace Policy Report," Nov. 2011, p. 2.
7. For a related distinction combined with a rather wide definition, see Lior Tabansky, "Basic Concepts in Cyber Warfare," *Military and Strategic Affairs*, vol. 3, 1 (2011), pp. 75–92.
8. Keith Alexander, "Cybersecurity Symposium Keynote Address," University of Rhode Island, 11 Apr. 2011, http://bitly.com/tNyDmX+

9. US Department of Energy, "Russian Hydroelectric Plant Accident: Lessons to be Learned," Office of Health, Safety and Security, 4 Aug. 2011, http://bitly.com/t4LDzy+

10. Steve Gutterman, "Negligence Factor in Russian Power Plant Accident," Associated Press, 3 Oct. 2009.

11. For a detailed discussion, see Geoffrey Blainey, *The Causes of War*, New York: Free Press, 1973, pp. 35–56.

12. An example of a definition that is too narrow is: "A cyber weapon is an information technology-based system that is designed to *damage* the structure or operations of some other information technology-based system." Peeter Lorents and Rain Ottis, "Knowledge Based Framework for Cyber Weapons and Conflict," *Conference on Cyber Conflict Proceedings*, 2010, pp. 129–42.

13. Anatoly Medetsky, "KGB Veteran Denies CIA Caused '82 Blast," *The Moscow Times*, 18 Mar. 2004.

14. David A Fulghum, Robert Wall, and Amy Butler, "Israel Shows Electronic Prowess," *Aviation Week & Space Technology*, 168, 25 Nov. 2007; David A Fulghum, Robert Wall, and Amy Butler, "Cyber-Combat's First Shot," *Aviation Week & Space Technology*, 167, 16 Nov. 2007, pp. 28–31.

15. John Markoff, "A Silent Attack, But Not a Subtle One," *The New York Times*, 26 Sep. 2010.

16. Sally Adee, "The Hunt for the Kill Switch," *IEEE Spectrum*, May 2008.

17. Geoff McDonald et al, "Stuxnet 0.5: The Missing Link," Symantec, 2013, p. 2.

18. Nicolas Falliere, Liam O Murchu, and Eric Chien, *W32.Stuxnet Dossier. Version 1.4*, Symantec, 2011, p. 3.

19. Ibid.

20. For more details on Stuxnet's infection mechanisms, see the chapter on espionage.

21. This is Ralph Langner's target theory. The question of whether Stuxnet's code 417 "warhead" was disabled or not is controversial among engineers. See ibid., p. 45 as well as Ralph Langner, "Matching Langner's Stuxnet Analysis and Symantec's Dossier Update," The Last Line of Cyber Defense, 21 Feb. 2011.

22. Ralph Langner, "Cracking Stuxnet," TED Talk, Mar. 2011.

23. William J. Broad, John Markoff, and David E. Sanger, "Israeli Test on Worm Called Crucial in Iran Nuclear Delay," *The New York Times*, 16 Jan. 2011, p. A1.

24. Falliere, Murchu, and Chien, *W32.Stuxnet Dossier. Version 1.4*, p. 3.

25. See Gary McGraw's discussion with Ralph Langner on Cigital's *Silver Bullet*, 25 Feb. 2011, http://www.cigital.com/silverbullet/show-059/

26. Falliere, Murchu, and Chien, *W32.Stuxnet Dossier. Version 1.4*

27. See for instance John Markoff, "A Silent Attack, But Not a Subtle One," p. A6.

28. David Fulghum, "Cyber Attack Turns Physical," *Aerospace Daily & Defense Report*, vol. 235, 61 (2010), p. 3.

29. A CBS news segment of the experiment is at http://youtu.be/rTkXgqK1l9A

30. Samuel M. Katz, *The Hunt for the Engineer*, New York: Fromm International, 1999, p. 260.

31. "Hezbollah Got Inside MI's Inner Sanctum," Ynet, 13 Sep. 2009.

32. It remained unclear how the work affected air-gapped secure systems, see "Virus Hits Secret Pentagon Network," BBC, 6 May 2000.

33. Tom Raum, "More CIA Employees May Be Disciplined in Computer Case," Associated Press, 6 May 2000.

34. D. Moore, V. Paxson, S. Savage, C. Shannon, S. Staniford, and N. Weaver, "Inside the Slammer Worm," *IEEE Security & Privacy*, vol. 1, 4 (2003), pp. 33–9.

35. Ibid., p. 33.

36. Kevin Poulsen, "Slammer Worm Crashed Ohio Nuke Plant Net," The Register, 20 Aug. 2003.

37. See ibid.

38. Letter from Edward J Markey to Nils Diaz, 20 Oct. 2003, http://bitly.com/PrRvow+

39. Dale Peterson, "Offensive Cyber Weapons: Construction, Development, and Employment," *Journal of Strategic Studies*, vol. 36, 1 (2012).

40. For an introduction into agent technology, see M. Luck, P. McBurney, and C. Preist, "A Manifesto for Agent Technology: Towards Next Generation Computing," *Autonomous Agents and Multi-Agent Systems*, vol. 9, 3 (2004), pp. 203–52.

41. David Sanger, "America's Deadly Dynamics with Iran," *The New York Times*, 6 Nov. 2011, p. SR1.

4. SABOTAGE

1. John Leyden, "Hack on Saudi Aramco Hit 30,000 Workstations, Oil Firm Admits," The Register, 29 Aug. 2012.

2. "Saudi-Aramco Emerges Stronger from Cyber Attack," *Arab News*, 1 Sep. 2012.

3. William J. Donovan, *Simple Sabotage Field Manual*, Washington, D.C.: Office of Strategic Services, 1944, p. 1.

4. Émile Pouget, *Le sabotage*, Paris: M. Rivière, 1910, p. 3.

5. Elizabeth Gurley Flynn, *Sabotage*, Cleveland, Ohio: IWW Publishing Bureau,

1916, p. 5, quoted in Ralph Darlington, *Syndicalism and the Transition to Communism*, Aldershot, England: Ashgate, 2008, p. 34.

6. Cited in Pouget, *Le sabotage*, p. 34, "Si vous êtes mécanicien, disait cet article, il vous est très facile avec deux sous d'une poudre quelconque, ou même seulement avec du sable, d'enrayer votre machine, d'occasionner une perte de temps et une réparation fort coûteuse à votre employeur. Si vous êtes menuisier ou ébéniste, quoi de plus facile que de détériorer un meuble sans que le patron s'en aperçoive et lui faire perdre ainsi des clients?" translation by Ralph Darlington.

7. Émile Pouget and Arturo M. Giovannitti, *Sabotage*, Chicago: C.H. Kerr & Co., 1913, p. 6.

8. Ibid.

9. Quoted in Darlington, *Syndicalism and the Transition to Communism*, p. 36.

10. Jim Finkle, "Exclusive: Insiders Suspected in Saudi Cyber Attack," Reuters, 7 Sep. 2012.

11. "The Shamoon Attacks," Symantec, 16 Aug. 2012.

12. "Shamoon/DistTrack Malware," US-CERT, 29 Aug. 2012, http://www.us-cert.gov/control_systems/pdf/JSAR-12-241-01.pdf

13. A Guest, "Untitled," Pastebin, 15 Aug. 2012, http://pastebin.com/HqAga QRj

14. A Guest, "Untitled," Pastebin, 17 Aug. 2012, http://pastebin.com/tztn RLQG

15. Nicole Perlroth, "Among Digital Crumbs from Saudi Aramco Cyberattack, Image of Burning U.S. Flag," The New York Times Bits, 24 Aug. 2012.

16. Dmitry Tarakanov, "Shamoon the Wiper in Details," Securelist, 21 Aug. 2012.

17. "Hackers Fail to Access Iranian Oil Ministry's Sensitive Data," Fars, 27 Apr. 2012.

18. "What Was That Wiper Thing?" Securelist, 29 Aug. 2012.

19. Camilla Hall and Javier Blas, "Aramco Cyber Attack Targeted Production," *Financial Times*, 10 Dec. 2012.

20. For an overview of SCADA networks, see Vinay M. Igure, Sean A. Laughter, and Ronald D. Williams, "Security Issues in SCADA Networks," *Computers & Security*, vol. 25 (2006), pp. 498–506.

21. Éireann P. Leverett, "Quantitatively Assessing and Visualising Industrial System Attack Surfaces," Cambridge: University of Cambridge, 2011.

22. Igure, Laughter, and Williams, "Security Issues in SCADA Networks," p. 500.

23. Brian Krebs, "Chinese Hackers Blamed for Intrusion at Energy Industry Giant Telvent," Krebs on Security, 26 Sep. 2012.

24. The US Air Force Office of Special Investigations (AFOSI) reportedly esta-

blished the link between the Comment Group and the PLA. The former US government codename is "Byzantine Candor," see the leaked cable: Secretary of State, "Diplomatic Security Detail," Reference ID 08STATE 116943, 30 Oct. 2008. See also Michael Riley and Dune Lawrence, "Hackers Linked to China's Army Seen from EU to DC," Bloomberg, 27 June 2012.

25. Shodan's URL is http://www.shodanhq.com

26. ICS-CERT, "Control System Internet Accessibility," Alert 10–301–01, 20 Oct. 2010.

27. Kim Zetter, "10K Reasons to Worry About Critical Infrastructure," *Wired*, 24 Jan. 2012.

28. Rubén Santamarta, "Reversing Industrial Firmware for Fun and Backdoors," Reversemode, 12 Dec. 2011, http://bitly.com/OsFWPI+

29. ICS-CERT, "Schneider Electric Quantum Ethernet Module Multiple Vulnerabilities," ICS-Alert 11–346–01, 12 Dec. 2011.

30. See Dillon Beresford, "Exploiting Siemens Simatic S7 PLCs," a paper prepared for Black Hat USA+2011, 8 July 2011, http://bitly.com/OtcuJx+

31. Elinor Mills, "SCADA Hack Talk Canceled after U.S., Siemens Request," CNet, 18 May 2011.

32. ICS-CERT, "Key Management Errors in RuggedCom's Rugged Operating System," ICS-Alert 11–346–01, 12 Dec. 2011.

33. See Dale Peterson, "Construction, Deployment and Use of Offensive Cyber Weapons," *Journal of Strategic Studies*, 2013, forthcoming.

34. For instance: Ralph Langner, "Enumerating Stuxnet's Exploits," Langner. com, 7 June 2011.

35. For instance: Dale Peterson, "Langner's Stuxnet Deep Dive S4 Video," Digital Bond, 31 Jan. 2012.

36. Dale Peterson, interview with author, by telephone, 11 Sep. 2012.

37. For a contrarian view, see Dusko Pavlovic, "Gaming Security by Obscurity," arXiv 1109.5542, 9, 2011.

38. For a more detailed discussion, see Bruce Schneier, "Secrecy, Security, and Obscurity," Crypto-Gram Newsletter, 15 May 2002.

39. See Eric Byres, and Justin Lowe, "The Myths and Facts Behind Cyber Security Risks for Industrial Control Systems," paper read at Proceedings of the VDE Congress, at VDE Association for Electrical Electronic & Information Technologies, Oct. 2004, p. 1.

40. Paul Quinn-Judge, "Cracks in the System," *Time*, 9 June 2002.

41. Jill Slay and Michael Miller, "Lessons Learned from the Maroochy Water Breach," in E. Goetz and S. Shenoi (eds), *Critical Infrastructure Protection*, vol. 253, pp. 73–82, Boston: Springer, 2008.

42. Garry Barker, "Cyber Terrorism a Mouse-Click Away," *The Age*, 8 July 2002.

43. Tony Smith, "Hacker Jailed for Revenge Sewage Attacks," *The Register*, 31 Oct. 2001.

44. "Arlington Security Guard Arrested on Federal Charges for Hacking into Hospital's Computer System," FBI, Dallas Office, 30 June 2009.

45. A screenshot is at Dan Goodin "Feds: Hospital Hacker's 'Massive' DDoS Averted," *The Register*, 1 July 2009.

46. United States Attorney James T. Jacks, "Press Release," US Department of Justice, Northern District of Texas, 18 Mar. 2011.

47. Joe Weiss, "Water System Hack—The System Is Broken," ControlGlobal. com, 17 Nov. 2011.

48. Ellen Nakashima, "Water-Pump Failure in Illinois Wasn't Cyberattack After All," *The Washington Post*, 25 Nov. 2011.

49. Ellen Nakashima, "Foreign Hackers Targeted U.S. Water Plant in Apparent Malicious Cyber Attack, Expert Says," *The Washington Post*, 18 Nov. 2011.

50. Byres and Lowe, "The Myths and Facts behind Cyber Security Risks for Industrial Control Systems," p. 2.

51. Dan Goodin, "Water Utility Hackers Destroy Pump, Expert Says," *The Register*, 17 Nov. 2011.

52. A Guest, "loldhs pr0f," Pastebin, 18 Nov. 2011, http://pastebin.com/Wx90LLum

53. Personal information on pr0f was reported by *The Washington Post*.

54. Robert O'Harrow Jr, "Cyber Search Engine Shodan Exposes Industrial Control Systems to New Risks," *The Washington Post*, 4 June 2012.

55. "Vulnerabilities in Tridium Niagara Framework Result in Unauthorized Access to a New Jersey Company's Industrial Control System", SIR-00000003417, FBI Newark Division, 23 July 2012, http://bit.ly/TULK6j+

56. Dan Goodin, "Intruders Hack Industrial Heating System Using Backdoor Posted Online," *Ars Technica*, 13 Dec. 2012.

57. A Guest, "#US #SCADA #IDIOTS part-II," 23 Jan. 2012, http://pastebin.com/eL9j3SE1

58. A Guest, "#US #SCADA #IDIOTS part-II," 23 Jan. 2012, http://pastebin.com/eL9j3SE1

59. A Guest, "#US #SCADA #IDIOTS part-II," 23 Jan. 2012, http://pastebin.com/eL9j3SE1

5. ESPIONAGE

1. Michael Polanyi's key book *Personal Knowledge*, Chicago: University of Chicago Press, 1962.

2. At the time of writing, the book had almost 28,000 citations on Google

Scholar, almost double the number of Karl Popper's classic *The Logic of Scientific Discovery*, for instance. See Ikujiro Nonaka, *The Knowledge-Creating Company*, New York: Oxford University Press, 1995, also Ikujiro Nonaka, "A Dynamic Theory of Organizational Knowledge Creation," *Organization Science*, vol. 5, 1 (1994), pp. 14–37.

3. For more details, see Justin Scheck and Evan Perez, "FBI Traces Trail of Spy Ring to China," *The Wall Street Journal*, 10 Mar. 2012.

4. Ben Elgin, Dune Lawrence, Michael Riley, "Coke Gets Hacked And Doesn't Tell Anyone," *Bloomberg*, 4 November 2012.

5. Tom Whitehead, "Cyber crime a global threat, MI5 head warns," *The Telegraph*, 26 Jun. 2012.

6. Siobhan Gorman, "Chinese Hackers Suspected In Long-Term Nortel Breach," *The Wall Street Journal*, 14 Feb. 2012.

7. Bradley Graham, "Hackers Attack Via Chinese Web Sites," *The Washington Post*, 25 Aug. 2005.

8. Dawn Onley and Patience Wait, "Red Storm Rising," *Government Computer News*, 17 Aug. 2006.

9. Joel Brenner, *America the Vulnerable*, New York: Penguin Press, 2011, p. 80.

10. Lynn, "Defending a New Domain," p. 97. Clarke says the spyware was of Russian origin, see the next footnote.

11. Richard A. Clarke and Robert A. Knake, *Cyber War*, New York: Ecco, 2010, p. 171.

12. A redacted version of the email can be found at Hon Lau, "The Truth Behind the Shady RAT," Symantec Blog, 4 Aug. 2011.

13. Ibid.

14. Ibid.

15. Dmitri Alperovitch, *Revealed: Operation Shady RAT*, Santa Clara, CA: McAfee, 2 Aug. 2011

16. Ibid., p. 4.

17. Greg Keizer, "'Shady RAT' Hacking Claims Overblown, Say Security Firms," *Computerworld*, 5 Aug. 2011.

18. Hon Lau, "The Truth Behind the Shady RAT."

19. Aliya Sternstein, "Attach on Energy Lab Computers was Isolated and Limited, Officials Say," Nextgov, 22 Apr. 2011.

20. Jack Date et al., "Hackers Launch Cyberattack on Federal Labs," ABC News, 7 Dec. 2007.

21. Symantec, "W32.Duqu," Oct. 2011, p. 1.

22. Ibid.

23. Dan Goodin, "Duqu Targeted Each Victim with Unique Files and Servers," The Register, 12 Nov. 2011.

24. Aleks Gostev, "The Duqu Saga Continues," Securelist, 11 Nov. 2011.

25. Symantec, "W32.Duqu," Oct. 2011, annex, p. 15.

26. Sean Sullivan, "Duqu: Questions and Answers," F-Secure, 3 Nov. 2011.

27. "sKyWIper: A Complex Malware for Targeted Attacks," Budapest University of Technology and Economics, 28 May 2012.

28. Alexander Gostev, "The Flame: Questions and Answers," Securelist, 28 May 2012, http://bitly.com/KnQYX5+

29. Ellen Nakashima, Greg Miller, and Julie Tate, "U.S., Israel Developed Flame Computer Virus to Slow Iranian Nuclear Efforts, Officials Say," *The Washington Post*, 19 June 2012.

30. "Flamer: Urgent Suicide," Symantec Connect, 6 June 2012.

31. "Resource 207: Kaspersky Lab Research Proves that Stuxnet and Flame Developers are Connected," Kaspersky Lab, 11 June 2012, http://bitly.com/Mzpv15+

32. "Full Analysis of Flame's Command & Control Servers," Securelist, 17 Sep. 2012.

33. Nakashima, Miller, and Tate, "U.S., Israel Developed Flame Computer Virus to Slow Iranian Nuclear Efforts, Officials Say."

34. "Computer Virus Briefly Hits Iran's Oil Industry," Associated Press, 30 May 2012.

35. Kaspersky Lab, "Gauss: Abnormal Distribution," 9 Aug. 2012, p. 5.

36. Ibid., p. 39.

37. Ibid., p. 4.

38. Ibid., p. 48.

39. Osama Habib, "No Proof Lebanese Banks Linked to Terrorist Financing: Sader," *The Daily Star*, 4 July 2012. See also Jeffrey Carr, "Was Flame's Gauss Malware Used to Uncover Hezbollah Money Laundering via Lebanese Banks?" Digital Dao, 9 Aug. 2012.

40. In English the malware is called R2D2, see Sean Sullivan, "More Info on German State Backdoor: Case R2S2," F-Secure, 11 Oct. 2011.

41. Chaos Computer Club, "Analyse einer Regierungs-Malware," Berlin, 8 Oct. 2011.

42. Lily Kuo, "Cyber Attacks Grow Increasingly 'Reckless,' U.S. Official Says," Reuters, 7 Sep. 2012.

43. Eli Lake, "Israel's Secret Iran Attack Plan: Electronic Warfare," *The Daily Beast*, 16 Nov. 2011. For an image of the dropper's copy, see http://bitly.com/NO4DdJ+

44. "The Madi Campaign—Part I," Securelist, 17 July 2012.

45. See "Mahdi—The Cyberwar Savior?" Seculert, 17 July 2012.

46. Dan Senor and Saul Singer, *Start-up Nation*, New York: Twelve, 2009, p. 11.

47. http://www.socialbakers.com/facebook-statistics/israel, statistics as of 18 Apr. 2011.

48. "Hezbollah Using Facebook to Kidnap Israeli Soldiers," *Ya Libnan*, 7 Sep. 2008.

49. Sarah Stricker, "Die schöne Facebook-Freundin der Elitesoldaten," *Spiegel*, 17 May 2010.

50. "Soldiers From 'Secretive' Israeli Base Set Up Facebook Group," *The Jerusalem Post*, 8 July 2010.

51. Peter Behr, "Chinese Company Accused of Economic Espionage in Wind Turbine Case," *Environment & Energy Publishing*, 26 Jan. 2012.

52. Eliza Strickland, "A Test Case for Intellectual Property in China," IEEE Spectrum, Mar. 2012.

53. Kid Möchel and Stefan Melichar, "Strafprozess gegen 'China-Spion'," *Wiener Zeitung*, 20 Sep. 2009.

54. Erin Ailworth and Eugen Freund, "Engineer Guilty in Software Theft," *The Boston Globe*, 24 Sep. 2011.

55. Ibid.

56. David Sanger, *Confront and Conceal*, New York: Crown, 2012, p. 196.

57. Ibid.

58. Information is taken from Siemens's now defunct Iran website, http://siemens.ir. An archived version of the "About us" section, dated 27 June 2009, is archived at the Wayback Machine, see http://bitly.com/Q79tBs+

59. Sanger, *Confront and Conceal*, p. 196.

60. Dan Raviv and Yossi Melman, *Spies Against Armageddon*, Sea Cliff, NY: Levant Books, 2012, p. 10.

61. See also Ralph Langner, "The Third Man Wears Black, Red, and Gold," Langner.com, 30 July 2012.

62. This author also endorsed that assumption, see Thomas Rid and Peter McBurney, "Cyber Weapons," *The RUSI Journal*, vol. 157, 1 (2012), pp. 6–13.

63. For a thoughtful historical essay on technology and intelligence, see Michael Warner, "Reflections on Technology and Intelligence Systems," *Intelligence and National Security*, vol. 27, 1 (2012), pp. 133–53.

64. Nigel Inkster, "Intelligence Agencies and the Cyber World," in *Strategic Survey*, London: International Institute for Strategic Studies, 2012.

65. Jonathan Evans, *The Threat to National Security*, London: The Worshipful Company of Security Professionals, 16 Sep. 2010.

66. Rhys Blakely, Jonathan Richards, James Rossiter, and Richard Beeston, "MI5 Alert on China's Cyberspace Spy Threat," *The Times*, 1 Dec. 2007, p. 1.

67. Office of the National Counterintelligence Executive, *Foreign Spies Stealing US Economic Secrets in Cyberspace*, Washington, D.C., October 2011.

68. Brenner, *America the Vulnerable*, p. 9.

69. Evans, "Worshipful Company of Security Professionals Speech," Sep. 2010.

70. See also Nigel Inkster, "Intelligence Agencies and the Cyber World," in *Strategic Survey*, London: International Institute for Strategic Studies, 2012.

71. Iain Lobban, *Iain Lobban Address*, London: International Institute of Strategic Studies, 12 Oct. 2010.

6. SUBVERSION

1. The Internet had yet to affect Islamic extremism significantly in 2001, but that drastically changed over the course of the decade. An entry point into the vast debate on online radicalization is Thomas Rid and Marc Hecker, *War 2.0: Irregular Warfare in the Information Age*, Westport: Praeger, 2009, Chapter 9, as well as Thomas Rid, "Cracks in the Jihad," *The Wilson Quarterly*, vol. 34, 1 (2010), pp. 40–8.

2. The curves reflect the frequency of the use of the word "subversion" in printed books and periodicals in the English language from 1750 to 2008.

3. Edmund Burke, *Reflections on the Revolution in France*, London: J. Dodsley, 1790, p. 243.

4. Samuel Johnson, *Dictionary of the English Language*, Dublin: G Jones, 1768.

5. James Leslie, *Dictionary of the Synonymous Words and Technical Terms in the English Language*, Edinburgh: John Moir, 1806.

6. William Belsham, *Memoirs of the Reign of George III to the Session of Parliament Ending A.D. 1793*, vol. I, London: J. Robinson, 1795, p. 123, see also p. 221; p. 303.

7. Charles James, *Military Dictionary, In French and English*, London: Egerton, 1810.

8. Quoted in Tim Weiner, *Enemies: A History of the FBI*, New York: Random House, 2012, Chapter 2.

9. Frank Kitson, *Low Intensity Operations: Subversion, Insurgency and Peacekeeping*, London: Faber and Faber, 2010, p. 3.

10. Ibid., pp. 82–3.

11. Carl von Clausewitz's may be the prime example of a military writer highlighting political aspects of war yet failing to analyze them in detail, see Clausewitz, *Vom Kriege*, Berlin: Ullstein, 1832 (1980), Book 1, Chapter 1.

12. One of Agnoli's students turned these lectures into a book, see Johannes Agnoli, *Subversive Theorie*, Freiburg: Ça ira, 1996.

13. Ibid., p. 29. Another example of an author with a positive notion of subversion was Diedrich Diederichsen, a leading German-language pop theorist and art historian who described subversion as an artistic method with political goals. Diedrich Diederichsen, "Subversion—Kalte Strategie und heiße Differenz," in Diedrich Diederichsen (ed.), *Freiheit macht arm: das*

Leben nach Rock'n'Roll 1990–1993, pp. 33–52, Köln: Kiepenheuer & Witsch, 1993, p. 35.

14. "Doch die Verhältnisse, sie sind nicht so" is Brecht's refrain from the *Dreigroschenoper*, Act 1, "Über die Unsicherheit menschlicher Verhältnisse."

15. Agnoli, *Subversive Theorie*, p. 12.

16. Consider Agnoli's haughty German, "Wer stattdessen das Ende der Utopie verkündet und nebenbei das Subversive kriminalisiert, will genau der Möglichkeit neuer Aufbrüche wehren," ibid., p. 13.

17. Ibid.

18. Hegel's original formulation, not quoted by Agnoli, is truly remarkable, "Das *Tiefe*, das der Geist von innen heraus, aber nur bis in sein *vorstellendes Bewußtsein* treibt und es in diesem stehen läßt,—und die *Unwissenheit* dieses Bewußtseins, was das ist, was es sagt, ist dieselbe Verknüpfung des Hohen und Niedrigen, welche an dem Lebendigen die Natur in der Verknüpfung des Organs seiner höchsten Vollendung, des Organs der Zeugung,—und des Organs des Pissens naiv ausdrückt.—Das unendliche Urteil als unendliches wäre die Vollendung des sich selbst erfassenden Lebens, das in der Vorstellung bleibende Bewußtsein desselben aber verhält sich als Pissen." G.W.F. Hegel, *Phänomenologie des Geistes*, Berlin: Duncker und Humblot, 1832, p. 263.

19. William Rosenau, *Subversion and Insurgency*, Santa Monica, CA: Rand, 2007, p. 5.

20. Kitson, *Low Intensity Operations: Subversion, Insurgency and Peacekeeping*, p. 3.

21. Clutterbuck and Rosenau develop a similar thought: "subversion needs to be conceptualized as one facet of a broader campaign that employs in a non-linear fashion a range of violent, less-violent, and non-violent instruments that serve to reinforce each other," Lindsay Clutterbuck and William Rosenau, "Subversion as a Facet of Terrorism and Insurgency," *Strategic Insights*, vol. 8, 3 (2009).

22. See Steven Best and Anthony J. Nocella, *Igniting a Revolution: Voices in Defense of the Earth*, Oakland, CA: AK Press, 2006.

23. Stefan H. Leader and Peter Probst, "The Earth Liberation Front and Environmental Terrorism," *Terrorism and Political Violence*, vol. 15, 4 (2003), pp. 37–58, p. 37.

24. Ibid.

25. http://earthliberationfront.org, 29 Apr. 2011.

26. Ibid.

27. The government's reaction to "more than 20 acts of domestic terrorism" was Operation Backfire. The nine-year joint investigation was sometimes referred to as the "Green Scare," and run by federal, state, and local law

enforcement agencies in several states, including Oregon, Colorado, Washington, and California, culminating in more than a dozen arrests starting in Dec. 2005 and continuing throughout 2006. US Department of Justice, *National Security Division*, "Progress Report," 2008, p. 48.

28. From the ELF's Frequently Asked Questions, reprinted in Leslie James Pickering, *The Earth Liberation Front, 1997–2002*, Portland, OR: Arissa Media Group, 2007, p. 61.

29. Leader and Probst, "The Earth Liberation Front and Environmental Terrorism," p. 37.

30. For a good overview, see Sean Parson, "Understanding the Ideology of the Earth Liberation Front," *Green Theory & Praxis*, vol. 4, 2 (2009), pp. 50–66.

31. "Die *Energie* des Handels drückt die Stärke des Motivs aus, wodurch das Handel hervorgerufen wird, das Motiv mag nun in einer Verstandesüberzeugung oder einer Gemütserregung seinen Grund haben. Die letztere darf aber schwerlich fehlen, wo sich eine große Kraft zeigen soll." Clausewitz, *Vom Kriege*, p. 69.

32. David Galula, *Counterinsurgency Warfare: Theory and Practice*, New York: Praeger, 1964, p. 71.

33. For a historical discussion of ideology's role in guerrilla war, see Walter Laqueur, *Guerrilla: A Historical and Critical Study*, vol. 4, Boston: Little, Brown, 1976.

34. See John Jordan, "Our Resistance is as Transnational as Capital," in David B. Solnit (ed.), *Globalize Liberation*, San Francisco, CA: City Lights Books, 2004, pp. 9–17.

35. Pope, quoted in Kirn et al., "The New Radicals," *Time*, 24 Apr. 2000, p. 21.

36. Mitch Frank, "Organized Chaos," *Time*, 24 Apr. 2000.

37. "Anti-Globalization—A Spreading Phenomenon," Canadian Security Intelligence Service, Ottawa, 22 Aug. 2000.

38. "Charter of Principles," World Social Forum Organizing Committee, São Paulo, 9 Apr. 2001, later approved with modifications by the World Social Forum International Council on 10 June 2001.

39. "The Anarchogeek Interview," Reader-List, http://bitly.com/SkUXCC+

40. For an overview of the literature, see R. Kelly Garrett, "Protest in an Information Society," *Information, Communication & Society*, vol. 9, 2 (2006), pp. 202–24.

41. Peter Van Aelst and Stefaan Walgrave, "New Media, New Movements? The Role of the Internet in Shaping the 'Anti-Globalization' Movement," ibid., vol. 5, 4 (2002), p. 466.

42. Ibid., p. 487.

43. For a balanced view, see W. Lance Bennett, "Communicating Global Activism," ibid., vol. 6, 2 (2003), pp. 143–68.

44. John D. Clark and Nuno S. Themudo, "Linking the Web and the Street: Internet-Based 'Dotcauses' and the 'Anti-Globalization' Movement," *World Development*, vol. 34, 1 (2005), pp. 50–74.

45. Clay Shirky, *Cognitive Surplus*, New York: Penguin Press, 2010.

46. An explanation and a good introduction into the sense of humor of that subculture is at http://ohinternet.com/lulz

47. Siobhan Courtney, "Pornographic Videos Flood YouTube," BBC News, 21 May 2009.

48. For some eye-popping examples, see Parmy Olson, *We Are Anonymous*, Little Brown & Co, 2012, pp. 371–8.

49. The video has since been viewed nearly 5 million times: "Message to Scientology," 21 Jan. 2008, http://youtu.be/JCbKv9yiLiQ

50. By far the best and most detailed book on Anonymous to date is Olson, *We Are Anonymous*.

51. For an overview of DDoS attack tools, see Curt Wilson, "Attack of the Shuriken: Many Hands, Many Weapons," Arbor Networks, 7 Feb. 2012.

52. The episode is masterly described by Parmy Olson, see Olson, *We Are Anonymous*, Chapter 7, "FIRE FIRE FIRE FIRE," pp. 101–24.

53. Gabriella Coleman, "Our Weirdness is Free," *May*, vol. 9, 6 (2012), pp. 83–95, p. 84.

54. Wael Ghonim, *Revolution 2.0*, Boston: Houghton Mifflin Harcourt, 2012.

55. See for instance ibid., p. 176.

56. Ibid., p. 184.

57. Kitson's and Rosenau's works, cited above, are examples of such a narrow conceptualization of subversion.

58. I would like to thank Josh Welensky for pointing out the relevance of time in this context.

59. For an excellent historical overview of this trend, see Barton L. Ingraham, *Political Crime in Europe*, Berkeley: University of California Press, 1979.

60. Thomas Kuhn, *Structure of Scientific Revolutions*, Chicago: Chicago University Press, 1962.

61. The author in a series of discussions with senior literary scholars, Konstanz, spring and summer 2011. See also, Thomas Ernst, "Subversion. Eine kleine Diskursanalyse eines vielfältigen Begriffs," *Psychologie & Gesellschaftskritik*, vol. 42, 4 (2009), pp. 9–34, pp. 26–7 and Thomas Ernst, *Literatur und Subversion: Politisches Schreiben in der Gegenwart*, Bielefeld: Transcript, 2012.

62. Irene Rima Makaryk, *Encyclopedia of Contemporary Literary Theory*, Toronto: University of Toronto Press, 1993, p. 636.

63. "Was ist also Wahrheit? Ein bewegliches Heer von Metaphern, Metonymien, Anthropomorphismen, kurz eine Summe von menschlichen Rela-

tionen, die, poetisch und rhetorisch gesteigert, übertragen, geschmückt wurden, und die nach langem Gebrauch einem Volke fest, kanonisch und verbindlich dünken: die Wahrheiten sind Illusionen, von denen man vergessen hat, daß sie welche sind, Metaphern, die abgenutzt und sinnlich kraftlos geworden sind, Münzen, die ihr Bild verloren haben und nun als Metall, nicht mehr als Münzen, in Betracht kommen," Friedrich Nietzsche, *Über Wahrheit und Lüge im außermoralischen Sinne. Unzeitgemässe Betrachtungen*, Leipzig: Alfred Kröner, 1873 (1921), p. 10.

64. Geoffrey Galt Harpham, *The Ascetic Imperative in Culture and Criticism*, Chicago: University of Chicago Press, 1987, p. 218.

65. Grundgesetz für die Bundesrepublik Deutschland, Art 20 (1) Die Bundesrepublik Deutschland ist ein demokratischer und sozialer Bundesstaat. (2) Alle Staatsgewalt geht vom Volke aus. Sie wird vom Volke in Wahlen und Abstimmungen und durch besondere Organe der Gesetzgebung, der vollziehenden Gewalt und der Rechtsprechung ausgeübt. (3) Die Gesetzgebung ist an die verfassungsmäßige Ordnung, die vollziehende Gewalt und die Rechtsprechung sind an Gesetz und Recht gebunden. (4) Gegen jeden, der es unternimmt, diese Ordnung zu beseitigen, haben alle Deutschen das Recht zum Widerstand, wenn andere Abhilfe nicht möglich ist.

66. "[D]ie Restauration der Ordnung [stellt] eine ständige Drohung dar, weil immer neue Götter und Götzen auftauchen. Und insofern wird die theoretische und praktische Arbeit der Subversion nie beendet sein." Agnoli, *Subversive Theorie*, p. 25.

7. ATTRIBUTION

1. Mike McConnell, "Mike McConnell on How to Win the Cyberwar We're Losing," *The Washington Post*, 28 Feb. 2010.

2. Leon Panetta, "Remarks by Secretary Panetta on Cybersecurity to the Business Executives for National Security," New York City, 11 Oct. 2012.

3. For a similar argument, see David D. Clark and Susan Landau, "Untangling Attribution," in Committee on Deterring Cyberattacks (ed.), *Proceedings of a Workshop on Deterring Cyberattacks*, Washington, D.C.: National Academies Press, 2011, p. 26.

4. Bruce Hoffman, "Why Terrorists Don't Claim Credit," *Terrorism and Political Violence*, vol. 9, 1 (1997), pp. 1–6.

5. A more detailed study of the attribution problem and the use of force has not been written, to the knowledge of the author.

6. Ron Deibert and Rafal Rohozinsky, *Tracking GhostNet*, Toronto: Munc Centre for International Studies, 2009, p. 47.

7. A sample email is at ibid., p. 20.

8. Shishir Nagaraja and Ross Anderson, *The Snooping Dragon*, Cambridge: University of Cambridge, Mar. 2009, p. 6.

9. Kim Zetter, "Electronic Spy Network Focused on Dalai Lama and Embassy Computers," *Wired*, 28 Mar. 2009.

10. For more details, including webcam shots of unsuspecting computer users, see Mikko Hypponen, "Behind GhostNet," F-Secure, 30 Mar. 2009.

11. Deibert and Rohozinsky, *Tracking GhostNet*, p. 48.

12. Nagaraja and Anderson, *The Snooping Dragon*, p. 3.

13. For a more detailed discussion, see W. Earl Boebert, "A Survey of Challenges in Attribution," in Committee on Deterring Cyberattacks (ed.), *Proceedings of a Workshop on Deterring Cyberattacks*, pp. 41–54, also Clark and Landau, "Untangling Attribution."

14. Jack Goldsmith and Tim Wu, *Who Controls the Internet? Illusions of a Borderless World*, Oxford: Oxford University Press, 2006

15. http://www.whois.net/ip-address-lookup, as queried on 5 Sep. 2012.

16. For a detailed description of a number of Anonymous cases, see Olson, *We Are Anonymous*.

17. Richard Clayton, *Anonymity and Traceability in Cyberspace*, vol. 653, *Technical Report*, Cambridge: University of Cambridge Computer Laboratory, 2005, p. 3.

18. Ibid., pp. 151–2.

19. One of the best sources on the case is Gary Cartwright, "Search and Destroy," *Texas Monthly*, Mar. 1989, pp. 122–71.

20. Richard E Overill, "Trends in Computer Crime," *Journal of Financial Crime*, vol. 2, 6 (1998), pp. 157–62.

21. Cartwright, "Search and Destroy," p. 171.

22. "Programmer Convicted After Planting a 'Virus'," *The New York Times*, 21 Sep. 1988, p. 15.

23. David Drummond, "A New Approach to China," Google Official Blog, 12 Jan. 2012.

24. McAfee, "Protecting Your Critical Assets. Lessons Learned from 'Operation Aurora'," White Paper, 3 Mar. 2010.

25. Ariana Eunjung Cha and Ellen Nakashima, "Google China Cyberattack Part of Vast Espionage Campaign, Experts Say," *The Washington Post*, 14 Jan. 2010.

26. John Markoff and David Barboza, "2 China Schools Said to Be Tied to Online Attacks," *The New York Times*, 18 Feb. 2010.

27. Ibid.

28. US Embassy Beijing, "Google Update: PRC Role in Attacks and Response Strategy," Cable reference ID #10BEIJING207, 26 Jan. 2010.

29. Gavin O'Gorman and Geoff McDonald, "The Elderwood Project," Symantec, 7 Sep. 2012.

30. Jeremy Kirk, "Irked by cyberspying, Georgia outs Russia-based hacker—with photos," *IT World*, 30 Oct. 2012. See also

31. See a blog post by Alexander Klink, "Evading AVs using the XML Data Package (XDP) format," *Shift or Die*, 9 Feb. 2011.

32. "Georbot Botnet," *Ministry of Justice of Georgia*, October 2012, http://bitly.com/Wp3E64+

33. Mandiant, "APT1. Exposing one of China's Cyber Espionage Units," Alexandria, Virginia, 19 February 2013, p. 52.

34. Mandiant, "APT1," p. 54.

35. The original source, with my emphasis: "(61398 Unit). The Second Bureau *appears to function* as the Third Department's premier entity targeting the United States and Canada, *most likely* focusing on political, economic, and military-related intelligence," Mark A. Stokes, Jenny Lin, L.C. Russell Hsiao, "The Chinese People's Liberation Army Signals Intelligence and Cyber Reconnaissance Infrastructure," *Project 2049 Institute*, 11 Nov. 2011, p. 8.

36. Mandiant, "APT1," p. 59–60.

37. Mandiant, "APT1," p. 60.

38. For a more detailed critical analysis of the report which points out other errors, see Jeffrey Carr, "More on Mandiant's APT1 Report," Digital Dao, 22 Feb. 2013

39. For a detailed discussion see the Butler Report, Lord Butler of Brockwell, "Review of Intelligence on Weapons of Mass Destruction," House of Commons, London, 14 Jul. 2004.

40. The classic text is Sherman Kent, "Words of Estimative Probability," *Studies in Intelligence*, 1964, vol 8, iss 4, 49–65.

41. See McAfee, "Global Energy Cyberattacks: 'Night Dragon'," White Paper, 11 Feb. 2011, p. 4.

42. Joseph Menn, "Chinese Hackers Hit Energy Groups," *Financial Times*, 11 Feb. 2011.

43. Ibid.

44. McAfee, "Global Energy Cyberattacks: 'Night Dragon'," White Paper, 11 Feb. 2011, p. 18, emphasis in original.

45. Ed Crooks, "Hackers Target US Natural Gas Pipelines," *Financial Times*, 8 May 2012.

46. Martin Libicki, *Cyberdeterrence and Cyberwar*, Santa Monica: RAND Corporation, 2009, p. 44.

47. Eli Jellenc, "Cyber Deterrence," *iDefense Weekly Threat Report*, Verisign, Apr. 2011.

48. Mohamad Saleh, "Al Qaeda Claims Responsibility for Power Blackout in US," *Dar Al Hayat*, 18 Aug. 2003, http://bitly.com/Q3jV9f+

49. Herbert Lin calls using all sources, not merely technical sources, at the scene

of an attack, "all-source attribution." See Herbert Lin, "Escalation Dynamics and Conflict Termination in Cyberspace," *Strategic Studies Quarterly* (2012), pp. 46–70, p. 49.

8. BEYOND CYBER WAR

1. I would like to thank David Betz for this reference. The article, which used cyberspace only once and without exploring it, was originally published in *Omni* magazine, July 1982. On the use of analogies, see David Betz and Tim Stevens, "Analogical Reasoning and Cyber Security," Security Dialogue, Vol. 44, No. 1, Apr. (2013).

2. William Gibson, *Neuromancer*, New York: Ace Books, 1984, pp. 10–11.

3. William Gibson, as quoted in Betz and Stevens, *Cyberspace and the State*, p. 36.

4. This three-step is inspired by W.H. Murray, "The Application of Epidemiology to Computer Viruses," *Computers & Security*, vol. 7 (1988), pp. 139–50.

5. "War in the Fifth Domain," *The Economist*, 1 July 2010.

6. The assertion was first made in 1996 and has since become part of the debate's standard lore, John Arquilla and David Ronfeldt, *The Advent of Netwar*, Santa Monica: RAND, 1996, p. 94.

7. Department of Defense, "Cyberspace Policy Report," Nov. 2011, p. 2.

8. See for instance, Libicki, *Cyberdeterrence and Cyberwar*, pp. 32–3.

9. Dale Peterson, interview with author, by telephone, 11 Sep. 2012.

10. Ralph Langner, "A Declaration of Bankruptcy for US Critical Infrastructure Protection," *The Last Line of Cyber Defense*, 3 June 2011.

11. An ongoing move towards open standards may affect the potential for generic attacks as well as the potential to gather target intelligence remotely, see Igure, Laughter, and Williams, "Security issues in SCADA networks," p. 500. Also Byres and Lowe, "The Myths and Facts behind Cyber Security Risks for Industrial Control Systems."

12. For a comparison between malware and car manufacturing, see Symantec, "W32.Duqu," Oct. 2011, p. 1.

13. Karl Frederick Rauscher and Andrey Korotkov, "Working Towards Rules for Governing Cyber Conflict," East West Institute, 4 Feb. 2011, p. 27.

14. Brent Scowcroft, "Cyber Security Issues Like Cold War," Georgetown University, 29 Mar. 2011.

15. Two useful articles are Joseph S. Nye, "Nuclear Lessons for Cyber Security?" *Strategic Studies Quarterly* (Winter 2011), pp. 18–38, Andrew F. Krepinevich, *Cyber Warfare: A Nuclear Option?* Washington, DC: Center for Strategic and Budgetary Assessments 2012.

16. An early and detailed example is Michael N. Schmitt, "Computer Network Attack and the Use of Force in International Law," *Columbia Journal of Transnational Law*, vol. 37 (1998), pp. 885–937. More recently, see Waxman, "Cyber-Attacks and the Use of Force," Marco Roscini, "World Wide Warfare-'Jus Ad Bellum' and the Use of Cyber Force," *Max Planck Yearbook of United Nations Law*, vol. 14 (2010), pp. 85–130.

17. For a pithy discussion of this problem, see Noah Shachtman and Peter W. Singer, "The Wrong War," *The Brookings Institution*, 15 Aug. 2011. See also Jerry Brito and Tate Watkins, "Loving the Cyber Bomb? The Dangers of Threat Inflation in Cybersecurity Policy," *Harvard National Security Journal* (2011).

18. I would like to thank Ron Tira for raising this point with me.

19. Ironically, Air Force General Lauris Norstad, Supreme Allied Commander Europe, was one of the most vocal opponents of this doctrine because it did not provide enough forces; he wanted a "shield," not a trip-wire. Howard D. Belote, *Once in a Blue Moon*, Maxwell, AL: Air University Press, 2000, p. 18.

20. See Ron Deibert, "Tracking the Emerging Arms Race in Cyberspace," *Bulletin of the Atomic Scientists*, vol. 67, 1 (2011), pp. 1–8.

21. Lynn, "The Pentagon's Cyberstrategy, One Year Later."

BIBLIOGRAPHY

The majority of primary sources that informed this book are not included in this bibliography. These sources are fully documented in the footnotes. Below is a selection of books, articles, and a few reports.

Adee, Sally, "The Hunt for the Kill Switch," *IEEE Spectrum*, May 2008.

Aelst, Peter Van and Stefaan Walgrave, "New Media, New Movements? The Role of the Internet in Shaping the 'Anti-Globalization' Movement," *Information, Communication & Society*, vol. 5, 4 (2002), pp. 465–93.

Agnoli, Johannes, *Subversive Theorie*, Freiburg: Ça ira, 1996.

Air Material Command, *Reconnaissance Aircraft and Aerial Photographic Equipment 1915–1945*, Wright Field: Historical Division, 1946.

Alperovitch, Dmitri, *Revealed: Operation Shady RAT*, Santa Clara, CA: McAfee, 2 Aug. 2011.

Arendt, Hannah, *On Violence*, New York: Harcourt, Brace, Jovanovich, 1970.

Arquilla, John and David Ronfeldt, *The Advent of Netwar*, Santa Monica: RAND, 1996.

——— "Cyberwar is Coming!" *Comparative Strategy*, vol. 12, 2 (1993), pp. 141–65.

Austin, John, *The Province of Jurisprudence Determined*, Plaistow: Curwen Press, 1832 (1954).

Belote, Howard D., *Once in a Blue Moon*, Maxwell, AL: Air University Press, 2000.

Belsham, William, *Memoirs of the Reign of George III to the Session of Parliament Ending A.D. 1793*, vol. I, London: J. Robinson, 1795.

Benjamin, Walter, "Critique of Violence," in *Reflections*, pp. 277–300, New York: Schocken Books, 1978.

Bennett, W. Lance, "Communicating Global Activism," *Information, Communication & Society*, vol. 6, 2 (2003), pp. 143–68.

BIBLIOGRAPHY

Best, Steven and Anthony J. Nocella, *Igniting a Revolution: Voices in Defense of the Earth*, Oakland, CA: AK Press, 2006.

Betz, David and Tim Stevens, *Cyberspace and the State*, Adelphi Series, London: IISS/Routledge, 2011.

Blainey, Geoffrey, *The Causes of War*, New York: Free Press, 1973.

Boebert, W. Earl, "A Survey of Challenges in Attribution," in Committee on Deterring Cyberattacks (ed.), *Proceedings of a Workshop on Deterring Cyberattacks*, pp. 41–54, Washington, DC: National Academies Press, 2011.

Brenner, Joel, *America the Vulnerable*, New York: Penguin Press, 2011.

Brito, Jerry and Tate Watkins, "Loving the Cyber Bomb? The Dangers of Threat Inflation in Cybersecurity Policy," *Harvard National Security Journal* (2011).

Broad, William J., John Markoff, and David E. Sanger, "Israeli Test on Worm Called Crucial in Iran Nuclear Delay," *The New York Times*, 16 Jan. 2011, p. A1.

Brusnitsin, Nikolai, *Openness and Espionage*, Moscow: Military Pub. House, USSR Ministry of Defense, 1990.

Burke, Edmund, *Reflections on the Revolution in France*, London: J. Dodsley, 1790.

Byres, Eric and Justin Lowe, "The Myths and Facts Behind Cyber Security Risks for Industrial Control Systems," paper read at Proceedings of the VDE Congress, at VDE Association for Electrical Electronic & Information Technologies, Oct. 2004.

Cartwright, Gary, "Search and Destroy," *Texas Monthly*, Mar. 1989, pp. 122–71.

Clark, David D. and Susan Landau, "Untangling Attribution," in Committee on Deterring Cyberattacks (ed.), *Proceedings of a Workshop on Deterring Cyberattacks*, pp. 25–40, Washington, DC: National Academies Press, 2011.

Clark, John D. and Nuno S. Themudo, "Linking the Web and the Street: Internet-Based 'Dotcauses' and the 'Anti-Globalization' Movement," *World Development*, vol. 34, 1 (2005), pp. 50–74.

Clarke, Richard A. and Robert K. Knake, *Cyber War*, New York: Ecco, 2010.

Clausewitz, Carl von, *Vom Kriege*, Berlin: Ullstein, 1832 (1980).

Clayton, Richard, *Anonymity and Traceability in Cyberspace*, vol. 653, *Technical Report*, Cambridge: University of Cambridge Computer Laboratory, 2005.

Clutterbuck, Lindsay and William Rosenau, "Subversion as a Facet of Terrorism and Insurgency," *Strategic Insights*, vol. 8, 3 (2009).

Coleman, Gabriella, "Our Weirdness is Free," *May*, vol. 9, 6 (2012), pp. 83–95.

Convertino, Sebastian M. II, Lou Anne DeMattei, and Tammy M. Knierim, "Flying and Fighting in Cyberspace," *Air War College Maxwell Paper*, 40 (2007).

Darlington, Ralph, *Syndicalism and the Transition to Communism*, Aldershot, England: Ashgate, 2008.

BIBLIOGRAPHY

Deibert, Ron, "Tracking the Emerging Arms Race in Cyberspace," *Bulletin of the Atomic Scientists*, vol. 67, 1 (2011), pp. 1–8.

Deibert, Ron and Rafal Rohozinsky, *Tracking GhostNet*, Toronto: Munc Centre for International Studies, 2009.

Deibert, Ron, Rafal Rohozinski and Masashi Crete-Nishihata, "Cyclones in Cyberspace: Information Shaping and Denial in the 2008 Russia-Georgia War," *Security Dialogue*, vol. 43, 1 (2012), pp. 3–24.

Department of Defense, *Cyberspace Policy Report*, Nov. 2011.

Diederichsen, Diedrich, "Subversion—Kalte Strategie und heiße Differenz," in Diedrich Diederichsen (ed.), *Freiheit macht arm: das Leben nach Rock'n'Roll 1990–1993*, pp. 33–52, Köln: Kiepenheuer & Witsch, 1993.

Dinstein, Yoram, "Computer Network Attacks and Self-Defense," *International Legal Studies*, vol. 76 (2002).

Donovan, William J., *Simple Sabotage Field Manual*, Washington, DC: Office of Strategic Services, 1944.

Ernst, Thomas, *Literatur und Subversion: Politisches Schreiben in der Gegenwart*, Bielefeld: Transcript, 2012.

———— "Subversion. Eine kleine Diskursanalyse eines vielfältigen Begriffs," *Psychologie & Gesellschaftskritik*, vol. 42, 4 (2009), pp. 9–34.

Evans, Jonathan, *The Threat to National Security*, London: The Worshipful Company of Security Professionals, 16 Sep. 2010.

Evron, Gadi, "Battling Botnets and Online Mobs," *Science & Technology* (Winter/Spring 2008), pp. 121–8.

Falliere, Nicolas, Liam O Murchu, and Eric Chien, *W32.Stuxnet Dossier. Version 1.4*, Symantec, 2011.

Filkins, Dexter, *The Forever War*, New York: Knopf, 2008.

Flynn, Elizabeth Gurley, *Sabotage*, Cleveland, Ohio: IWW Publishing Bureau, 1916.

Fulghum, David, "Cyber Attack Turns Physical," *Aerospace Daily & Defense Report*, vol. 235, 61 (2010), p. 3.

Galula, David, *Counterinsurgency Warfare: Theory and Practice*, New York: Praeger, 1964.

Garrett, R. Kelly, "Protest in an Information Society," *Information, Communication & Society*, vol. 9, 2 (2006), pp. 202–24.

Gellner, Ernest, "Trust, Cohesion, and the Social Order," in Diego Gambetta (ed.), *Trust: Making and Breaking Cooperative Relations*, pp. 142–57, London: Wiley-Blackwell, 1990.

Ghonim, Wael, *Revolution 2.0*, Boston: Houghton Mifflin Harcourt, 2012.

Gibbs, Jack P., "Deterrence Theory and Research," in Gary Melton, Laura Nader, and Richard A. Dienstbier (eds), *Law as a Behavioral Instrument*, Lincoln: University of Nebraska Press, 1986.

BIBLIOGRAPHY

Gibson, William, *Neuromancer*, New York: Ace Books, 1984.

Giraudoux, Jean, *Tiger at the Gates (La guerre de Troie n'aura pas lieu)*, translated by Christopher Fry, New York: Oxford University Press, 1955.

Goldsmith, Jack and Tim Wu, *Who Controls the Internet? Illusions of a Borderless World*, Oxford: Oxford University Press, 2006.

Gross, Michael Joseph, "A Declaration of Cyber-War," *Vanity Fair*, Apr. 2011.

Hardin, Russell, *Trust and Trustworthiness*, New York: Russell Sage Foundation, 2002.

Harpham, Geoffrey Galt, *The Ascetic Imperative in Culture and Criticism*, Chicago: University of Chicago Press, 1987.

Hayden, Michael V., "The Future of Things 'Cyber'," *Strategic Studies Quarterly*, vol. 5, 1 (2011), pp. 3–7.

Hegel, G.W.F., *Phänomenologie des Geistes*, Berlin: Duncker und Humblot, 1832.

Hobbes, Thomas, *Leviathan*, London: Penguin, 1651 (1996).

Hoffman, Bruce, "Why Terrorists Don't Claim Credit," *Terrorism and Political Violence*, vol. 9, 1 (1997), pp. 1–6.

Igure, Vinay M., Sean A. Laughter, and Ronald D. Williams, "Security Issues in SCADA Networks," *Computers & Security*, vol. 25 (2006), pp. 498–506.

Ingraham, Barton L., *Political Crime in Europe*, Berkeley: University of California Press, 1979.

Inkster, Nigel, "Intelligence Agencies and the Cyber World," in *Strategic Survey*, London: International Institute for Strategic Studies, 2012.

James, Charles, *Military Dictionary, In French and English*, London: Egerton, 1810.

Johnson, Samuel, *Dictionary of the English Language*, Dublin: G Jones, 1768.

Jordan, John, "Our Resistance is as Transnational as Capital," in David B. Solnit (ed.), *Globalize Liberation*, pp. 9–17, San Francisco, CA: City Lights Books, 2004.

Kalyvas, Stathis, *The Logic of Violence in Civil War*, Cambridge: Cambridge University Press, 2006.

Kaspersky Lab, "Gauss: Abnormal Distribution," 9 Aug. 2012.

Katz, Samuel M., *The Hunt for the Engineer*, New York: Fromm International, 1999.

Kelsen, Hans, *Pure Theory of Law* (Second Edition), Berkeley: University of California Press, 1984.

Kitson, Frank, *Low Intensity Operations: Subversion, Insurgency and Peacekeeping*, London: Faber and Faber, 2010.

Kraus, Jürgen, *Selbstreproduktion bei Programmen*, Dortmund: Universität Dortmund, 1980.

Krepinevich, Andrew F., *Cyber Warfare: A Nuclear Option?* Washington, DC: Center for Strategic and Budgetary Assessments 2012.

Kuhn, Thomas, *Structure of Scientific Revolutions*, Chicago: Chicago University Press, 1962.

Laqueur, Walter, *Guerrilla: A Historical and Critical Study*, vol. 4, Boston: Little, Brown, 1976.

Leader, Stefan H. and Peter Probst, "The Earth Liberation Front and Environmental Terrorism," *Terrorism and Political Violence*, vol. 15, 4 (2003), pp. 37–58.

Leslie, James, *Dictionary of the Synonymous Words and Technical Terms in the English Language*, Edinburgh: John Moir, 1806.

Leverett, Éireann P., *Quantitatively Assessing and Visualising Industrial System Attack Surfaces*, Cambridge, UK: University of Cambridge, 2011.

Lewis, J. David and Andrew J. Weigert, "Social Atomism, Holism, and Trust," *The Sociological Quarterly*, vol. 26, 4 (1985), pp. 455–71.

——— "Trust as a Social Reality," *Social Forces*, vol. 63, 4 (1985), pp. 967–85.

Libicki, Martin, *Cyberdeterrence and Cyberwar*, Santa Monica: RAND Corporation, 2009.

Lin, Herbert, "Escalation Dynamics and Conflict Termination in Cyberspace," *Strategic Studies Quarterly* (2012), pp. 46–70.

Lobban, Iain, *Iain Lobban Address*, London: International Institute of Strategic Studies, 12 Oct. 2010.

Locke, John, *Two Treatises of Government*, Cambridge: Cambridge University Press, 1689 (1988).

Lorents, Peeter and Rain Ottis, "Knowledge Based Framework for Cyber Weapons and Conflict," *Conference on Cyber Conflict Proceedings*, 2010, pp. 129–42.

Luck, M., P. McBurney, and C. Preist, "A Manifesto for Agent Technology: Towards Next Generation Computing," *Autonomous Agents and Multi-Agent Systems*, vol. 9, 3 (2004), pp. 203–52.

Lynn, William J., "Defending a New Domain," *Foreign Affairs*, vol. 89, 5 (2010), pp. 97–108.

——— "The Pentagon's Cyberstrategy, One Year Later," *Foreign Affairs*, 28 Sep. 2011

Mahnken, Thomas G., "Cyber War and Cyber Warfare," in Kristin Lord and Travis Sharp (eds), *America's Cyber Future: Security and Prosperity in the Information Age*, vol. 2, pp. 53–62, Washington, DC: CNAS, 2011.

Makaryk, Irene Rima, *Encyclopedia of Contemporary Literary Theory*, Toronto: University of Toronto Press, 1993.

Mandiant, "APT1. Exposing one of China's Cyber Espionage Units," Alexandria, Virginia, 19 February 2013.

Mark A. Stokes, Jenny Lin, L.C. Russell Hsiao, "The Chinese People's Liberation Army Signals Intelligence and Cyber Reconnaissance Infrastructure," *Project 2049 Institute*, 11 Nov. 2011.

Moore, D., V. Paxson, S. Savage, C. Shannon, S. Staniford, and N. Weaver, "Inside the Slammer Worm," *IEEE Security & Privacy*, vol. 1, 4 (2003), pp. 33–9.

Murray, W.H., "The Application of Epidemiology to Computer Viruses," *Computers & Security*, vol. 7 (1988), pp. 139–50.

Nagaraja, Shishir and Ross Anderson, *The Snooping Dragon*, Cambridge: University of Cambridge, Mar. 2009.

Nietzsche, Friedrich, *Über Wahrheit und Lüge im außermoralischen Sinne. Unzeitgemässe Betrachtungen*, Leipzig: Alfred Kröner, 1873 (1921).

Nonaka, Ikujiro, "A Dynamic Theory of Organizational Knowledge Creation," *Organization Science*, vol. 5, 1 (1994), pp. 14–37.

———— *The Knowledge-Creating Company*, New York: Oxford University Press, 1995.

Nye, Joseph S., "Nuclear Lessons for Cyber Security?" *Strategic Studies Quarterly* (Winter 2011), pp. 18–38.

Office of the National Counterintelligence Executive, *Foreign Spies Stealing US Economic Secrets in Cyberspace*, Washington, DC, October 2011.

Olson, Parmy, *We Are Anonymous*, Little Brown & Co, 2012.

Onley, Dawn and Patience Wait, "Red Storm Rising," *Government Computer News*, 17 Aug. 2006.

Overill, Richard E., "Trends in Computer Crime," *Journal of Financial Crime*, vol. 2, 6 (1998), pp. 157–62.

Parson, Sean, "Understanding the Ideology of the Earth Liberation Front," *Green Theory & Praxis*, vol. 4, 2 (2009), pp. 50–66.

d'Entrèves, Alessandro Passerin, *The Notion of the State*, Oxford: Oxford University Press, 1967.

Pavlovic, Dusko, "Gaming Security by Obscurity," *arXiv 1109.5542*, 9, 2011.

Pickering, Leslie James, *The Earth Liberation Front, 1997–2002*, Portland, OR: Arissa Media Group, 2007.

Polanyi, Michael, *Personal Knowledge*, Chicago: University of Chicago Press, 1962.

Popitz, Heinrich, *Phänomene der Macht*, Tübingen: Mohr Siebeck, 2004.

Pouget, Émile, *Le sabotage*, Paris: M. Rivière, 1910.

Pouget, Émile and Arturo M. Giovannitti, *Sabotage*, Chicago: C.H. Kerr & Co., 1913.

Prins, J.R., *DigiNotar Certificate Authority Breach 'Operation Black Tulip'*, Delft: Fox-IT 2011.

Raviv, Dan and Yossi Melman, *Spies Against Armageddon*, Sea Cliff, NY: Levant Books, 2012.

Reed, Thomas C., *At the Abyss*, New York: Random House, 2004.

BIBLIOGRAPHY

Rid, Thomas, "Cracks in the Jihad," *The Wilson Quarterly*, vol. 34, 1 (2010), pp. 40–8.

——— "Cyber War Will Not Take Place," *Journal of Strategic Studies*, vol. 35, 1 (2012).

——— *War and Media Operations. The U.S. Military and the Press from Vietnam to Iraq*, London: Routledge, 2007.

Rid, Thomas and Marc Hecker, *War 2.0: Irregular Warfare in the Information Age*, Westport: Praeger, 2009.

Rid, Thomas and Peter McBurney, "Cyber Weapons," *The RUSI Journal*, vol. 157, 1 (2012), pp. 6–13.

Roscini, Marco, "World Wide Warfare—'Jus Ad Bellum' and the Use of Cyber Force," *Max Planck Yearbook of United Nations Law*, vol. 14 (2010), pp. 85–130.

Rosenau, William, *Subversion and Insurgency*, Santa Monica, CA: Rand, 2007.

Sanger, David, *Confront and Conceal*, New York: Crown, 2012.

Schmitt, Michael N., "Computer Network Attack and the Use of Force in International Law," *Columbia Journal of Transnational Law*, vol. 37 (1998), pp. 885–937.

Schneier, Bruce, *Liars and Outliers*, Indianapolis, IN: Wiley, 2012.

Senor, Dan and Saul Singer, *Start-up Nation*, New York: Twelve, 2009.

Shirky, Clay, *Cognitive Surplus*, New York: Penguin Press, 2010.

Slay, Jill and Michael Miller, "Lessons Learned from the Maroochy Water Breach," in E. Goetz and S. Shenoi (eds), in: *Critical Infrastructure Protection*, vol. 253, pp. 73–82, Boston: Springer, 2008.

Sofsky, Wolfgang, *Traktat über die Gewalt*, Frankfurt am Main: Fischer, 1996.

Tabansky, Lior, "Basic Concepts in Cyber Warfare," *Military and Strategic Affairs*, vol. 3, 1 (2011), pp. 75–92.

Tikk, Eneken, Kadri Kaska, Kristel Rünnimeri, Mari Kert, Anna-Maria Talihärm, and Liis Vihul, *Cyber Attacks Against Georgia*, Tallinn: CCDCOE, 2008.

Tikk, Eneken, Kadri Kaska, and Liis Vihul, *International Cyber Incidents*, Tallinn: CCDCOE, 2010.

Tzu, Sun, *The Art of War*, translated by Samuel B Griffith, Oxford: Oxford University Press, 1963.

Warner, Michael, "Reflections on Technology and Intelligence Systems," *Intelligence and National Security*, vol. 27, 1 (2012), pp. 133–53.

Waxman, Matthew C., "Cyber-Attacks and the Use of Force," *The Yale Journal of International Law*, vol. 36 (2011), pp. 421–59.

Weber, Max, *Politik als Beruf*, Berlin: Duncker & Humblot, 1968 (1919).

Weiner, Tim, *Enemies: A History of the FBI*, New York: Random House, 2012.

Wynne, Michael, "Flying and Fighting in Cyberspace," *Air & Space Power Journal* (2007), pp. 5–9.

INDEX

4chan: /b/, 129; terminology of, 129

A16 (2000): participants in, 125
Aaviksoo, Jaak: Estonian Minister of Defense, 30
AC/DC: 172; 'Hells Bells', 34
Adobe: targeted in Operation Aurora (2010), 149
Adobe Flash Player: zero-day exploit in, 92
Afghanistan: 102; Soviet Invasion of (1979–89), 141
Agnoli, Johannes: 138; background of, 119; theories of subversion, 119–20, 134
Alexander, Keith: 38
Alibo: 27–8
Alperovitch, Dmitri: 157; Vice President for Threat Research at McAfee, Inc., 90–1
American Superconductor Corp. (AMSC): legal damages sought by, 104; personnel of, 104; Windtec Solutions, 105
Anonymous: activities of, 128; origins of, 128–9; Project

Chanology, 129–30; protests conducted by, 129–30; use of DDoS attacks by, 129–31; use of IRC by, 130
Ansip, Andrus: Estonian Prime Minister, 7
Apple, Inc.: iPhone, 70, 92, 95, 146
Arab Spring: 63, 113; Egyptian Revolution (2011), 22, 116, 132–3; Libyan Civil War (2011), 35, 132; Tunisian Revolution (2010–11), 132; use of social media in, 132–3; Yemeni Uprising (2011–12), 132
Arendt, Hannah: 24
Arquilla, John: xiii
al-Assad, Bashar: regime of, 34
Assange, Julian: 130
Australia: Queensland, 74
Austria: 105; Vienna, 32
Ayyash, Yahya Abd-al-Latif: assassination of (1999), 47

Bacon, Kenneth: 48
Bahrain: 55
Bangladesh: 142
Barbados: 142

INDEX

Battle of Seattle (1999): 124, 127
Belgium: Brussels, 142
Benjamin, Walter: *Critique of Violence* (1921), 24
Beresford, Dillon: discovery of vulnerability in Siemens S7 PLC, 71
Bhutan: 142
big data: concept of, 109–10
Bluetooth: exploitation by Flame virus, 94
Boden, Vitek: role in Maroochy incident (2000), 74
Bosnian War (1992–5): Srebrenica Massacre (1995), 29
Brazil: Porto Alegre, 125
British Broadcasting Corporation (BBC): 129
British Columbia Institute of Technology: Industrial Security Incident Database, 76
Brunei: 142
Brusnitsin, Lt. Gen. Nikolai: *Openness and Espionage* (1990), 5
Bryant, Janelle: 75
Bulletin de la bourse du travail de Montpellier (1900): political impact of, 59–60
Bundestrojaner: 100
Burke, Edmund: *Reflections on the Revolution in France* (1790), 117
Burleson, Donald Gene: conviction of for Burleson case (1985), 147
Burleson case (1985): 146–8, 156; perpetrators in, 147; significance of, 156
Bush, George H.W.: administration of, 170
Bush, George W.: administration of, xiv, 139

Canada: 102, 142; Canadian

Security Intelligence Service (CSIS), 125; government of, 91; Ontario, 85
Carnival Against Capital (J18) (1999): 124
Carter, Jimmy: signing of FISA (1978), 112
Changchun, Li: role in Operation Aurora (2010), 150
Chaos Computer Club (CCC): *Bundestrojaner* report (2011), 100
China: 35, 84, 92, 114, 148, 154, 161, 170–1; Baidu, 150; Beijing, 19, 91, 144, 153, 157, 160; government of, 108, 142, 144, 154; Lanxinag Vocational School, 149–50; Lingshui Air Base, 144; Olympic Games (2008), 91; Politburo Standing Committee, 150; Shanghai, 69, 110, 154–5; Shanghai Jiatong University, 149; State Council Information Office, 150; suspected use of cyber espionage by, 85–7, 108, 160
China Huiyuan Juice Group: attempted acquisition of (2009), 85, 154
China Telecom: supply of high-speed fiber-optic line to Unit 61398 facilities, 154–5
Church of Scientology: opposition to, 129–30
Citibank: 97
Citizen Lab: personnel of, 142
Clarke, Justin: discovery of vulnerability in RuggedCom products, 71
Clarke, Richard: xiii; *Cyber War*, 174
von Clausewitz, Carl: 10; *On War*, 1–2, 24; theories of, 25–6, 123

208

Coca-Cola Corporation: Comment Group hacking incident (2009), 85, 154

Cold War: 116, 170, 172

Comodo Hacker: 29–30; cyber attack on DigitNotar (2011), 27, 29, 31

Cruise, Tom: 129

Cutting Sword of Justice: claim of responsibility for Saudi Aramco Shamoon attack (2012), 63–4, 159

cyber espionage: 103, 109, 113, 142, 167, 171; attribution issue of, 142, 144, 156–7; economic impact of, 85; limitations of, 82–3, 85, 112

cyber warfare: 26, 30, 52, 56, 79; concept of, 3; limitations of, 20, 24–5, 82; non-violent, 61–2; political, 161; use in sabotage, 56–7, 82, 113, 171–2; use in subversion, 113, 123, 167, 170–3; violence in context of, 12–14, 17

cyber weaponry: 36, 38–9, 161, 169; definition of, 46–7; targeting of, 51; terminology of, 37, 51

cyberspace: concept of, 164–5; origin of term, 163–4

Dalai Lama: escape to Tibet (1959), 142; targeted during GhostNet incident (2008), 142–3

Deibert, Ron: head of Citizen Lab, 142

denial of service (DoS) attacks: 155; concept of, 6; shortcomings of, 40

DigiNotar: bankruptcy of (2011), 28, 30, 32; certificates issued by, 27–8; Comodo Hacker attack on (2011), 27, 29, 31; purpose of, 26–7

Digitial Bond: S4 Conference, 70, 72

Distributed Control Systems (DCS): concept of, 66–7; use in Industrial Control Systems, 67

distributed denial of service (DDoS) attacks: 6, 40; examples of, 6–8, 30–2, 40, 129–30

Dow Chemical: targeted in Operation Aurora (2010), 149

drones: potential hijacking of, 14–15

Dupont: 84

Duqu: 83; code of, 66; customisation potential of, 93–4; discovery of (2011), 93, 97; use of, 93–4

Earth Liberation Front (ELF): 128; launch of (1992), 121; ideology of, 121–2; limitations of, 121–2; organisational model of, 121–3; 'The Family', 122

Egypt: Alexandria, 132; Cairo, 22, 133; Revolution (2011), 22, 116, 132–3

Emerson Electric Company: 71

Ergma, Ene: Speaker of Estonian Parliament, 31

Estonia: 8; DDoS attacks (2007), 6–7, 31–2, 40; internet usage figures for, 6; Reform Party, 6; Tallinn, 6, 8

European Commission: 7

European Union (EU): 170

Evans, Jonathan: 108–9

Facebook: 102, 110, 129, 132; founding of, 127; prevalence of use of, 102–3; use in Arab Spring, 132–3

Farewell Dossier: contents of, 5–6

Federal Republic of Germany (West Germany): Berlin, 119; *Grundgesetz* (basic law), 137–8; US military presence in, 172

Finland: 33

FirstEnergy: personnel of, 49; targeting of business network of (2003), 48–9

First World War (1914–18): 61

Flame: 33, 83, 96, 99–100, 144; development and potential deployment of (2006), 95; discovery of (2012), 94; significance of, 168; suicide functionality of, 95; systems targeted by, 95

Flynn, Elizabeth Gurly: 59

Ford, Gerald: administration of, 170

France: 22, 35, 61; Direction Générale de la Sécurité Extérieure (DGSE), 99; Paris, ix, xiii, 59, 117; Revolution (1789–99), 116–17, 119

F-Secure: 29; personnel of, 44

Galula, David: 123

Gauss: 99; code of, 97–8; discovery of (2012), 96–8; modules of, 97–8; purpose of, 97; significance of, 156

Gazprom: insider breach (2000), 74; SCADA systems of, 74

Georbot (2011): 151–2, 156; Georgian response to, 151–2; significance of, 152

George III, King: 117

Georgia: 7, 9; 'Dr. WEB', 151; government of, 8, 152; military of, 7; Ministry of Foreign Affairs, 8; Ministry of Justice, 152; National Bank, 8

German (language): 24

Germany: 22; Berlin, viii, ix, 100; Bundesnachrichtendienst (BND), 99, 106; Cologne, 124; Fall of Berlin Wall (1989), 138; government of, 100

Ghonim, Wael: 133–4; background of, 132; *Revolution 2.0.*, 132

GhostNet: significance of, 160; use of, 142–3; use of spear phishing, 143

Gibson, William: *Burning Chrome* (1982), 163; *Neuromancer* (1984), 163–4; role in origin of term 'cyberspace', 163–4

Giovannitti, Arturo: 60

Giraudoux, Jean: background of, xiii; *La guerre de Troie n'aura pas lieu* (The Trojan War Will Not Take Place) (1914), xiii, 174

globalization: economic, 124; opposition to, 113, 115–16, 123–7

Google Inc.: 28, 30, 78; Chrome, 27–8; Gmail, 27–8, 102; personnel of, 148; software configuration management system (SCM), 148; targeted in Operation Aurora (2010), 148–9; use of 'public key pinning' by, 28

Gostev, Alex: Chief Security Expert for Kaspersky Lab, 91

Greece: 157

Greenpeace: presence at A16 (2000), 125

Guoqiang, He: family of, 150

De Guzman, Onel: programmer of ILOVEYOU worm, 48

Hamas: 47

Hebrew (language): 101, 104

Hegel, Georg Wilhelm Friedrich: 120

Henshaw-Plath, Evan: interview with (2001), 126

Hezbollah: 17, 47; listed as Foreign Terrorist Organizations by US State Department, 99; supporters of, 141; use of cyber espionage by, 103

Hitler, Adolf: 8

Hobbes, Thomas: *Leviathan*, 15–16; theories of, 16, 23

Honeywell International, Inc.: 71

Hotmail: 102

human intelligence (HUMINT): 81, 83, 110

human machine interface (HMI): concept of, 67

Hungary: 93

Idaho National Laboratory: 164; test of 'Aurora' vulnerability (2006), 46

Illinois Statewide Terrorism and Intelligence Center: 76

ILOVEYOU worm: damage inflicted by, 48, 53; use of (2000), 48

India: Calcutta, 106; Delhi, viii; Dharamsala, 142; government of, 91

Indonesia: 142

Industrial Control Systems: 57; as example of master devices, 67; software written for, 43; use of DCS systems by, 67; use of SCADA systems by, 56, 67

Industrial Control Systems Cyber Emergency Response Team (ICS-CERT): 70–1, 158

Industrial Workers of the World: members of, 59, 61

Inkster, Nigel: 108

International Atomic Energy Agency: 32

International Business Machines (IBM) Corporation: 147; sponsorship of Battle of the Brains (1997), 149; System/38, 146

International Committee of the Red Cross (ICRC): 14; personnel of, 165

International Institute for Strategic Studies: 108

International Monetary Fund (IMF): 124

internet protocols (IPs): 63, 70, 76–8, 90, 92, 143–5, 154, 157; random generation of, 49; tracing of, 7, 145–6; use in SCADAs, 69

Internet Relay Chat (IRC): 130

internet service providers (ISPs): 30, 146; examples of, 100, 145; use of log files by, 145

Interstate Natural Gas of America: personnel of, 158

Iran: xiv, 27–9, 64–5, 101, 114, 141–2; Atomic Energy Organization of Iran (AEOI), 33; Green Movement, 29; Kashmar, 15; military of, 96; Ministry of Oil, 64, 94; Natanz, 32, 42–4, 72, 106; nuclear enrichment program of, 44, 172; seizure of CIA drone in (2011), 15; Stuxnet attacks (2009–10), 32–4, 42–5, 106; Tehran, 29, 106

Iraq: Operation Iraqi Freedom (2003–11), 34, 156

Ireland: Irish Rebellion (1798), 116

Islam: concept of Mahdi, 101; Eid ul-Fitr, 55; Ramadan, 55; Shia, 101

Islamic Jihad: 47
Israel: 34, 41, 54, 98, 102, 161; Air
    Force, 11, 42; economy of, 102;
    Mossad, 27, 106; Operation
    Orchard, 11, 34, 41–2; popula-
    rity of Facebook in, 102–3; Sami
    Shamoon College of Engineering,
    62; Shin Bet, 47; Tel Aviv, 47
Israeli Defence Force (IDF): digital
    training regimen of, 103;
    Facebook security breach (2010),
    103–4; Unit 8200, 42, 47, 96

Jackson, Rosemary: *Fantasy: The
    Literature of Subversion* (1981),
    136–7
Jalali, Gholam Reza: 96
James, Major Charles: 117
Japan: 91; Osaka, 84
JavaScript: 148
Jellenc, Eli: 156
Jiabao, Wen: Chinese Prime
    Minister, 150
Jintao, Hu: President of China, 150
JMicron: 94
Judaism: 24

Kahn, Herman: 170
Karabasevic, Dejan: cracked AMSC
    software, 105
Kaspersky Lab: discovery of Gauss
    (2012), 96–8; personnel of, 64,
    91; research into Flame, 94–6;
    research into Mahdi incident,
    102; research into Wiper, 64–6
Kaufmann, Bill: 170
Kazakhstan: 4, 157
Kennedy, Ted: FISA Bill introduced
    by, 112
Kenya: Mau Mau Uprising (1952–
    60), 118

Kerchkoffs, Auguste: Kerchoffs's
    Principle, 73–4
Kelsen, Hans: *Pure Theory of Law,
    The*, 24
Khamenei, Ayatollah Ali: 29
Kitson, Frank: military career of,
    118; theories of subversion,
    118–20, 134
Kosovo War (1998–9): 17; Opera-
    tion Allied Force (1999), 18
Kraus, Jürgen: 'Reproduktion bei
    Programmen' (1980), 14
Kremslehner, Florian: 105
Kubrick, Stanley: *2001: A Space
    Odyssey* (1968), vii
Kuhn, Thomas: concept of 'para-
    digm shifts', 136

Laboratory of Cryptography and
    System Security (CrySys Lab):
    discovery of Duqu (2011), 93–4,
    97; 'Flame' Report (2012), 94
Lake, Eli: 'Israel's Secret Iran Attack
    Plan: Electronic Warfare' (2011),
    101
Langner, Ralph: 45, 72
Latvia: 142
Lau, Hon: 91
Lawrence Livermore National
    Laboratory: cyber attack on
    (2007), 92
Lebanon: 98; banking sector of, 97,
    99; Beirut, 18; Israeli Invasion of
    (2006), 17–18
legacy systems: concept of, 51
Leverett, Éireann: use of Shodanhq.
    com by (2010), 70
Libicki, Martin: 156
Libya: Civil War (2011), 35, 132
LinkedIn: data harvested from, 87
Lobban, Iain: head of GCHQ, 111

Locke, John: 23
logic bombs: 6, 147; timed, 73
Lord, Major General William: 86
Los Alamos National Laboratory: cyber attack on (2007), 92
Low Orbit Ion Cannon (LOIC): hive option, 131; use of, 131
Lynn, William: US Deputy Secretary of Defense, 35, 173

Mahdi incident (2012): 100–2; languages used by, 101–2
Makaryk, Irene Rima: *Encyclopaedia of Contemporary Literary Theory*, 137
Malayan Emergency (1948–50): 118
malware: 66, 96, 106; concept of, 39–40, 52–3; examples of, 94, 97, 101–2, 143, 147
De Man, Paul: 137
Mandiant: APT1 report (2013), 155–6
Maroochy incident (2000): 74–5; significance of, 74
Marx, Karl: 24
Mason, Thom: Director of Oak Ridge National Laboratory, 92
master devices: examples of, 67
Matherley, John: creator of Shodanhq,com, 69–70, 78–9
Matsushita Electrical Company: personnel of, 84
McAfee, Inc.: 99; discovery of ShadyRAT by (2011), 87, 90–1; personnel of, 90–1; research on Night Dragon (2011), 154
McCain, John: 173
McConnell, Admiral Mike: 141; US Director of National Intelligence, xiv, 139–40

McCown, Davis: Tarrant County District Attorney, 147
McGraw, Jesse William: role in W.B. Carrell Memorial Clinic incident (2009), 75–6
McKinley, William: assassination of (1901), 118
McVeigh, Timothy: role in Oklahoma City Bombing (1995), 141–2
Microsoft Corporation: 28; SQL Server, 49; vulnerabilities in security of, 88, 95
Microsoft Internet Explorer: zero-day exploit in, 92, 148–9
Microsoft Office: Excel, 88; file formats of, 87, 143–4; Outlook, 90, 143; PowerPoint, 101; Word, 90, 93, 101, 144, 151
Microsoft Windows: 43, 48, 55–6, 99; kernel vulnerabilities of, 93–4; registry hives of, 65; rootkit, 45
Mitsubishi: 71
Moonlight Maze (1999): 85; events of use of, 9
Mozilla: 27–8
Mubarak, Hosni: 133
Murchu, Liam: 61–2

Netherlands: 26, 59; government of, 26, 29–30; Ministry of Interior, 30; Rijksdienst voor het Wegverkeer (DigiD), 27; Tax and Customs Administration, 27
Niagara AX framework: 78
Night Dragon (2011): systems targeted by, 157
Nietzsche, Friedrich: 137
Nikzad, Alireza: spokesman for Iranian Ministry of Oil, 64

Nixon, Richard: Watergate Scandal (1972), 112

Nonaka, Ikujiro: 83–4; *Knowledge Creating Company, The* (1995), 83

Nortel Networks Corp: liquidation of (2009), 85

North Atlantic Treaty Organization (NATO): 151; Cooperative Cyber Defence Centre for Excellence, 6, 8; members of, 30, 35

Northern Ireland: The Troubles (1966–98), 118

Northrop Grumman: targeted in Operation Aurora (2010), 149

NSS Labs: personnel of, 71

Oak Ridge National Laboratory: cyber attack on (2007), 92; cyber attack on (2011), 91–2; personnel of, 92

Obama, Barack: 32; administration of, 45

Occupy Wall Street movement: 113; significance of, 136

Online Certificate Status Protocol (OCSP): 28

Operation Aurora (2010): 150, 156–7; companies targeted by, 148–9; individuals involved in, 150

Osaka International Hotel: 84

packet: concept of, 163

Paet, Urmas: Estonian Foreign Minister, 31

paintball pistol effect: concept of, 40

Palestinian Territories: 98

Panetta, Leon: 140, 152; Director of CIA, xiv

Passerin, d'Entrèves, Alexander: *Notion of the State, The*, 22–3

Pastebin: 63, 78, 155

PayPal: 130; collective DDoS attack against (2010), 131

Pchelintsev, Vasily: 4

Penland, Barbara: Deputy Director of Communications at Oak Ridge National Laboratory, 92

Pentagon: vii, 35, 37, 167; personnel of, xiii, xiv, 173; Secret Internet Protocol Router Network (SIPRNET), 86–7; targeted by ILOVEYOU virus (2000, 48; targeted by Titan Rain (2003), 86; unclassified network (NIPRNET), 86–7; use of Niagara AX framework by, 78

People's Liberation Army (PLA) of China: 108; Comment Group/Advanced Persistent Threat 1 (APT1), 69, 85, 155–6; General Staff Department (GSD), 154; National Defense University, 153; Third Technical Department, 144; Unit 61398, 154–6

Persian (language): 102

Persian Gulf War (1990–1): 17

Peters, Ralph: 31

Peterson, Dale: 72; classification of attack on industrial control system variants, 51–2

Philippines: 48, 142; Manila, 48

Plunkett, Debora: Director of Information Assurance Directorate of NSA, 100

Polanyi, Michael: influence of, 83

Pope, Carl: Executive Director of Sierra Club, 124–5

Pouget, Émile: 59; *Sabotage*, 60

Programmable Logic Controller (PLC): 43, 52, 72, 106; as example of master devices, 67;

manufacturers of, 69–72; rootkit, 45

al-Qaeda: 113; claim of responsibility for Egyptian power blackout (2003), 156
Qatar: RasGas, 64

RAND Corporation: personnel of, xiii, 159
Reed, Thomas: 4
Register, The: 77
Remote Access Tool (RAT): 87; examples of, 87, 93
remote shell: concept of, 90
Remote Terminal/Telemetry Units (RTUs): 67; as example of slave devices, 68
Rockwell Automation: 71
Rolls Royce: 108
Ronfeldt, David: xiii
Roosevelt, Theodore: 118
rootkit: concept of, 45
Round Robin Domain Name Service: concept of, 98
RuggedCom: 71
Russia-Georgia War (2008): 151; causes of, 7; cyber attacks during, 7–9
Russian Federation: 35, 76, 114, 145, 151, 170; Federal Security Service (FSB), 151; government of, 7; Institute of Space Research, 31; Kremlin, 7–8, 31; Ministry of Inetrior, 74; Moscow, 6, 110, 151–2; Shushenskaya dam attack (2009), 38; Victory Day, 6

al-Saadan, Abdullah: Saudi Aramco Vice President for Corporate Planning, 66

Saakashvili, Mikheil: President of Georgia, 8
sabotage: 67, 139–40, 167; concept of, 58–60; examples of, 55–6; use in cyber warfare, 56–7, 82, 113, 171–2
Sader, Makram: Secretary-General of Associated Banks of Lebanon, 99
Saint John, Vincent: 61
Santamarta, Rubén: discovery of flaw in firmware of NOE 771 module (2011), 70–1
Saudi Arabia: 102; Dhahran, 55; oil reserves of, 55
Saudi Aramco: personnel of, 66; Shamoon attack (2012), 55–6, 61–4, 66, 159
Schmitt, Carl: 24
Schneider Electric: 71; NOE 771 module, 71; subsidiaries of, 69
Schweitzer: 70
Scowcroft, Brent: 166
Second World War (1939–45): 6, 9, 140; Atomic bombing of Hiroshima and Nagasaki (1945), xiv, 174; belligerents of, 58; Blitz (1940–1), 18; Bombing of Dresden (1945), 18; Holocaust, 107; Pearl Harbor attack (1941), 31, 174
secure sockets layer (SSL): 28, 95
Serbia: Belgrade, 18
Shady RAT: 83; discovered by McAfee, Inc. (2011), 87, 90–1; networks targeted by, 91; processes used by attackers, 87–90; suspected creator of, 87; use of Trojan virus, 88–90
Shamoon: 55–6, 61–2, 74, 159; shortcomings of, 66; systems affected by, 63–4

Shannon, Claude: 74
Shell Oil: 108
Shriky, Clay: 127
Siemens AG: 106; Field PGs, 43–4;
    hardware manufactured by, 33,
    43–4; Indo-European telegraph
    line, 106; personnel of, 106–7;
    Simatic HMI software, 77;
    Simatic PCS 7 software, 72;
    Simatic S7 PLC, 71–2, 107;
    vulnerabilities in products of,
    71–2
Sierra Club: members of, 124–5
signal intelligence (SIGINT):
    109–10; requirement of specialists
    for, 81
Sinovel: use of cracked AMSC
    software, 104
Skype: 27, 30, 94, 100, 110
Slammer Worm (SQL Slammer):
    52; code of, 49; damage inflicted
    by, 50; targeting of Davis-Besse
    nuclear power plant (2003),
    48–50, 53
slave devices: examples of, 68
social media: growth of, 116, 127;
    political use of, 116
Sofsky, Wolfgang: 18; *Trakat über
    die Gewalt* (Pamphlet on Vio-
    lence), 16–17
South Korea: 91; Seoul, 93
South Ossetia: 7
Soviet Union (USSR): 41, 116, 172;
    Committee for State Security
    (KGB), 4; cyber attack targeting
    Urengoy-Surgut-Chelyabinsk
    pipeline (1982), 4–5, 41; Invasion
    of Afghanistan (1979–89), 141;
    State Technical Commission, 5;
    Tobolsk, 4
spear phishing: examples of, 87–8,
    143

Stuxnet: 32, 45–6, 50, 96, 99–100,
    105–6; code of, 66, 107; PLC
    used in, 43; political impact of, 9,
    79, 161, 168, 172; purpose of,
    xiv, 32, 53–4, 72; use of (2009–
    10), 32–4, 42–5
subversion: 128, 136–7, 138–40,
    155; concept of, 114–16;
    language of, 136; non-violent,
    120, 122, 135; purpose of,
    119–21; theories of, 118–19,
    134–5; use in cyber warfare, 113,
    123, 163, 166–7
Sun Tzu: *Art of War, The*, 1, 13
Switzerland: Davos, 125; Geneva,
    97
Supervisory Control and Data
    Acquisition (SCADA) software: 4,
    51, 73–4, 76; attacks targeting,
    66; fieldbus protocol-based, 68;
    potential vulnerabilities of,
    68–70; urban legends regarding
    attacks on, 76; use in Industrial
    Control Systems, 56; use of
    communication infrastructure by,
    68; use of IPs in, 69
Symantec: 93, 99, 159; observations
    of ShadyRAT events, 88; observa-
    tions of *W32.Stuxnet Dossier*, 44,
    46; personnel of, 61–2, 91;
    targeted in Operation Aurora
    (2010), 149
Syria: borders of, 11; Israeli
    bombing of Dayr ez-Zor reactor
    (2007), 11, 34, 41–2; Tall
    al-Abuad, 11, 42

Taiwan: 91, 144, 148, 157
Tanaka, Ikuko: 84, 110
Tarakanov, Dmitry: 64
Telvent: OASyS, 69

INDEX

Third Position: presence at A16 (2000), 125
Third Reich (1933–45): 6, 58
Tibet: 142, 144
Titan Rain (2003): networks targeted by, 85–6
Trojan virus: 108–9; backdoor, 100, 143; examples of, 88–90, 95, 97
Tunisia: Revolution (2010–11), 132
Turkey: borders of, 11, 42
Twitter: 1, 78; founding of, 127; use in Arab Spring, 132; use in coordination of subversive activities, 131

United Arab Emirates (UAE): 102; Dubai, 132, 171
United Kingdom (UK): 22, 35, 48, 54, 85; Brighton, 121; Centre for the Protection of the National Infrastructure, 108; Government Communication Headquarters (GCHQ), 99, 111–12; legal system of, 153; Lockerbie Bombing (1988), 141; London, 106, 142, 144–5; military of, 117; Scotland Yard, 145; Secret Intelligence Service (MI6), 27; Security Services (MI5), 85, 108; Virgin Media, 145
United Nations (UN): 32; personnel of, 170
United States of America (USA): 34, 54, 116, 118, 135, 151, 157; 9/11 attacks, xiii–xiv, 77, 113; Air Force, xiii, 4, 9, 165–6; Central Intelligence Agency (CIA), xiv, 4–5, 15, 27, 41, 48, 53, 58, 96, 110, 151; Constitution of, 26; Cyber Command, 38; Department of Defense (DoD), 9, 20, 31, 35, 37, 48, 86; Department of Energy, 9, 86, 91–2; Department of Homeland Security (DHS), 70–1, 76–7, 86, 92, 158; Federal Bureau of Investigation (FBI), 9, 75–8, 85, 96; Federal Trade Commission, 92; Foreign Intelligence Surveillance Act (FISA), 112; government of, 42–3, 62, 71, 85, 91, 96, 108, 140, 173; Grabow Riot (1912), 61; Internal Revenue Service, 78; legal system of, 153; military of, 86; National Aeronautics and Space Administration (NASA), 9; National Nuclear Safety Administration, 86; National Security Agency (NSA), 4, 9, 38, 42, 96, 100, 110–11, 139, 149, 161; National Security Council, 4; navy of, 140; New York, viii, 19, 102, 142; Office of the National Counterintelligence Executive (NCIX), 109; Oklahoma City Bombing (1995), 141–2; Operation Olympic Games, 156; Oregon, 122, 124; State Department, 86, 99; Washington DC, ix, 35, 46, 86, 109, 159
US Cyber Emergency Response Team (US-CERT): 92
US Office of Strategic Services: *Simple Sabotage Field Manual* (1963), 57–8, 73
US Planning Association: Independent Research Agency for Life Insurance, 146; offices of, 146; personnel of, 146-7

VASCO: owner of DigiNotar, 28
Verisign: 150; personnel of, 160
Vietnam War (1955–75): 17

violence: containment of, 61; in context of cyber warfare, 12–14, 17; indiscriminate, 25; instruments of, 18; political, 21–2, 25, 57

virtual private network (VPN): 33

voice over internet protocols (VoIP): 70, 100

Wang, Jack: alias of 'UglyGorilla' 153–5; background of, 153

W.B. Carrell Memorial Clinic incident (2009): 75–6

Web Intellects: 100

Web 2.0.: 116

Weber, Max: 24

Weiss, Joe: 'Water System Hack— The System Is Broken' (2011), 76

Wightman, Reid: 72

WikiLeaks: 131; publication of diplomatic cables by (2010), 130

Wiper: purpose of, 65; research conducted on, 64–5; shortcomings of, 66

Wohlstetter, Albert: 174

Wolfexp: 143–4

Words of Estimative Probability: concept of, 156

World Anti-Doping Agency: targeted by ShadyRAT, 91

World Bank: 124

World Conference on International Telecommunications (WCIT) (2012): 171

World Economic Forum: Davos Conference, 125

World Social Forum: charter of principles, 125–6; Porto Alegre Conference (2001), 125

World Trade Organization: protests against, 124

worm virus: examples of, 94

Worshipful Company of Security Professionals: 108, 110

Wynne, Michael: US Secretary of the Air Force, xiii

Yahoo! Inc.: 30; targeted in Operation Aurora (2010), 149

Yemen: cultural weaponry of, 19; Uprising (2011–12), 132

Yokogawa Electric Corporation: 71

Yongkang, Zhou: role in Operation Aurora (2010), 150

YouTube: 75, 129–30

Zappa, Frank: 'Cheepnis', 31

Zhaozhong, Zhang: 153–4; *Network Warfare*, 153